Instant Pot Pressure Cooker Cookbook

550 Recipes for Any Budget

By

Jessica Taylor

Table of contents

Instant Pot Rice Dishes 73

Seafood and Fish Recipes 247

Instant Pot Stocks and Sauces 312

Vegetables Recipes 329

Instant Pot Dessert Recipes 368

Introduction

Instant Pot is quite popular these days. It has managed to impress many consumers around the world, and it has become one of the most-appreciated tools in the kitchen.

This book contains proven steps and strategies on how to use your Instant Pot to make wonderfully delicious and healthy meals faster than ever!

This cookbook is created for those who want to learn more about different ways to use their pressure cookers Instant Pot to make tasty meals.

This book focuses primarily on recipes; it delivers different kinds of recipes, so you'll be able to find those that need just a few ingredients as well as those that need more. Regardless of the number of ingredients, all the meals are super easy to make, taste divine, and deliver a multitude of nutrients to your body, keeping you healthy and happy.

According to the common belief, handling a pressure cooker requires an advanced level of cooking skills, but that's far from the truth. This book shows that you don't really have to be expert to use this practical appliance and prepare food faster.

The **Instant Pot** Pressure Cooker is the answer to your kitchen needs.

This introduction cookbook is packed with many VEGAN (marked as V) recipes that will astonish and surprise you.

Many recipes will be good for beginners, because they are EASY & SIMPLE and marked with an E&S sign.

How to Use the Control Panel

There are 18 buttons on the Instant Pot DUO (16 on the LUX – I've noted the buttons not present on the LUX) and here is what happens when you push each of them:

Soup

- *Purpose* – A programmed setting designed for cooking soups.
- *Type* – Preset button
- *Default Setting* – 30 minutes high pressure.
- *How To Change* – Pressing Adjust will increase or decrease the time. Press the Adjust button to navigate to the Less setting to cook for 20 minutes or navigate to the More setting to cook for 40 minutes. Press the Plus or Minus buttons to navigate to a time other than those programmed. Press Pressure to change the pressure setting from high to low (remember low pressure is on the DUO only).

Meat/Stew

- *Purpose* – A programmed setting designed for cooking meat and stews.
- *Type* – Preset button
- *Default Setting* – 35 minutes high pressure.
- *How To Change* – Pressing Adjust will increase or decrease the time. Press the Adjust button to navigate to the Less setting to cook for 20 minutes or navigate to the More setting to cook for 45 minutes. Press the Plus or Minus buttons to navigate to a time other than those programmed. Press Pressure to change the pressure setting from high to low (remember low pressure is on the DUO only).

Bean/Chili

- *Purpose* – A programmed setting designed for cooking beans and chili.
- *Type* – Preset button
- *Default Setting* – 30 minutes high pressure.

- *How To Change* – Pressing Adjust will increase or decrease the time. Press the Adjust button to navigate to the Less setting to cook for 25 minutes or navigate to the More setting to cook for 40 minutes. Press the Plus or Minus buttons to navigate to a time other than those programmed. Press Pressure to change the pressure setting from high to low (remember low pressure is on the DUO only).

Poultry

- *Purpose* – A programmed setting designed for cooking poultry.
- *Type* – Preset button
- *Default Setting* – 15 minutes high pressure.
- *How To Change* – Pressing Adjust will increase or decrease the time. Press the Adjust button to navigate to the Less setting to cook for 5 minutes or navigate to the More setting to cook for 30 minutes. Press the Plus or Minus buttons to navigate to a time other than those programmed. Press Pressure to change the pressure setting from high to low (remember low pressure is on the DUO only).

Slow Cook

- *Purpose* – To cook food slowly at a lower temperature.
- *Type* – Function button
- *Default Setting* – 4 hours at normal temperature (about 200°F).
- *How To Change* – Pressing Adjust will increase or decrease the temperature. Press the Adjust button to navigate to the Less setting to cook at a lower temperature (about 190°F) or navigate to the More setting increase the temperature (about 210°F). Press the Plus or Minus buttons to navigate to a time other than those programmed. On this setting the Instant Pot goes up or down in increments of 30 minutes.

Saute

- *Purpose* – To brown meat or for stir frying.
- *Type* – Function button
- *Default Setting* – 30 minutes at normal temperature (320°F).
- *How To Change* – Pressing Adjust will increase or decrease the temperature. Press the Adjust button to navigate to the

Less setting to cook at a lower temperature (about 221°F) or navigate to the More setting increase the temperature (about 338°F). Pressing the Plus or Minus buttons have no effect with this setting and the cycle is set to 30 minutes.

Note – Never place the lid on when using this function as pressure could build inside the Instant Pot.

Pressure (DUO only)

- *Purpose* – To increase or low pressure.
- *Type* – Utility button
- *Default Setting* – High pressure (10.2-11.6psi) when using manual.
- *How To Change* – Press this button to change pressure from high to low (5.8-7.2 psi).

Manual

- *Purpose* – To pressure cook food.
- *Type* – Function button (pressure cooking).
- *Default Setting* – 30 minutes high pressure.
- *How To Change* – Press the Plus or Minus buttons to navigate to a time other than 30 minutes. Press Pressure to change the pressure setting from high to low (low pressure-DUO only).

Note – Pressing Adjust has no effect using this setting.

Plus

- *Purpose* – To add time to the default or preset time.
- *Type* – Utility button
- *Default Setting* – None
- *How To Change* – Press to increase time.

Minus

- *Purpose* – To subtract time to the default or preset time.
- *Type* – Utility Button
- *Default Setting* – None
- *How To Change* – Press to subtract time.

Adjust

- *Purpose* – To adjust temperature from the default or preset mode. Also used to navigate to different preset time once a preset has been selected.
- *Type* – Utility button
- *Default Setting* – Normal
- *How To Change* – Press to go between the Less, Normal and More modes.

Timer

- *Purpose* – To delay the start of the cooking setting and time you enter.
- *Type* – Utility button
- *Default Setting* – Start cooking in 6 hours.
- *How To Change* – Press the Plus or Minus buttons to navigate to a time other than 6 hours.

Note – Pressing Adjust has no effect using this setting.

Rice

- *Purpose* –To cook white or parboiled rice.
- *Type* – Function button
- *Default Setting* – 12 minutes low pressure.
- *How To Change* – This function is automatic and depending how much moisture and rice the machine senses the time and pressure could fluctuate to make sure all the rice if fully cooked. The remaining pressure should be released after 10 minutes.

Notes –This is the only function setting that is completely automatic. You can not adjust the time or the pressure with the Adjust, or Plus or Minus buttons. If you'd like more control over your rice, you can use the Manual button and program in your own time.

Multigrain

- *Purpose* – A programmed setting designed for cooking harder grains like wild rice and split corn.

24

- *Type* – Preset button
- *Default Setting* – 40 minutes high pressure.
- *How To Change* – Pressing Adjust will increase or decrease the time. Press Adjust button to navigate to the Less setting to cook for 20 minutes or navigate to the More setting to cook for 60 minutes. Press the Plus or Minus buttons to navigate to a time other than those programmed. Press Pressure to change the pressure setting from high to low (remember low pressure is on the DUO only).

Notes – The More setting has a 45 minute warm soak period as well

Porridge (Congee in the LUX)

- *Purpose* – A programmed setting designed for recipes involving grains that have a porridge texture. In other words, only use this setting if you'd like to have your grains mushy like porridge.
- *Type* – Preset button
- *Default Setting* – 20 minutes high pressure.
- *How To Change* – Pressing Adjust will increase or decrease the time. Press Adjust button to navigate to the Less setting to cook for 15 minutes or navigate to the More setting to cook for 30 minutes. Press the Plus or Minus buttons to navigate to a time other than those programmed. Press Pressure to change the pressure setting from high to low (remember low pressure is on the DUO only).

Steam

- *Purpose* – To steam food with water or other liquid
- *Type* – Function button
- *Default Setting* – 10 minutes high pressure.
- *How To Change* – Pressing Adjust will increase or decrease the time. Press the Adjust button to navigate to the Less setting to cook for 3 minutes or navigate to the More setting to cook for 15 minutes. Press the Plus or Minus buttons to navigate to a time other than those programmed. Press Pressure to change the pressure setting from high to low.

Notes – The steam function is the only setting that heats food at full power continuously. This will probably cause food that is in direct contact with the bottom to burn. Always use the proper amount of water and a tiviot with this setting.

Yogurt (DUO only)

- *Purpose* – To pasteurize milk, make yogurt or make Jiu Niang.
- *Type* – Function button
- *Default Setting* – 8 hours at the incubate temperature which is between 100 and 115 degrees Fahrenheit.
- *How To Change* – Pressing Adjust will increase the incubation period or boil the milk. Press Adjust button to navigate to the Less setting to increase the incubation period to 24 hours. Press Adjust button to navigate to the More setting to boil your yogurt. Press the Plus or Minus buttons to navigate to a time other than those programmed when on the Normal or Low setting. Pressing the Plus or Minus buttons on the More (boil setting) setting has no effect.

Notes – When making yogurt in smaller bottles you can steam them with the Steam (function) button for 1 minute (don't forget to put water in the bottom). After letting your bottles cool and adding your starter you can place them back in the Instant Pot and for the proper incubation period.

Keep Warm/Cancel

- *Purpose* – To keep food warm after cooking.
- *Type* – Function button
- *Default Setting* – 10 hours on low temperature (145-172°F)
- *How To Change* – Press the Plus or Minus buttons to navigate to a time other than 10 hours.

Notes – Pressing Adjust has no effect using this setting. When in the Keep Warm mode the Instant Pot counts up (instead of down like in it does when cooking). Also, the Instant Post goes into Keep Warm mode after any pressure cooking setting or slow cooking setting is complete. This is also the button you press to turn the Instant Pot off.

Cooking Measurement Conversion Chart

Dry Measurements	
Measurement	Equivalent
1 pound	16 ounces
1 cup	16 tablespoons
3/4 cup	12 tablespoons
2/3 cup	10 tablespoons plus 2 teaspoons
1/2 cup	8 tablespoons
3/8 cup	6 tablespoons
1/3 cup	5 tablespoons plus 1 teaspoon
1/4 cup	4 tablespoons
1/6 cup	2 tablespoons plus 2 teaspoons
1/8 cup	2 tablespoons
1/16 cup	1 tablespoon
1 tablespoon	3 teaspoons
1/8 teaspoon	Pinch
1/16 teaspoon	Dash
1/2 cup butter	1 stick of butter

Liquid Measurements	
Measurement	Equivalent (rounded for ease of use)
4 quarts	1 gallon
2 quarts	1/2 gallon
1 quart	1/4 gallon
2 pints	1 quart
4 cups	1 quart
2 cups	1/2 quart
2 cups	1 pint
1 cup	1/2 pint
1 cup	1/4 quart
1 cup	8 fluid ounces
3/4 cup	6 fluid ounces
2/3 cup	5.3 fluid ounces
1/2 cup	4 fluid ounces
1/3 cup	2.7 fluid ounces
1/4 cup	2 fluid ounces
1 tablespoon	0.5 fluid ounces

Abbreviations

(V) – Recipes that vegans can use too

(E&S) – Recipes for beginners, very easy and simple

oz = ounce

tsp = teaspoon

tbsp = tablespoon

ml = milliliter

c = cup

qt = quart

Banana Bread Steel Cut Oatmeal (V, E&S)
(Prep + Cook Time: 25 minutes | Servings: 4)

Ingredients:
- 2 cups steel cut oatmeal
- 1 tsp cinnamon
- 1 tsp vanilla
- ¼ tsp nutmeg
- 2 ripe bananas, mashed
- 3 1/3 cups water
- ½ cup walnuts, chopped
- ¼ cup honey
- ¼ tsp salt

Directions:
1. With a potato masher or a fork, mash the bananas at the bottom of the Instant Pot container.
2. Add the oats, water, nutmeg, cinnamon, vanilla, and salt; stir to combine. Close the lid and make sure the valve is closed.
3. Set the pot to PORRIDGE and the timer to 10 minutes.
4. When the timer beeps, let the pressure release for 10 minutes naturally.
5. Stir in the walnuts and honey.
6. Serve and enjoy.

Peaches & Cream Oatmeal (E&S)
(Prep + Cook Time: 20 minutes | Servings: 4)

Ingredients:
- 2 cups rolled oats
- 4 cups water

Optional:
- ½ cup chopped almonds
- 2 tbsp flax meal
- Splash of cream, milk, or non-diary milk
- Maple syrup
- 1 tsp vanilla
- 1 chopped peach

Directions:
1. Combine the water, peaches, oats, and vanilla in the Instant Pot.
2. Set to HIGH pressure using the MANUAL setting. Be sure the valve is Sealed. Adjust the time to 3 minutes.
3. When the timer beeps, allow the pressure to release naturally for 10 minutes; then perform a quick release for the remainder of the pressure.
4. Garnish as desired and enjoy

Carrot Cake Breakfast Oatmeal

(Prep + Cook Time: 20 minutes | Servings: 6)

Ingredients:

1 cup grated carrots

1 cup steel cut oats

1 tbsp butter

4 cups water

1 tsp pumpkin pie spice

¼ cup chia seeds

¼ tsp salt

2 tsp cinnamon

3 tbsp maple syrup

¾ cup raisins

Directions:

1. Put the butter into the Instant Pot; select SAUTE.
2. When the butter is melted, add the oats; toast, constantly stirring for about 3 minutes or until the oats are nutty.
3. Add the water, carrots, cinnamon, maple syrup, salt, and pumpkin pie spice. Close the lid of the pot.
4. Set the pressure to HIGH and the timer to 10 minutes.
5. When the timer beeps, turn off the pot, let the pressure release naturally for 10 minutes, then turn the steam valve to release remaining pressure.
6. When the valve drops, carefully open the lid. Stir in the oats, chia seeds, and raisins.
7. Close the lid and let sit for about 5-10 minutes or until the oats are cooked in the heat to desired thickness.
8. Serve topped with milk, chopped nuts, and additional raisins and maple syrup.

Notes: You can cook a batch ahead of time; just freeze individual portions. When ready to serve, add a bit of milk and serve cold or microwave until heated.

Cinnamon Roll Oats

(Prep + Cook Time: 30 minutes | Servings: 4)

Ingredients:

- 3 ½ cups water
- 1 cup steel cut oats
- ¾ cup raisins
- ¼ cup light brown sugar
- 1 tbsp butter
- 1 tsp cinnamon
- ¼ tsp salt
- 2-ounces softened cream cheese
- 2 tbsp powdered sugar
- 1 tsp milk

Directions:

1. Turn your cooker to SAUTE and melt the butter.
2. When melted, pour in the oats and stir until they're toasty and nutty.
3. Pour water and salt into the cooker. Close and seal the lid.
4. Choose MANUAL and then adjust time for 10 minutes on HIGH pressure.
5. When time is up, press CANCEL and wait 5 minutes before quick-releasing the rest of the pressure. Open the lid and stir in raisins. Cover again, but just let it sit for 5-10 minutes to thicken.
6. In the meantime, mix the brown sugar and cinnamon together.
7. Also, for the cream cheese topping, mix milk, cream cheese, and powdered sugar. If the cream cheese icing is too thick, add a bit more milk.
8. Serve the oats with a healthy sprinkle of brown sugar and cinnamon, with a drizzle of the cream cheese icing.

Creamy Peaches Steel Cut Oats (V, E&S)
(Prep + Cook Time: 10 minutes | Servings: 4)

Ingredients:
- 2 peaches, diced
- 1 cup steel cut oats
- 1 cup coconut milk, full fat
- 2 cups water
- ½ of a vanilla bean, scraped, seeds and pod

Directions:
1. Put all of the ingredients into the bowl of the Instant Pot.
2. Close the lid and the vent. Set the pressure to HIGH and the timer to 3 minutes.
3. When the timer beeps, let the pressure release naturally for 10 minutes.
4. Turn the steam valve to release remaining pressure.
5. Sweeten the oats, if desired.

Creamy Strawberry Rolled Oats (E&S)
(Prep + Cook Time: 20 minutes | Servings: 2)

Ingredients:
- 2 cups water
- 2/3 cup whole milk
- 2 tbsp strawberries, freeze-dried (or your favorite dried or frozen fruit)
- 1/3 cup rolled oats
- ½ tsp white sugar
- 1 pinch salt

Directions:
1. Pour 2 cups of water into the Instant Pot container and then put a steamer basket or a rack with a handle in the pot.
2. In a small-sized, heat-safe mug or bowl, add the oats, strawberries, milk, and salt.
3. Close and lock the pot lid. Set the pressure to HIGH and the timer to 10 minutes.
4. When the timer beeps, unplug the pot. Let the pressure release for about 7-10 minutes naturally or until the pressure indicator is down and then open the lid. You can turn the steam valve to release remaining pressure before opening. Carefully remove the bowl from the pot.
5. Mix the contents vigorously and then sprinkle with sugar to taste. Serve.

Coconut and Creamy Steel Cut Oats
(Prep + Cook Time: 20 minutes | Servings: 4)

Ingredients:
- ½ cup unsweetened coconut flakes
- 1 cup coconut milk, plus additional for topping (full-fat canned or lighter varieties)
- 1 cup steel cut oats
- 1 pinch salt
- 1 cinnamon stick or ½ tsp ground cinnamon, optional
- 2 cups water
- 2 tbsp brown sugar

Directions:
1. Put the coconut flakes into the Instant Pot container.
2. Press SAUTE and cook the coconut flakes, frequently stirring and closely watching to avoid burning.
3. When the flakes starts to lightly brown, remove 1/2 and reserve for topping.
4. Add the oats and cook for a couple of minutes until both the coconut flakes and the oats are fragrant.
5. Add 1 cup of milk and the remaining ingredients; stir to combine. Press CANCEL to stop SAUTÉ mode.
6. Close the lid, press MANUAL, set the pressure to HIGH and the timer to 2 minutes.
7. When the timer beeps, let the pressure release for 10 minutes naturally and then turn the valve to release remaining pressure. Carefully open the lid.
8. Divide the oatmeal between 4 bowls.
9. Drizzle each serving with coconut milk, 1 tablespoon of toasted coconut, and your desired toppings.

Steel Cut Oatmeal (E&S)
(Prep + Cook Time: 30 minutes | Servings: 4)

Ingredients:
- 1 cup steel cut oats (use gluten free as needed)
- 3 cups almond milk or water

Optional:
- Cinnamon, sweetener (honey, maple syrup)
- vanilla extract
- pinch of salt

Toppings of your choice:
- Berries, chia seeds, nut butter, splash of milk

Directions:

1. Add oats into the Instant Pot followed by milk. (please see note on sticking)
2. Secure the lid and close the vent.
3. Select MANUAL and cook at HIGH pressure for 3 minutes.
4. After the oats finish cooking, allow the pressure to release naturally (about 10-15 minutes).
5. After the pressure releases, open the lid and give the oatmeal a good stir. Any extra liquid will absorb as it cools.
6. Add cinnamon, sweetener or other additions you like.
7. Top oatmeal with fresh fruit, nut butter, a splash of milk, or any other toppings you like.

Notes: If you are worried about the oatmeal sticking, you can lightly grease the bottom of the POT with nonstick cooking spray or oil (I use coconut).

Pear Oats with Walnuts (V, E&S)
(Prep + Cook Time: 10 minutes | Servings: 4)

Ingredients:

- 2 cups almond milk
- 2 cups peeled and cut pears
- 1 cup rolled oats
- ½ cup chopped walnuts
- ¼ cup sugar
- 1 tbsp melted coconut oil
- ¼ tsp salt
- Dash of cinnamon

Directions:

1. Mix everything except the walnuts and cinnamon in an oven-safe bowl that you know fits in the Instant Pot.
2. Pour 1 cup of water into the pressure cooker and lower in steamer rack.
3. Put the bowl on top and lock the lid. Select MANUAL and then HIGH pressure for 6 minutes.
4. When time is up, quick-release the pressure.
5. Carefully remove the bowl, divide into 4 servings, and season with salt and cinnamon.

Breakfast Quinoa (E&S)

(Prep + Cook Time: 10 minutes | Servings: 6)

Ingredients:

- 2 ¼ cups water
- 1 ½ cups quinoa, uncooked, well rinsed
- 2 tbsp maple syrup
- ½ tsp vanilla
- Pinch salt
- ¼ tsp ground cinnamon

Optional toppings:

- Fresh berries
- Milk
- Sliced almonds

Directions:

1. Put all of the ingredients into the Instant Pot and close the lid.
2. Set the pressure to HIGH and the timer to 1 minute.
3. When the timer beeps, turn the Instant Pot off, let the pressure release for 10 minutes naturally and then turn the steam valve to release remaining pressure.
4. Carefully open the lid. Fluff the cooked quinoa.
5. Serve with berries, milk, and almonds.

Quinoa Salad

(Prep + Cook Time: 30 minutes | Servings: 6)

Ingredients:

- 1 cup quinoa
- 2 cups chicken stock
- 1 can red beans
- 1 tsp salt
- 2 tbsp tomato paste
- 1 tsp olive oil
- 1 yellow onion
- 5 tomatoes
- 2 cucumbers
- 1 tsp sour cream

Directions:

1. Place the quinoa in the Instant Pot.
2. Add chicken stock and red beans. Stir the mixture gently and close the lid.
3. Cook the dish at the Instant Pot mode at HIGH pressure for 20 minutes.

4. Then remove the quinoa mixture from the Instant Pot and chill it well.
5. Slice the cucumbers and chop the onion and tomatoes.
6. Then place the vegetables together in the mixing bowl.
7. Add the sour cream, tomato paste, and olive oil. Stir the mixture carefully and add the quinoa mixture.
8. Then sprinkle the dish with salt and mix up the salad until you get homogenous mass.
9. Serve the salad. Enjoy!

Cranberry-Almond Quinoa (V, E&S)

(Prep + Cook Time: 10 minutes | Servings: 4)

Ingredients:
- 2 cups water
- 1 cup quinoa
- 1 cup dried cranberries
- ½ cup slivered almonds
- ¼ cup salted sunflower seeds

Directions:
1. Rinse quinoa before putting in the pot with water.
2. Seal the lid. Select MANUAL and cook at HIGH pressure for 10 minutes.
3. When time is up, press CANCEL and quick-release the pressure.
4. Mix in sunflower seeds, almonds, and dried cranberries.
5. Serve.

Perfect Quinoa (V, E&S)

(Prep + Cook Time: 15 minutes | Servings: 4)

Ingredients:
- 2 cups quinoa (any color)
- 3 cups vegetable broth or water
- 2 pinches salt
- Juice of one lemon
- Handful your choice of fresh herbs, minced

Directions:
1. Rinse the quinoa well.
2. Preferably, you should soak it overnight in filtered water mixed with 1 tablespoon apple cider vinegar or lemon juice.
3. Strain and put into the Instant Pot. Add the broth, lemon juice, salt, and, if using, herbs.
4. Close and lock the lid. Press MANUAL and set the time to 1 minute.
5. When the timer beeps, let the pressure release naturally for 10 minutes. Turn the steam valve to Venting. Carefully open the lid and serve the quinoa.

Quinoa with Garden Vegetables (V)

(Prep + Cook Time: 20 minutes | Servings: 4)

Ingredients:
- 1 cup quinoa
- 1½ cups water
- 8 oz sweet green peas
- ½ zucchini, medium-sized, cut in lengthwise into halves and then sliced thin (about 2 cups)
- 3-4 large Swiss chard leaves, stems removed and leaves chopped (about 2 cups)
- 1 red onion, sliced thin
- 1 tbsp balsamic vinegar
- 1 tbsp pure maple syrup
- ¼ cup vegetable broth
- 1/8 tsp salt, or to taste
- 2 cloves garlic, minced
- 2 tbsp Dijon mustard
- ½ lime, juiced
- Salt and pepper to taste

Directions:
1. Put the quinoa in a fine sieve and rinse under running cold water. Put into the Instant Pot.
2. Add the water and the lime juice. Close and lock the lid. Select MANUAL and cook at HIGH pressure for 1 minute.
3. When the timer beeps, press CANCEL. Let the quinoa sit for 10 minutes. Use a natural release.

4. Open the lid and fluff the quinoa.
5. While the quinoa is sitting, heat a sauté pan over medium heat.
6. When hot, pour the broth in the pan and the onion. Cook for about 3-4 minutes, stirring occasionally until the onions starts to soften.
7. If the pan gets too dry, add 1 tablespoon additions of vegetable broth so the onions do not stick to the pan.
8. Add the zucchini and the garlic in the pan. Sprinkle with salt, pepper, and sauté for 2 minutes, occasionally stirring until the veggies starts to soften.
9. Add the green peas, Swiss chard, and dressing, and stir for 2 minutes or until heated.
10. To serve, place the quinoa topped with the veggie mix.
11. Alternatively, you can just mix the quinoa and veggies together. Serve immediately.

Cherry and Farro Salad
(Prep + Cook Time: 55 minutes | Servings: 6)

Ingredients:
- 1 cup whole grain farro raw
- 1 tbsp apple cider vinegar
- 1 tsp lemon juice freshly squeezed
- 1 tbsp olive oil
- ¼ tsp sea salt
- ½ cup dried cherries coarsely chopped
- ¼ cup chives or green onions, finely minced
- 8-10 leaves mint minced
- 2 cups cherries pitted and cut in half

Directions:
1. Rinse the farro. Put in the Instant Pot with 3 cups water.
2. Lock the lid in place. Select HIGH Pressure and set the timer for 40 minutes.
3. When the beep sounds, quick release the pressure by pressing CANCEL, and twisting the steam handle to Venting position. The grain should be plump and tender, but chewy.
4. Drain the farro (If you wish, save the extra liquid for soup stock).
5. Put the cooked farro in a bowl. Stir in vinegar, lemon juice, oil, salt, dried cherries, chives and mint.
6. Refrigerate until cold. Just before serving, stir in fresh cherries. Enjoy!

Buckwheat Porridge (V, E&S)

(Prep + Cook Time: 35 minutes | Servings: 4)

Ingredients:
- 1 cup raw buckwheat groats
- 3 cups rice milk
- ¼ cup raisins
- 1 banana, sliced
- ½ tsp vanilla
- 1 tsp ground cinnamon
- Chopped nuts, optional

Directions:
1. Rinse the buckwheat and then put in the Instant Pot container.
2. Add the rice milk, raisins, banana, vanilla, and cinnamon. Close the lid and make sure the valve is closed.
3. Set to MANUAL, the pressure is HIGH, and the timer to 6 minutes. When the timer beeps, unplug the pot, and let the pressure release naturally for 20 minutes.
4. With a long handled spoon, stir the porridge.
5. Divide the porridge between 4 bowls.
6. Add more milk into each serving to desired consistency. If desired, sprinkle with chopped nuts.

Softly Millet Porridge (E&S)

(Prep + Cook Time: 20 minutes | Servings: 3)

Ingredients:
- 2 cups of millet flakes
- 1 cup of water
- 2 cups of heavy cream
- 3 tbsp of maple syrup
- 1 tbsp of coconut oil
- 1 tsp of vanilla extract
- 1 cup of almond butter
- 1 tsp of cinnamon

Directions:
1. Toss all of your ingredients in your Instant Pot.
2. Select the pressure cooker setting to MANUAL and cook at HIGH pressure for 2 minutes.
3. Once cooked, wait for 10 minutes and release the pressure naturally.
4. Once done, take out your dish and serve it with some walnuts and pour in some maple syrup as a topping.

Special Vegan Polenta (V, E&S)

(Prep + Cook Time: 30 minutes | Servings: 2)

Ingredients:
- 1½ cups very hot water
- 1 bunch green onion, thinly sliced
- 2 cups veggie stock
- 2 tsp garlic, minced
- 1 tbsp chili powder
- 1 cup corn meal
- ¼ cup cilantro, finely chopped
- Salt and black pepper to taste
- 1 tsp cumin
- 1 tsp oregano
- A pinch of cayenne pepper
- ½ tsp smoked paprika

Directions:
1. Heat up a pan over medium heat. Add a splash of water, the green onion and garlic, stir and sauté for 2 minutes.
2. Transfer this to your Instant Pot, add stock, hot water, corn meal, cilantro, salt, pepper, chili powder, cumin, oregano, paprika and a pinch of cayenne pepper.
3. Close the pot and cook on HIGH pressure for 10 minutes.
4. Release pressure naturally for 10 minutes.
5. Divide amongst plates and serve. Enjoy!

Corn Chowder (V)

(Prep + Cook Time: 35 minutes | Servings: 6)

Ingredients:
- 4 cups veggie broth
- 3 ½ cups of corn
- 1 cup coconut milk
- 3 minced garlic cloves
- 3 big chopped carrots
- 3 chopped Yukon Gold potatoes
- 1 tbsp coconut oil
- 1 diced onion
- flakes
- 1 tbsp potato starch Juice of
- 1 lime
- 1 tsp smoked paprika
- 1 tsp salt
- 1 tsp black pepper
- ½ tsp cumin
- ⅛ tsp crushed red pepper

Directions:
1. Set SAUTE setting and preheat your Instant Pot.

2. Add oil. Cook carrots, onion, corn, and red pepper flakes until the carrots begin to turn clear.
3. Add garlic and cook for 1 minute.
4. Pour in broth, along with potatoes, salt, and pepper. Select MANUAL and cook at HIGH pressure for 6 minutes.
5. When time is up, set CANCEL and let the pressure release naturally for 15 minutes. In a small bowl, mix coconut milk with potato starch until smooth.
6. Add lime juice before pouring into the pot. Turn your cooker back to SAUTE to activate the thickening process.
7. With a hand blender, process until smooth.
8. If you need to use a regular blender, puree the chowder before you add the coconut milk/ starch/ lime mixture.
9. Season to taste if necessary.

Bulgar Pilaf
(Prep + Cook Time: 25 minutes | Servings: 4-6)

Ingredients:
- 1 tbsp olive oil
- 1 tbsp butter
- 3 tbsp onion finely chopped
- 2 tbsp celery finely chopped
- 1 cup medium bulgur wheat uncooked
- 2 cups chicken broth
- ½ tsp table salt
- ½ tsp Italian seasoning

Optional Garnishes:
- Lime wedges
- Chopped cashews
- Fresh chives

Directions:
1. Remove the lid from a 6-quart Instant Pot. Add olive oil and butter to inner pot. Press SAUTÉ. Cook until butter melts.
2. Add onion and celery. Cook, stirring constantly, 2 minutes. Add bulgur, stirring to coat with oil. Stir in chicken broth, salt, and Italian seasoning.
3. Close and lock the lid. Turn the steam release handle to Sealing position. Select the RICE function and cook at LOW pressure for 12 minutes.
4. When time is up, remove lid using quick pressure release. Fluff pilaf with a fork. Garnish, if desired.

Israeli Couscous

(Prep + Cook Time: 10 minutes | Servings: 8)

Ingredients:
- 1 package (16-ounce) Israeli Couscous (I used Harvest Grains Blend)
- 2 ½ cups chicken broth
- 2 tbsp butter
- Salt and pepper to taste

Directions:
1. Set the Instant Pot to SAUTE mode. Add the butter and melt.
2. Add the broth and the couscous blend; stir to combine. Close and lock the lid. Cook on HIGH pressure for 5 minutes.
3. If using a different brand, adjust the cooking time to 1/2 of the recommended time on the package.
4. When the timer beeps, press CANCEL and quick release the pressure.
5. With a fork, fluff the couscous and season to taste with salt and pepper.

Cheesy Grits

(Prep + Cook Time: 35 minutes | Servings: 4)

Ingredients:
- 3 cups water
- 1 ¾ cups cream
- 1 cup stone-ground grits
- 4-ounces cheddar cheese
- 2-3 tbsp butter
- 2 tbsp coconut oil
- 1½ tsp salt

Directions:
1. On the SAUTE setting, heat your oil.
2. Add grits and stir to toast for 3 minutes.
3. Add the rest of the ingredients.
4. Close and seal the lid. Select MANUAL and adjust time to 10 minutes at HIGH pressure.
5. When time is up, press CANCEL and wait 15 minutes. Quick-release any remaining pressure.
6. Serve hot!

Bulgar Pilaf

(Prep + Cook Time: 25 minutes | Servings: 4-6)

Ingredients:

- 1 tbsp olive oil
- 1 tbsp butter
- 3 tbsp onion finely chopped
- 2 tbsp celery finely chopped
- 1 cup medium bulgur wheat uncooked
- 2 cups chicken broth
- ½ tsp table salt
- ½ tsp Italian seasoning

Optional Garnishes:

- Lime wedges
- Chopped cashews
- Fresh chives

Directions:

5. Remove the lid from a 6-quart Instant Pot. Add olive oil and butter to inner pot. Press SAUTÉ. Cook until butter melts.
6. Add onion and celery. Cook, stirring constantly, 2 minutes. Add bulgur, stirring to coat with oil. Stir in chicken broth, salt, and Italian seasoning.
7. Close and lock the lid. Turn the steam release handle to Sealing position. Select the RICE function and cook at LOW pressure for 12 minutes.
8. When time is up, remove lid using quick pressure release. Fluff pilaf with a fork. Garnish, if desired.

Instant Pot Beans and Legumes Dishes

Quick Soaking Dry Beans (V)
(Prep + Cook Time: 15 minutes | Servings: 3)

Ingredients:
- 4 cups water
- 1 cup beans
- 1 tsp salt, optional

Directions:
1. Place water, beans and salt into the Instant Pot
2. Set Instant Pot to MANUAL and cook for 2-8 minutes at HIGH pressure.
3. Once time is up, slow release the pressure from the Instant Pot.
4. Strain, rinse and drain the beans.
5. You are now able to use these beans in any recipe at normal cooking time!

Notes: You can double, triple, or half this recipe as long as you keep the ratio of beans to water at 1:4.

Italian Cannellini Beans and Mint Salad (V)
(Prep + Cook Time: 15 minutes | Servings: 4)

Ingredients:
- 1 cup cannellini beans, soaked overnight
- 4 cups water
- 1 clove garlic smashed
- 1 bay leaf
- 1 sprig mint fresh
- 1 dash vinegar
- Olive oil
- Salt to taste
- Pepper to taste

Directions:
1. Add soaked beans, water, garlic clove and bay leaf to the Instant Pot.
2. Close and lock the lid. Press MANUAL and cook at HIGH pressure for 8 minutes.
3. When time is up, open the Instant Pot using natural release.
4. Strain the beans and mix with mint, vinegar, olive oil, salt and pepper. Enjoy!

Spice Black Bean and Brown Rice Salad (V)

(Prep + Cook Time: 35 minutes | Servings: 8)

Ingredients:

- 1 can (14 oz) black beans, drained and rinsed
- 1 cup brown rice
- 1 avocado, diced
- 1½ cups water
- ¼ cup cilantro, minced
- ¼ tsp salt
- 12 grape tomatoes, quartered

For the spicy dressing:

- 3 tbsp lime juice, fresh squeezed
- 3 tbsp extra-virgin olive oil
- 2 tsp Tabasco or Cholula
- 2 garlic cloves, pressed or minced
- 1/8 tsp salt
- 1 tsp agave nectar

Directions:

1. Combine the rice with the water and salt in the Instant Pot. Close and lock the lid. Select MANUAL and cook at HIGH pressure for 24 minutes.
2. When the timer beeps, release the pressure naturally for 10 minutes. Turn the steam valve to release any remaining pressure. Carefully open the lid.
3. Using a fork, fluff the rice and let cool to room temperature.
4. When cool, refrigerate until ready to use. In a large-sized bowl, stir the brown rice with the black beans, avocado, tomato, and cilantro.
5. In a small-sized bowl, except for the olive oil, whisk the dressing ingredients together. While continuously whisking, slowly pour in the olive oil.
6. Pour the dressing over the brown rice mix and stir to combine.

Refried Beans (V)

(Prep + Cook Time: 55 minutes | Servings: 8)

Ingredients:

- 2 tsp dried oregano
- 2 pounds pinto beans, dried, sorted
- 1-2 tsp sea salt
- 3 tbsp vegetable OR shortening lard
- ½ tsp ground black pepper
- 4 cups vegetable broth
- 1 jalapeno, seeds removed and chopped
- 4 cups water
- 1½ tsp ground cumin
- 4-5 garlic cloves, roughly chopped
- 1 ½ cups onion, chopped

Directions:

1. Put the sorted pinto beans into a large-sized mixing bowl.
2. Fill the bowl with just enough water to cover the beans by several inches. Set aside to soak for 15 minutes.
3. Meanwhile, put the garlic cloves, onion, dried oregano, jalapeno, cumin, lard, vegetable broth, black pepper, and water in the Instant Pot. Stir to mix.
4. Put the soaked beans in a colander to strain. Discard the soaking liquid. Rinse the beans with fresh water.
5. Add the beans into the pot. Stir to mix. It's ok if the lard is still a lump. It will melt as the pot heats up. Cover and lock the lid.
6. Press the BEAN/CHILI button and adjust the time to 45 minutes.
7. When the timer beeps, let the pressure down naturally, about 40 minutes.
8. When the pressure is released, carefully open the lid and season the beans with sea salt to taste.
9. With an immersion blender, blend the beans to desired consistency. It will appear soupy, but as the beans cool, it will thicken.

Easy Aloo Beans (V)

(Prep + Cook Time: 25 minutes | Servings: 3)

Ingredients:

- 1 tbsp oil
- ½ tsp cumin seeds or Jeera
- 4 cloves garlic chopped
- 1 green chili chopped (optional)
- 2 cup green beans chopped in ½ inch pieces
- 1 potato cubed into small pieces

Spices:

- 2 tsp coriander or Dhania powder
- ¼ tsp turmeric or Haldi powder
- ¼ tsp red chili or Mirchi powder
- 1½ tsp salt
- 1 tsp dry mango or Amchur powder, can also be replaced with lemon juice

Directions:

1. Start the Instant Pot in SAUTÉ mode, heat it and then add oil. Heating the pot first helps later, so the veggies don't stick to the bottom. Then add cumin seeds, garlic and green chili.
2. When the cumin seeds start to splutter, add chopped green beans and potatoes. Add spices except dry mango powder and mix properly. Sprinkle water with your hand.
3. Close the instant pot lid, and change setting to MANUAL mode and cook at HIGH pressure for 2 minutes. When the instant pot beeps, let the pressure release naturally.
4. Mix in the dry mango powder or lemon juice. If there is any water, change the setting to SAUTÉ mode and get it to your desired consistency. Aloo Beans are ready to be served with roti or naan.

Notes:

If you like firm beans do a 5 minute NPR, which means release the pressure manually 5 minutes after the instant pot beeps.

Steamed Green Beans (V)

(Prep + Cook Time: 20 minutes | Servings: 4)

Ingredients:
- 1 pound green beans, washed
- 1 cup water
- 2 tbsp fresh parsley, chopped, for garnish

For the dressing:
- 1 pinch ground black pepper
- 1 pinch salt
- 2 tbsp white wine vinegar
- 3 tbsp
- 3 tbsp olive oil
- 3 cloves garlic, sliced

Directions:
1. Pour the water into the Instant Pot and set the steamer basket. Put the green beans in the basket.
2. Press MANUAL, set the pressure to HIGH and the timer to 1 minute.
3. When the timer beeps, turn the valve to Venting to quick release the pressure.
4. Transfer the beans into a serving bowl.
5. Toss with the dressing Ingredients and let stand for 10 minutes.
6. Remove the slices of garlic and then garnish with the parsley. Serve.

Green Bean Casserole

(Prep + Cook Time: 30 minutes | Servings: 4)

Ingredients:
- 16 ounces green beans (I used Frozen)
- 12 ounces mushroom, sliced
- ½ cup French's onions, for garnishing
- 1 onion, small-sized
- 1 cup heavy cream
- 1 cup chicken broth
- 2 tbsp butter

Directions:
1. Press SAUTE key of the Instant Pot.

2. Put the butter in the pot and melt. Add the onion and mushrooms; sauté for about 2-3 minutes or until the onions are soft.
3. Add the green beans, heavy cream, and chicken broth. Press the CANCEL key to stop the SAUTÉ function. Cover and lock the lid.
4. Press the MANUAL key, set the pressure to HIGH, and set the timer for 15 minutes.
5. When the Instant Pot timer beeps, press the CANCEL key and unplug the Instant Pot. Turn the steam valve to quick release the pressure. Unlock and carefully open the lid.
6. While the dish is still hot, add 2 tablespoons cornstarch to thicken. Serve topped with French's onions.

Refried Bean Nachos (V)
(Prep + Cook Time: 35 minutes | Servings: 6)

Ingredients:
- 2 cups pinto beans dried, (rinsed well, but not soaked)
- 1 onion, large-sized, cut into fourths (or diced if you like to leave your beans chunky)
- 4 cloves garlic, peeled and roughly chopped
- 1 jalapeno pepper, seeded (more or less to taste, optional)
- 1 tsp salt
- 1 tsp paprika
- 1 tsp chili powder
- 1 tsp cumin
- ½ tsp black pepper
- ½ cup salsa Cilantro, to taste (optional)
- 3 cups vegetable broth OR water OR combination of the two

Directions:
1. Put all of the ingredients in the Instant Pot and stir well to incorporate. Close and lock the lid. Press MANUAL and cook at HIGH pressure for 28 minutes.
2. When the timer beeps, let the pressure release naturally for 10 minutes. Turn the valve to release any remaining pressure. Carefully open the lid and stir the dish.
3. With a potato masher or in a blender, mash or blend the beans to desired consistency – be careful because the beans are hot.
4. If you prefer your beans thick, drain some of the water before mashing or blending.
5. Serve warm.

Black Bean + Sweet Potato Hash (V)

(Prep + Cook Time: 15 minutes | Servings: 4)

Ingredients:
- 1 cup chopped onion
- 2 cups peeled, chopped sweet potatoes
- 2 tsp hot chili powder
- 1 minced garlic clove
- ⅓ cup veggie broth
- 1 cup cooked and drained black beans
- ¼ cup chopped scallions

Directions:
1. Prep your veggies.
2. Turn your Instant Pot to SAUTE and cook the chopped onion for 2-3 minutes, stirring so it doesn't burn.
3. Add the garlic and stir until fragrant. Add the sweet potatoes and chili powder, and stir.
4. Pour in the broth and give one last stir before locking the lid. Select MANUAL and cook at HIGH pressure for 3 minutes.
5. When time is up, quick-release the pressure carefully.
6. Add the black beans and scallions, and stir to heat everything up.
7. Season with salt and more chili powder if desired.

Bacon-y Black Beans (V)

(Prep + Cook Time: 60 minutes | Servings: 4)

Ingredients:
- 3 strips bacon, cut into halves
- 1 pound dried black beans
- 1 small onion, cut in half
- 6 garlic cloves, crushed
- 1 orange, cut in half
- 2 bay leaves
- 2 quarts chicken stock, low-sodium
- 2 tsp kosher salt, more for seasoning

Directions:
1. Press the SAUTE key. Put the bacon in the pot and sauté for 2 minutes or until crisp and the fat is rendered.
2. Add the rest of the ingredients in the pot. Cover and close the lid.
3. Set the pressure to HIGH and the timer to 40 minutes.

4. When the timer beeps, quick release the pressure – the beans will cooked, but still firm.
5. If you want a creamier and tender beans, let the pressure release naturally. Open the lid.
6. Discard the bay leaves, orange, and onion.
7. Season with salt to taste and serve.

Notes: If you want texture and flavor in your dish, serve with orange zest, green onions, and orange slices.

White Bean Dip with Tomatoes (V)
(Prep + Cook Time: 15 minutes | Servings: 8)

Ingredients:
- 1 can cannellini beans, soaked overnight
- 1 small white onion, peeled and diced
- 1½ tsp minced garlic, divided
- 6 sun-dried tomatoes
- 3 tbsp chopped parsley
- 1¼ cups water
- 1 tsp salt
- 1/8 tsp ground black pepper
- 1 tsp paprika
- 3 tbsp olive oil
- 2 tbsp lemon juice
- 1 tbsp capers

Directions:
1. Drain beans and place in the Instant Pot. Pour in water and add 1 teaspoon garlic, salt, and black pepper.
2. Plug in and switch on the Instant Pot and secure with lid. Then position pressure indicator, select MANUAL and cook at HIGH pressure for 14 minutes.
3. When the timer beeps, switch off the Instant Pot and let pressure release naturally for 10 minutes and then do quick pressure release.
4. In the meantime, place a small non-stick frying pan over medium heat, add oil and let heat.
5. Then add onion and remaining garlic and cook for 3-5 minutes or until onions are nicely golden brown.
6. When the onions are done, set pan aside until required. Then uncover the pot and drain beans, reserve ½ cup of cooking liquid.

7. Let beans cool slightly and then transfer to a food processor and add onion-garlic mixture, paprika, and lemon juice.
8. Pulse until smooth; slowly blend in reserved cooking liquid until dip reaches to desired thickness. Tip mixture into a serving bowl.
9. Dice tomatoes and stir together with capers and parsley.
10. Add this mixture into bean dip and stir until mixed well.
11. Adjust the seasoning and serve immediately.

White Bean with Greens and Lemon (V)
(Prep + Cook Time: 20 minutes | Servings: 4-6)

Ingredients:
- 1 onion, chopped
- 2 tsp olive oil
- 1 cup white beans, soaked overnight
- 2 bay leaves
- ½ - ¾ cup vegetable stock or water
- 3 cloves garlic minced
- 3-4 cups greens kale, chard or spinach (stems removed), chopped
- 1 tsp lemon zested,
- 1-2 tbsp lemon juice
- Salt to taste
- Pepper to taste

Directions:
1. Press SAUTÉ to pre-heat the Instant Pot. When the display says "Hot", add the olive oil and sauté the onion.
2. Turn off SAUTÉ function. Add beans, vegetable stock and bay leaves to the Instant Pot. Select MANUAL and cook at HIGH pressure for 7 minutes.
3. Begin preparing greens while contents of Instant Pot continue to cook (If using kale, remove stems and finely chop).
4. Zest and juice lemon. Peel and mince the garlic.
5. When pressure cooking is complete, allow for natural pressure release. Open up the Instant Pot and add greens, lemon zest, and garlic.
6. Close up the Instant Pot, press MANUAL and cook at HIGH pressure for 1 minute.
7. Quick release pressure, open the lid add lemon juice, and remove bay leaves
8. Serve alone or with your favorite noodles or grain. Enjoy!

Stewed Tomatoes and Green Beans (V)

(Prep + Cook Time: 15 minutes | Servings: 10)

Ingredients:
- 1 pound trimmed green beans
- 2 cups fresh, chopped tomatoes
- 1 crushed garlic clove
- 1 tsp olive oil
- ½ cup water
- Salt to taste

Directions:
1. Set SAUTE setting and preheat your Instant Pot.
2. When warm, add 1 teaspoon of olive oil and garlic.
3. When the garlic has become fragrant and golden, add tomatoes and stir. If the tomatoes are dry, add ½ cup water.
4. Fill the steamer basket with the green beans and sprinkle on salt. Lower into cooker.
5. Close and seal the lid. Select MANUAL and cook at HIGH pressure for 5 minutes.
6. When the timer beeps, turn off cooker and quick-release the pressure.
7. Carefully remove the steamer basket and pour beans into the tomato sauce.
8. If the beans aren't quite tender enough, simmer in sauce for a few minutes. Serve.

Not Re-Fried Beans (V)

(Prep + Cook Time: 25 minutes | Servings: 6-8)

Ingredients:
- 1 tbsp vegetable oil
- 1 onion chopped
- 1 bunch cilantro or parsley, stems and leaves divided and chopped
- ¼ tsp chipotle powder
- ½ tsp cumin
- 2 cups Borlotti beans dried, pinto or kidney beans, soaked
- 2 cups water
- 1 tsp salt

Directions:
1. Press SAUTÉ to pre-heat the Instant Pot. When the display says "Hot", add the oil and sauté the onion, cilantro stems, chipotle and cumin until the onions just begin to soften.

2. Add the beans and water.
3. Close and lock the lid of the Instant Pot. Press MANUAL and cook at HIGH pressure for 10 minutes.
4. When time is up, open the Instant Pot using natural pressure release.
5. Remove a heaping spoonful of beans (for garnish) and sprinkle the rest in the cooker with salt and mash with a potato masher to the desired consistency.
6. Serve sprinkled with whole beans, parsley and an optional dollop of sour cream. Enjoy!

Beans Stew (V)
(Prep + Cook Time: 1 hour 25 minutes | Servings: 8)

Ingredients:
- 1 pound red beans, dry
- Water as needed
- 2 carrots, chopped
- 1 plantain, chopped
- Salt and black pepper to taste
- 1 tomato, chopped
- 2 green onions stalks, chopped
- 1 small yellow onion, diced
- ¼ cup cilantro leaves, chopped
- 2 tbsp vegetable oil

Directions:
1. Put the beans in your Instant Pot, add water to cover, cook on HIGH pressure for 35 minutes and release pressure for 10 minutes naturally.
2. Add plantain, carrots, salt and pepper to the taste, cover Instant Pot again and cook on HIGH pressure for 30 more minutes.
3. Meanwhile, heat up a pan with the vegetable oil over medium high heat, add yellow onion, stir and cook for 2 minutes.
4. Add tomatoes, green onions, some salt and pepper, stir again, cook for 3 minutes more and take off the heat.
5. Release pressure naturally from your Instant Pot, divide cooked beans amongst plates, top with tomatoes and onions mix, sprinkle cilantro at the end and serve right away.
6. Serve.

Tex Mex Pinto Beans

(Prep + Cook Time: 55 minutes | Servings: 6)

Ingredients:
- 20 oz package pinto beans with ham
- 5 cups chicken broth
- 1 clove garlic, diced
- ½ cup Salsa Verde
- 1 packet taco seasoning
- 1 onion
- 1 jalapeno, diced
- ¼ cup cilantro, chopped
- Salt and pepper to taste

Directions:
1. Rinse and sort out the dried beans. Put into the Instant Pot. Pour the broth in the pot.
2. Add garlic, onion, and jalapeno. Stir in the taco seasoning. Close and lock the lid.
3. Select MANUAL and cook at HIGH pressure for 42 minutes.
4. When the timer beeps, let the pressure release naturally for about 15 minutes.
5. Drain excess liquid from the pot. Stir in the Salsa Verde, ham seasoning, and cilantro. Taste and season with salt to taste.
6. Serve in tacos, over rice, or as a side dish.

Great Northern Bean Dip (V)

(Prep + Cook Time: 25 minutes | Servings: 2)

Ingredients:
- ¾ cup soaked overnight Gr. Northern white beans
- ⅓ cup extra virgin olive oil
- 2 garlic cloves
- 3 tbsp lemon juice
- 3 tbsp minced cilantro
- 2 tsp ground cumin
- 1½ tsp chili powder
- Pinch of red pepper flakes
- Salt and pepper to taste
- Water as needed

Directions:
1. Drain the beans before putting them in the Instant Pot. Cover with 1 inch of fresh water. Close and seal the lid.
2. Press MANUAL and cook for 13 minutes at HIGH pressure.
3. When time is up, press CANCEL and wait 10 minutes for a natural pressure release.
4. When the pressure is gone, drain the beans and run under cold water. In a food processor, chop up the garlic.
5. Add the rest of the ingredients (except cilantro) and puree till smooth. Serve with cilantro on top.

Smokey Sweet Black Eyed Peas and Greens (V)
(Prep + Cook Time: 30 minutes | Servings: 4-6)

Ingredients:
- 1 tsp oil, optional
- 1 onion, thinly sliced
- 2-3 cloves garlic, minced
- 1 cup red pepper, diced
- 1 jalapeno or other hot chili, minced
- 1-2 tsp smoked paprika
- 1-2 tsp chili powder mild or medium
- 1½ cups black-eyed peas dried, soaked overnight and drained
- 4 dates chopped fine
- 1 cup water or vegetable broth
- 1 can Fire Roasted Tomatoes with green chilies, 15 ounce can
- 2 cups greens chopped, kale, collards or Swiss chard
- Salt to taste

Directions:
1. Set your Instant Pot to SAUTÉ. Dry sauté the onion for a few minutes, adding some of the water if the onion starts to stick.
2. Add the garlic and peppers and sauté for another minute. Add the smoked paprika and chili powder along with the peas and dates. Stir to coat them with the spices.
3. Add the water, stirring well to be sure that nothing is stuck to the bottom of the pot.
4. Close and lock the lid. Select MANUAL and cook at HIGH pressure for 3 minutes. Let the pressure come down naturally when time is up.
5. Once pressure has released, carefully open the lid, tilting it away from you. Add the tomatoes and greens and lock the lid on the pressure cooker for 5 minutes.
6. Open the Instant Pot. Taste and adjust seasonings. Add salt to taste. Enjoy!

Chili Con Carne

(Prep + Cook Time: 30 minutes | Servings: 6)

Ingredients:

- 1 can (28 ounce) ground and peeled tomatoes
- 1 can (14 ounce) kidney beans, rinsed and drained
- 1 can (14 ounce) black beans, rinsed and drained
- 1½ pounds ground beef
- 1½ tsp ground cumin
- 1½ tsp salt
- 1½ cups onion, large diced
- 1 tbsp chili powder
- 1 tbsp Worcestershire Sauce
- 1 tsp dry oregano
- ½ cup fresh water
- ½ cup sweet red bell pepper, large dice
- ½ tsp freshly ground black pepper
- 1-2 jalapeños, medium-sized, stems and seeds removed, finely diced
- 2 tbsp garlic, minced
- 3 tbsp extra-virgin olive oil

Directions:

1. Press the SAUTE button. Let the Instant Pot heat. Put the oil in the pot.
2. Add the ground beef, sauté, breaking up using a wooden spoon, until the beef is slightly brown. Remove excess fat.
3. Add the onions, jalapenos, and bell pepper. Sauté for 3 minutes.
4. Add the garlic, chili powder, cumin, oregano, salt, and pepper. Sauté for 1 minute.
5. Add the beans, tomatoes, water, and Worcestershire sauce. Stir to combine. Close and lock the lid.
6. Select MANUAL and cook at HIGH pressure for 10 minutes.
7. When the timer beeps, let the pressure release for 10 minutes.
8. Turn the steam valve to release remaining pressure.
9. Serve immediately or simmer on less SAUTÉ for a thicker chili.

Delightful Rainbow Beans

(Prep + Cook Time: 35 minutes | Servings: 6)

Ingredients:

- 1 cup chicken stock
- 1 cup water
- 1 cup black beans, cooked
- ½ cup red beans, cooked
- ½ cup white beans, cooked
- 1 yellow sweet pepper
- 1 red sweet pepper
- 1 red onion
- 3 tbsp tomato paste
- 1 tbsp salt
- 1 tsp turmeric
- 3 tbsp sour cream

Directions:

1. Place the chicken stock and water in the Instant Pot. Add the black beans, red beans, and white beans.
2. Remove the seeds from the sweet yellow pepper and red pepper.
3. Peel the onion. Chop the vegetables into the medium pieces.
4. Add the chopped vegetables in the Instant Pot. After this, sprinkle the mixture with the tomato paste, salt, turmeric, and sour cream.
5. Mix up it carefully and close the lid.
6. Set the STEW mode and cook the dish for 20 minutes.
7. When the time is over – chill the dish little.
8. Then transfer it to the serving bowls.
9. Serve the dish immediately. Enjoy!

Stewed Chickpeas (V)

(Prep + Cook Time: 45 minutes | Servings: 4)

Ingredients:

- 1 ½ tbsp smoked paprika
- 1 jar (680 grams or 24 ounces) tomatoes, strained
- ½ tsp ground cumin
- ½ tsp rounded sea salt
- 1/8-1/4 tsp ground allspice
- 2 cans chickpeas (14 or 15 ounces each rinsed and drained)
- 2 large-sized or
- 3 small-sized-medium-sized onions, chopped (about 3 - 3½ cups)
- 2/3 cup dates, pitted, chopped
- 2-3 tbsp water, more as needed

Directions:

1. Press the SAUTE key of the Instant Pot.
2. Add the onions, cumin, paprika, salt, and allspice.
3. Cook for about 6 to7 minutes, occasionally stirring, adding more water if sticking.
4. Add the tomatoes, chickpeas, and dates, and stir until mixed through. Press the CANCEL key to stop the sauté function. Cover and lock the lid.
5. Press the MANUAL key, set the pressure to HIGH, and set the timer for 20 minutes.
6. When the Instant Pot timer beeps, press the CANCEL key. Turn the steam valve to quick release the pressure.
7. Alternatively, you can naturally release the pressure. Unlock and carefully open the lid.
8. Stir and mix through and, if desired, add seasoning.
9. Serve over cooked whole-grain, such with quinoa, millet, and brown rice.
10. You can also serve over mashed potatoes, roasted squash, and steamed kale.

Notes: Use jarred strained tomatoes – it gives a better texture than crushed tomatoes and lets the base cook down to a more uniform sauce.

Chickpea Curry (V)

(Prep + Cook Time: 20 minutes | Servings: 4-6)

Ingredients:

- 2 tbsp extra-virgin olive oil
- 1 onion diced
- 1 small green bell pepper diced
- 2 cloves garlic minced
- 1 tbsp curry powder
- 2 cans chickpeas rinsed and drained, 15-ounce cans
- 1 can tomatoes crushed or diced, with juice, 14.5-ounce
- 1 cup corn frozen
- 1 cup okra frozen and sliced
- 1 packed cup kale chopped
- 1 cup vegetable broth
- 1 tbsp sugar or honey
- 1 tsp kosher salt
- ¼ tsp black pepper freshly ground
- 1 lime juiced
- 2 tbsp Cilantro leaves

Directions:

1. Preheat the Instant Pot by selecting SAUTÉ. Once hot, add the oil and onion and stir.
2. Cook for 4 minutes until the onion is translucent and starting to brown. Add the bell pepper and garlic and cook for 2 minutes more.
3. Add the curry powder and stir. Cook for 30 seconds before adding the chickpeas, tomatoes with juice, corn, okra, kale, broth, and sugar or honey.
4. Stir and secure the lid. Select MANUAL and cook at HIGH pressure for 5 minutes. Once cooking is complete, use a natural release.
5. Add the salt, pepper, and lime juice. Stir and taste, adding more salt as needed.
6. Top with cilantro leaves and serve. Enjoy!

Falafel

(Prep + Cook Time: 30 minutes | Servings: 6)

Ingredients:

- 1 cup chickpea, cooked
- 1 tsp cumin
- ½ tsp coriander
- 1 tbsp sesame seeds
- 1 tsp salt
- ½ cup parsley
- 1 tsp paprika
- 1 tsp chili flakes
- 3 garlic cloves
- 1 tsp garlic powder
- 4 oz shallots
- 3 tbsp tahini
- ½ cup olive oil
- 2 tsp water
- 1 tbsp lemon juice
- ½ tsp sea salt

Directions:

1. Place the chickpea, cumin, coriander, salt, parsley, paprika, chili flakes, garlic powder, and water in the blender.
2. Blend the mixture carefully until you get smooth mass.
3. Slice the garlic cloves and shallot and add the shallot to the chickpea mixture.
4. Continue to blend it for 1 minute more. Combine the sesame seeds and sea salt together in the mixing bowl and stir the mixture.
5. Make the medium balls from the chickpea mixture and coat them with the sesame mixture.
6. Pour the olive oil in the Instant Pot and SAUTE it until the oil is boiled.
7. Then toss the falafel into the hot oil and cook them for 1 minute or until they get a crust.
8. Then transfer the cooked falafel into the paper towels and remove the excess oil.
9. Combine the tahini, sliced garlic, and lemon juice together.
10. Whisk the mixture carefully until you get homogenous mass.
11. Sprinkle the cooked falafel with the tahini sauce. Enjoy!

Classic Hummus (V)

(Prep + Cook Time: 35 minutes | Servings: 6)

Ingredients:

- 6 cups water
- 1 cup soaked chickpeas
- 3-4 crushed garlic cloves
- 1 bay leaf
- ¼ cup chopped parsley
- 2 tbsp tahini
- 1 juiced lemon
- ½ tsp salt
- ¼ tsp cumin
- Dash of paprika

Directions:

1. Soak your chickpeas overnight in water.
2. When you're ready to make the hummus, rinse them and put them in the Instant Pot.
3. Pour 6 cups of water. Add the bay leaf and garlic cloves.
4. Close and seal the lid. Select MANUAL and cook for 18 minutes at HIGH pressure.
5. When the beeper goes off, hit CANCEL and wait for the pressure to come down on its own.
6. When the cooker is safe to open, drain the chickpeas, but save 1 cup of cooking liquid.
7. Remove the bay leaf before pureeing the chickpeas.
8. Add tahini, lemon juice, cumin, and ½ cup of cooking liquid to start.
9. Keep pureeing, and if the mixture isn't creamy enough, keep adding ½ cup of liquid at a time.
10. When it's the right level of creaminess, salt, and puree once more.
11. Serve with a sprinkle of paprika and fresh chopped parsley!

Creole Peas

(Prep + Cook Time: 25 minutes | Servings: 4)

Ingredients:

- 2 cups fresh peas, shelled, rinsed
- 2 slices bacon, chopped into ½ inch pieces
- 1 ½ tsp Creole seasoning
- 1 cup tomatoes, oven-roasted (or canned tomatoes)
- 1 small onion, chopped (about 1/3 cup)
- ½ tsp granulated garlic
- ½ tsp kosher salt
- ½ tsp Spanish paprika, hot, smoked
- 2 tsp Worcestershire sauce
- ¾ cup chicken broth
- Fresh ground pepper to taste
- Olive oil or your choice of cooking oil

Directions:

1. Set the Instant Pot to SAUTE. Add a bit of olive oil in the pot.
2. Add bacon and cook until the edges start to crisp and fat is rendered.
3. Add the onion and sauté until soft. Pour in the broth.
4. Add the tomatoes, peas, sauce and the seasoning. Stir well and bring to boil. Turn off the SAUTÉ function. Close and lock the lid.
5. Press MANUAL and cook at HIGH pressure for 5 minutes.
6. When the timer beeps, let the pressure release naturally for 15 minutes. Open the pot and stir in the peas.
7. If needed, adjust the seasoning. Serve.

Notes: If you want a hot dish, add a bit of hot sauce or cayenne. You can even add in a few okra pods before closing the lid. You can even use a variety of peas, such as pink-eyed, black-eyed, field peas, purple hulls, and Crowder peas.

Ham and Peas (E&S)

(Prep + Cook Time: 55 minutes | Servings: 10)

Ingredients:
- 5 ounces ham, diced
- 1 pound dried peas, use black-eyed (rinse, but do not pre-soak)
- 6 ½ cups stock (vegetable, chicken, or ham OR 6½ cups water mixed with 2 tbsp chicken bouillon).

Directions:
1. Put all of the ingredients into the pot. Cover and lock the lid. Press the MANUAL key, set the pressure to HIGH, and set the timer to 30 minutes.
2. When the Instant Pot timer beeps, press the CANCEL key and unplug the Instant Pot. Let the pressure release naturally for 10-15 minutes or until the valve drops. Release remaining pressure. Unlock and carefully open the lid.
3. Taste and season with salt and pepper as needed.

Notes: The cooking time indicated for this dish cooked the peas well-done and soft, with a couple falling apart. If you want the peas to be more firm, then reduce the cooking time for a couple of mins.

Lentil Sloppy Joe's (V)

(Prep + Cook Time: 55 minutes | Servings: 6)

Ingredients:
- 3 cups veggie broth
- 2 cups green lentils
- 1 chopped yellow onion
- 1 stemmed and chopped red bell pepper
- One, 14-ounce can of crushed tomatoes
- 2 tbsp soy sauce
- 1 tbsp Dijon mustard
- 1 tbsp olive oil
- 1 tbsp dark brown sugar
- 1 tsp black pepper

Directions:
1. Turn your Instant Pot to SAUTE and add oil. Cook the pepper and onion until they've turned softened.
2. Pour in broth before adding soy sauce, lentils, mustard, brown sugar, tomatoes, and pepper. Stir until the sugar has dissolved. Close and seal the lid.
3. Select MANUAL and cook at HIGH pressure for 27 minutes.
4. When time is up, press CANCEL and wait for 15 minutes the pressure to come down on its own.
5. Stir before serving on hamburger buns.

Lentils and Farro (V, E&S)

(Prep + Cook Time: 20 minutes | Servings: 2)

Ingredients:

Lentils:

- ½ cup lentils black, brown, or green
- 1¼ cup water or vegetable stock
- ½ tsp dried oregano
- ½ tsp medium chili powder
- ½ tsp dried basil
- ½ tsp salt
- ¼ tsp cumin powder
- ¼ tsp smoked paprika
- ¼ tsp onion powder
- ¼ tsp garlic powder
- ¼ tsp black pepper

Farro:

- ½ cup Farro
- 1 cup water
- ½ tsp Italian herbs
- ½ tsp onion powder
- ½ tsp salt

Directions:

1. Add lentils ingredients to 3-quart inner pot. Place trivet on top of lentils.
2. Add farro ingredients to small stainless steel inner bowl. Place bowl on top of trivet.
3. Secure lid in place. Turn valve to Sealing. Press MANUAL and cook at HIGH pressure for 12 minutes.
4. Once pressure cooking is complete, use a natural release. This will take about 15 minutes.
5. Serve with your favorite veggies and sauce.

Lentil Tacos (V, E&S)

(Prep + Cook Time: 25 minutes | Servings: 8)

Ingredients:

- 2 cups dry brown lentils
- 4 cups water
- 4 oz tomato sauce
- ½ tsp cumin
- 1 tsp salt
- 1 tsp onion powder
- 1 tsp garlic powder
- 1 tsp chili powder

Directions:

1. Put all of the ingredients in the Instant Pot. Stir to mix.
2. Close and lock the lid. Select MANUAL and cook at HIGH pressure for 15 minutes.
3. When the timer beeps, turn off the pot. Let the pressure release naturally. Carefully open the lid.
4. Let sit for a few minutes before serving.
5. This dish is great as part of a taco or burrito salad. It's great with soft or crunchy tacos.

Lentil and Wild Rice Pilaf (V)

(Prep + Cook Time: 50 minutes | Servings: 4)

Ingredients:

For the lentils and rice:

- (soak for 30 minutes before cooking):
- ¼ cup brown rice
- ¼ cup black/ wild rice
- ½ cup black or green lentils

For the vegetables:

- 1 cup mushrooms, sliced
- 1 stalk celery, finely chopped
- ½ onion, medium-sized, finely chopped
- 3 cloves garlic, pressed/ minced

65

For the spices:
- 1 bay leaf
- 1 tbsp Italian seasoning blend (no-salt added)
- 1 tsp dried coriander
- 1 tsp fennel seeds
- ½ tsp ground black pepper
- ¼ tsp red pepper flakes
- 2 cups vegetable broth

Directions:
1. Combine the rice and the lentils in a medium-sized bowl. Let soak for 30 minutes.
2. Drain and then rinse thoroughly. Set the Instant Pot to SAUTE.
3. Put the veggies in the inner pot and sauté for 3-5 minutes. If needed, add a bit of water to prevent the veggies from burning.
4. Add the rice and lentils, vegetable broth, and spices into the pot. Close and lock the lid. Press MANUAL, set the pressure to HIGH, and set the timer to 9 minutes.
5. When the timer beeps, let the pressure release naturally. Open the lid. Stir in the pilaf.
6. If liquid remains, let sit for 5 minutes uncovered to allow the pilaf to absorb more liquid.
7. Serve this dish with steamed or fresh veggies.

Notes: If you don't like fennel seeds, then use 1 tablespoon of your preferred dried herbs, such as thyme, rosemary, parsley, basil, or oregano. If you don't have black or wild rice on hand, you can use all brown rice.

Lentil Bisque (V)

(Prep + Cook Time: 35 minutes | Servings: 4)

Ingredients:

- 1 cup dry lentils, rinsed
- 2 tbsp olive oil
- 2 tbsp shallots, diced
- 2 tsp flour
- 2 tbsp dry white wine
- 1 cup apple, peeled and diced
- 1 tsp lemon zest
- 1 tsp lemon juice
- ½ tsp curry powder
- ½ tsp cinnamon
- 1 tsp salt
- 1 tsp coarse ground black pepper
- 1 cup vegetable juice
- 3 cups vegetable stock
- ½ cup coconut milk
- Fresh parsley for serving

Directions:

1. Add the olive oil to the pressure cooker and turn on the SAUTE setting.
2. Add in the shallots and sauté for 2 minutes.
3. Sprinkle the shallots with flour and stir.
4. Add the white wine and let reduce for 2 minutes.
5. Add in the lentils and apples. Season with the lemon zest, lemon juice, curry powder, cinnamon, salt and black pepper.
6. Combine the vegetable juice and vegetable stock and add them to the pressure cooker.
7. Close and lock the lid. Select MANUAL and cook at HIGH pressure for 15-20 minutes. Use a quick release
8. Take one half of the soup mixture and place it in a blender with the coconut milk.
9. Blend until smooth.
10. Add the blender mixture back into the rest of the soup.
11. Serve immediately, garnished with fresh parsley, if desired.

Three Lentil Chili (V)

(Prep + Cook Time: 35 minutes | Servings: 6)

Ingredients:
- 1 cup split red lentils, rinsed
- 2/3 cup brown lentils, rinsed
- 1 cup French green lentils, rinsed
- 1 medium-sized white onion, peeled and chopped
- 2 tsp minced garlic
- 2 medium-sized green bell peppers, seeded and chopped
- 28 ounce diced tomatoes
- 2 tbsp olive oil
- 1 tbsp salt
- ½ tsp ground black pepper
- 1 tsp red chili powder
- 1 tbsp ground cumin
- 7 cups vegetable stock

Directions:
1. Plug in and switch on a 6-quarts Instant Pot, select SAUTE option and add oil.
2. When the oil is heated, add onion and pepper and cook for 3-5 minutes or until onion is tender.
3. Then add garlic and sauté for 1 minute or until fragrant.
4. Add remaining ingredients into the pot, press CANCEL, select MULTIGRAIN option, secure pot with lid and then position pressure indicator.
5. When the timer beeps, switch off the Instant Pot and let pressure release naturally for 10 minutes and then do quick pressure release.
6. Then uncover the pot, stir and serve immediately.

Red Lentil Chili (V, E&S)

(Prep + Cook Time: 50 minutes | Servings: 6)

Ingredients:
- 2 red peppers, diced
- 1 onion, diced
- 5 garlic cloves, minced
- 2 cups red lentils
- 7 cups water
- 1 tbsp chili powder
- 1 tbsp paprika
- 1 tsp cayenne
- ¼ cup brown sugar
- 2 tbsp apple cider vinegar
- 1 can (6oz) tomato paste
- 1 can (14oz) diced tomatoes

Directions:

1. Prepare and place all of your ingredients into the Instant Pot.
2. Close and lock the lid. Select MANUAL and cook at HIGH pressure for 17 minutes.
3. Once the time is complete, let it naturally release for 15 minutes. Serve and enjoy!

Mixed Lentils and Vegetables Khichdi
(Prep + Cook Time: 45 minutes | Servings: 6)

Ingredients:

- 2 tbsp ghee
- 1 tsp cumin seeds
- 1 tbsp Ginger
- 1 carrot peeled and sliced
- ¼ cup green beans, chopped
- ¼ cup green peas, frozen
- 1 red potato, cubed
- 1 tomato, diced
- 1 cup cauliflower, chopped
- 1 cup cabbage, chopped
- 1 cup spinach, chopped
- ½ tsp turmeric
- 2 tsp red chili powder mild
- 2 tsp salt
- 1 cup white rice
- 1 cup mixed lentils (moong, masoor, toor and chana daal)
- 6 cups water
- ¼ cup cilantro chopped, for garnish

Directions:

1. Turn Instant Pot to SAUTÉ Mode. Once the 'Hot' sign displays, add ghee, cumin seeds and ginger.
2. Cook for 30 seconds. Add all the vegetables (carrots, beans, peas, tomato, potato, cauliflower, cabbage and spinach). Mix well.
3. Add turmeric, red chili powder and salt. Mix well. Add rice and mixed lentils.
4. Add 6 cups of water. Give everything a quick stir and close the Instant Pot lid with pressure valve to Sealing.
5. Press the RICE button and cook for 12 minutes. Once pressure cooking is complete, use a natural release.
6. Open the lid, garnish with cilantro. Serve hot with roasted papad and pickle. Enjoy!

Barbecue Lentils over Baked Potato Wedges (V)

(Prep + Cook Time: 30 minutes | Servings: 4)

Ingredients:
- 3 cups water
- 1 cup brown lentils dry, rinsed and drained
- 1 small onion chopped
- ½ cup ketchup organic preferred
- 2 tsp molasses
- 2 tsp liquid smoke
- 2 large potatoes baked, cut into 6 wedges each

Directions:
1. Place the water, lentils, and onion in the Instant Pot.
2. Cover the lid, press MANUAL and cook at HIGH pressure for 10 minutes.
3. When cooking time is finished, press CANCEL. Let pressure release naturally for 10 minutes and then do quick pressure release.
4. Add ketchup, molasses and liquid smoke to the lentils.
5. Press SAUTÉ and decrease heat to Less. Simmer until barbecue sauce begins to thicken, about 5 minutes.
6. Press CANCEL once to stop SAUTÉ function. Serve barbecue lentils over baked potato wedges. Enjoy!

Apple and Spiced Lentils (V)

(Prep + Cook Time: 30 minutes | Servings: 4)

Ingredients:
- 1 cup red lentils, soaked for 30 minutes
- 2 medium-sized apples, cored
- 1 tbsp ground cinnamon
- 1 tsp turmeric powder
- ¼ tsp ground cinnamon
- 1 tsp ground cloves
- 1 tbsp maple syrup
- 1 cup coconut milk, divided
- 3 cups red rooibos tea, brewed

Directions:

1. Drain lentils and place in a 6-quarts Instant Pot along with remaining ingredients except for maple syrup and milk.
2. Stir until combine, then plug in and switch on the Instant Pot.
3. Close and lock the lid. Select MANUAL and cook at HIGH pressure for 10 minutes.
4. When the timer beeps, switch off the Instant Pot and let pressure release naturally for 10 minutes and then do quick pressure release.
5. Then uncover the pot, stir until well mixed and then divide equally among serving bowl.
6. Serve with a generous amount of milk and maple syrup.

Mung Bean Dahl (V, E&S)

(Prep + Cook Time: 35 minutes | Servings: 2-4)

Ingredients:

- ½ cup mung beans dry
- 2 cups vegetable stock
- 2 tsp curry powder
- ½ tsp salt
- ½ tsp onion powder
- ¼ tsp garlic powder
- ¼ tsp black pepper

Directions:

1. Add mung beans, stock, curry powder, salt, onion, and garlic to the Instant Pot.
2. Secure lid in place, turn the valve to sealing. Press MANUAL and cook at HIGH pressure for 25 minutes.
3. When time is up, use a natural pressure release for 10 minutes. Quick release the remaining pressure after 10 minutes.
4. With a fork, smash about 1/4 to 1/3 of the beans and stir to thicken the sauce.
5. Add spinach, stir and allow to cook in the residual heat. Enjoy!

Delicious Dhal (V)

(Prep + Cook Time: 25 minutes | Servings: 10)

Ingredients:

- 1 cup green lentils
- 6 cups hot water
- 1½ cups channa dal
- 2 tbsp ginger, minced
- Salt and black pepper to taste
- 8 medium yellow onions, minced
- 1½ tsp turmeric
- 10 garlic cloves, minced
- 3 tsp cumin
- 2 tsp chili powder
- 2 tsp garam masala
- 1 tbsp sultana
- 1 tbsp extra virgin olive oil
- 15 oz potatoes, cut in small chunks
- 15 oz sweet potatoes, chopped

Directions:

1. Heat up a pan with the oil over medium high heat, add all garlic and onions, stir, cook for 3-4 minutes and then transfer to your Instant Pot.
2. Add water, channa dal, lentils, ginger, turmeric, cumin, potatoes and sweet potatoes, stir and cook on HIGH pressure for 10 minutes.
3. Release pressure naturally, leave aside for 10 minutes, add salt and pepper to the taste, garam masala, chili powder and sultana, stir well and divide amongst plates.
4. Serve right away and enjoy.

Perfect Basmati Rice (V, E&S)

(Prep + Cook Time: 15 minutes | Servings: 4)

Ingredients:
- 1 cup white basmati rice
- 1¼ cups water
- Salt to taste

Directions:
1. Put the rice in a colander.
2. Rinse until the water is clear.
3. Transfer into the Instant Pot and then add the water.
4. Set the pot to MANUAL, set the pressure to LOW, and the timer to 8 minutes.
5. When the timer beeps, quick release the pressure.
6. Fluff the rice using a fork and serve.

Instant Pot Brown Rice (V, E&S)

(Prep + Cook Time: 30 minutes | Servings: 6)

Ingredients:
- 2 cups brown rice
- ½ tsp of sea salt
- 2 ½ cups any kind vegetable broth or water

Directions:
1. Put the rice into the Instant Pot.
2. Pour in the broth or water and salt. Close and lock the lid. Press the MANUAL and set the pressure to HIGH and the timer to 22 minutes.
3. When the timer beeps, naturally release the pressure for 10 minutes.
4. Carefully open the lid. Serve.

Brown Rice Medley (V, E&S)

(Prep + Cook Time: 35 minutes | Servings: 4)

Ingredients:
- 3-4 tbsp red, wild or black rice
- ¾ cup (or more) short grain brown rice
- 1½ cups water
- 3/8-1/2 tsp sea salt, optional

Directions:
1. Put as much as 3-4 tablespoons of red, wild, or black rice or use all three kinds in 1-cup measuring cup.
2. Add brown rice to make 1 cup total of rice. Put the rice in a strainer and wash. Put the rice in the Instant Pot.
3. Add 1½ cups water in the pot. If desired, add salt.
4. Stir and then check the sides of the pot to make sure the rice is pushed down into the water. Close and lock the lid. Press MULTIGRAIN and set the time to 23 minutes.
5. When the timer beeps, let the pressure release naturally for 5 minutes, then turn the steam valve and release the pressure slowly.
6. If you have time, let the pressure release naturally for 15 minutes. Stir and serve.

Brown Rice-Stuffed Cabbage Rolls with Pine Nuts and Currants (V)

(Prep + Cook Time: 35 minutes | Servings: 4)

Ingredients:
- 1 large head green cabbage cored
- 1 tbsp olive oil
- 1½ cups onion finely chopped
- 3 cups brown rice cooked
- 3 ounces feta cheese crumbled, about ¾ cup
- ½ cup currants dried
- 2 tbsp pine nuts toasted
- 2 tbsp parsley fresh chopped
- ¼ tsp salt
- ½ tsp black pepper freshly ground
- ½ cup apple juice
- 1 tbsp cider vinegar
- 1 can crushed tomatoes undrained, 14.5-ounce
- Parsley additional, chopped and fresh, optional

Directions:
1. Steam cabbage head 8 minutes; cool slightly. Remove 16 leaves from cabbage head; discard remaining cabbage. Cut off raised portion of the center vein of each cabbage leaf (do not cut out vein); set trimmed cabbage leaves aside.
2. Heat oil in a large nonstick skillet over medium heat; swirl to coat. Add onion; cover and cook 6 minutes or until tender.
3. Remove from heat; stir in brown rice, add feta cheese, currants dried, pine nuts and parsley. Stir in 1/4 teaspoon of the salt and 1/8 teaspoon of the pepper.
4. Place cabbage leaves on a flat surface; place about 1/3 cup rice mixture into center of each cabbage leaf. Fold in edges of leaves over rice mixture; roll up. Arrange cabbage rolls in bottom of the inner pot of a 6-quart Instant Pot.
5. Combine the remaining 1/4 teaspoon salt, remaining 1/8 teaspoon pepper, apple juice, vinegar, and tomatoes; pour evenly over cabbage rolls.
6. Close and lock the lid of the Instant Pot. Turn the steam release handle to Venting position. Press SLOW cook, and select 2 hours cook time.
7. Serve sprinkled with parsley, if desired. Enjoy!

Portuguese Tomato Rice with Shrimp
(Prep + Cook Time: 35 minutes | Servings: 4)

Ingredients:
- 2 tbsp olive oil
- 1 large onion finely chopped
- 2 tbsp tomato paste
- 4 cloves garlic finely chopped
- 2 bay leaves
- 1½ cups Arborio rice
- 2 ¾ cups passata or thin tomato puree (if the passata is very thick use 2¼ cups passata and 1¼ cups of stock)
- ¾ cup chicken stock
- 2 tsp paprika
- Kosher salt to taste
- Black pepper to taste
- 1 cup tomato diced, heaping cup
- 3-4 tbsp butter
- 1 handful parsley freshly chopped
- 24 raw shrimp shelled and deveined, optional

Directions:
1. Hit the SAUTÉ button on your Instant Pot and when says it's 'Hot', add in the oil and the onions and sauté for 3 or 4 minutes, until the onions are nice and soft.
2. Add in the tomato paste and cook for another couple of minutes, stirring constantly so the tomato paste doesn't burn.
3. Now add the garlic and bay leaves, stir another minute before adding in the rice.
4. Pour in the stock, the tomatoes, paprika and good pinch of kosher salt (start with 1 teaspoon and taste) and a few grinds of black pepper. Lastly, stir in the chopped tomatoes
5. Close up the lid, seal the vent and program your Instant Pot to cook for 6 minutes at HIGH pressure.
6. When the time is up, quick release the pressure, open the lid and give the rice a good stir. It will be quite soupy.
7. If you are adding shrimp, add them now, stir them into the rice and add the lid back on and let the rice sit for 3 or 4 minutes to cook them. If you are NOT adding shrimp, you can leave the lid off but continue to stir the rice occasionally for another minute or so to thicken the rice up a bit.
8. Just before serving, stir in the butter and parsley. Enjoy!

Rice and Lentils (V)

(Prep + Cook Time: 55 minutes | Servings: 4)

Ingredients:

For the sauté:

- 1 tbsp oil, OR dry sauté (or add a little water/vegetable broth)
- ½ cup onion, chopped
- 2 cloves garlic, minced

For the porridge:

- 1½ cups brown rice
- 1 cup rutabaga, peeled and diced, OR potato OR turnip
- 1 cup brown lentils
- 1 tbsp dried marjoram (or thyme)
- 2-inch sprig fresh rosemary
- 3½ cups water
- Salt and pepper to taste

Directions:

1. Press the SAUTÉ key of the Instant Pot and select the Normal option.
2. Put the oil/ broth in the pot and, if using oil, heat. When the oil is hot, add the onion and sauté for 5 minutes or until transparent.
3. Add the garlic and sauté for 1 minute.
4. Add the lentils, brown rice, rutabaga, marjoram, rosemary, and pour in the water into the pot and stir to combine. Press the CANCEL key to stop the SAUTÉ function.
5. Press the MANUAL key, set the pressure to HIGH, and set the timer for 23 minutes.
6. When the Instant Pot timer beeps, press the CANCEL key. Let the pressure release naturally for 10-15 minutes or until the valve drops. Release remaining pressure. Unlock and carefully open the lid.
7. Taste and, if needed, season with pepper and salt to taste.
8. If needed, add more ground rosemary and more marjoram.

Rice &Chickpea Stew (V)

(Prep + Cook Time: 35 minutes | Servings: 6)

Ingredients:

- 3 medium-sized onions, peeled and sliced
- 1 pound sweet potato, peeled and diced
- 6 oz brown basmati rice, rinsed
- 30 oz cooked chickpeas
- ¼ tsp salt
- ¼ tsp ground black pepper
- 2 tsp ground cumin
- 2 tsp ground coriander
- 8 fluid oz orange juice
- 1 tbsp olive oil
- 4 cups vegetable broth
- 4 oz chopped cilantro

Directions:

1. Plug in and switch on a 6-quarts Instant Pot, select SAUTE option, add oil and onion and let cook for 8-10 minutes or until browned.
2. Stir in coriander and cumin and continue cooking for 15 seconds or until fragrant.
3. Add remaining ingredients into the pot except for black pepper and cilantro and stir until just mixed.
4. Press CANCEL and secure pot with lid. Then position pressure indicator, select MANUAL option and adjust cooking time on timer pad to 5 minutes and let cook on HIGH pressure.
5. Instant Pot will take 10 minutes to build pressure before cooking timer starts.
6. When the timer beeps, switch off the Instant Pot and let pressure release naturally for 10 minutes and then do quick pressure release.
7. Then uncover the pot and stir in pepper until mixed.
8. Garnish with cilantro and serve.

Mexican Rice (V, E&S)

(Prep + Cook Time: 25 minutes | Servings: 4)

Ingredients:
- 1 tbsp olive oil
- ¼ cup onion, diced
- 2 cups long grain white rice
- 2⅓ cups chicken stock
- 1 cup salsa
- 1 tsp salt

Directions:
1. Set the Instant Pot to SAUTÉ setting.
2. Sauté olive oil and onion until translucent about 1 to 2 minutes
3. Add in rice and sauté for 2 to 3 minutes.
4. Stir in chicken stock, salsa, and salt into the rice.
5. Close and lock the lid. Select MANUAL and cook at HIGH pressure for 10 minutes.
6. Once the time is up, let the pressure release naturally.
7. Fluff the rice with a fork and serve.

Spanish Rice (E&S)

Ingredients:
- 2 tbsp butter
- 2 cups long grain rice
- 1½ cups chicken stock or water
- 8 oz tomato sauce
- 1 tsp cumin
- 1 tsp chili powder
- ½ tsp garlic powder
- ½ tsp onion powder
- ½ tsp salt

Directions:
1. Set the Instant Pot to SAUTÉ setting.
2. Sauté butter and dry rice together for 4 minutes.
3. Stir in chicken stock, tomato sauce, cumin, chili powder, garlic powder and onion powder into the rice.
4. Close and lock the lid. Select MANUAL and cook at HIGH pressure for 10 minutes.
5. Once the time is up, let the pressure release naturally.
6. Fluff the rice with a fork and serve.

Delicious Rice and Artichokes

(Prep + Cook Time: 30 minutes | Servings: 4)

Ingredients:
- 6 ounces graham crackers, crumbled
- 6 ounces arborico rice
- 16 ounces vegan cream cheese, soft
- 14 ounces artichoke hearts, chopped
- 1½ tbsp vegan cheese, grated
- 8 ounces veggie stock
- 8 ounces water
- 2 tbsp white wine
- Salt and black pepper to taste
- 1 tbsp vegetable oil
- 2 garlic cloves, minced
- 1 ½ tbsp thyme, finely chopped

Directions:
1. Heat up a pan with the oil over medium high heat, add rice and garlic, stir and cook for 3 minutes.
2. Transfer everything to your Instant Pot, add stock, wine, water, cover and cook on HIGH pressure for 10 minutes.
3. Release pressure naturally for 5 minutes.
4. Add crackers, add artichokes, vegan cheese, vegan cream cheese, salt, pepper and thyme, stir well, divide into bowls and serve right away.
5. Enjoy!

Multi-Grain Rice Millet Blend (V, E&S)

(Prep + Cook Time: 15 minutes | Servings: 8)

Ingredients:
- 2 cups jasmine rice OR long-grain white rice
- ½ cup millet
- 3¼ cups water
- ½ tsp sea salt (optional)

Directions:
1. Put all the ingredients in the Instant Pot and stir.
2. Cover and lock the lid.
3. Press the RICE button and let the pot do all the cooking, about 10 minutes.
4. When the timer beeps, quick release the pressure. Carefully open the lid. Serve.

Fried Rice

(Prep + Cook Time: 15 minutes | Servings: 4)

Ingredients:
- 1 tbsp butter (or oil)
- 1 medium onion, diced
- 2 cloves garlic, minced
- 1 egg
- 1 cup basmati rice, uncooked
- ¼ cup soy sauce
- 1½ cups chicken stock
- ½ cups peas, frozen OR your preferred vegetable

Directions:
1. Select SAUTE mode and preheat the Instant Pot. Put the oil in the pot.
2. Add the garlic and the onion. Sauté for 1 minute.
3. Add the egg, scramble with the garlic mix for about 1-2 minutes.
4. Add the rice, stock, and soy sauce in the pot. Press CANCEL. Close and lock the lid. Press RICE and set the time for 10 minutes.
5. When the timer beeps, quick release the pressure. Carefully open the lid. Stir in the frozen peas or veggies.
6. Let sit until the peas/ veggies are warmed through.

Delicious Risotto

(Prep + Cook Time: 30 minutes | Servings: 6)

Ingredients:
- 1 finely chopped medium onion
- 1½ cups Arborio rice
- 1½ tbsp olive oil
- 3½ cups chicken stock
- 3 tbsp Romano or Parmesan cheese
- Salt and pepper to taste

Directions:
1. Press the SAUTE key of the Instant Pot. Put the oil in the pot and heat.
2. Sauté the onion until soft and nearly translucent.
3. Add the rice and chicken stock.
4. Close the lid and select the RICE function. Set the timer for 15 minutes.
5. When the Instant Pot timer beeps, press the CANCEL key and let the pressure release naturally for 10-15 minutes.
6. Open the lid and stir in a little bit of black pepper.
7. Add the Romano or Parmesan cheese.
8. Serve immediately.

Mushroom Risotto (V)

(Prep + Cook Time: 25 minutes | Servings: 4)

Ingredients:

- 4 oz mushrooms, chopped or broken into small pieces
- 3 cups vegetable broth, at room temperature
- 3 cloves garlic, minced
- 2 cups fresh spinach
- ¼ cup lemon juice
- ½ cup white onion, minced
- ½ cup dry white wine, at room temperature
- 1 tsp thyme
- 1 tsp salt
- 1 tbsp vegan butter
- 1 tbsp olive oil, optional
- 1 cup Arborio rice
- 1 ½ tbsp nutritional yeast
- Black pepper to taste

Directions:

1. Press the SAUTE key of the Instant Pot. Put the oil in the pot and heat.
2. When hot, add the garlic and onion; sauté for 3 minutes.
3. Add the rice and stir well to mix. Pour in the veggie broth, add the mushrooms, wine, thyme, and salt.
4. Press the CANCEL key to stop the SAUTÉ function. Cover and lock the lid. Press the MANUAL key, set the pressure to HIGH, and set the timer for 5 minutes.
5. When the Instant Pot timer beeps, press the CANCEL key. Using an oven mitt or a long handled spoon, turn the steam valve to quick release the pressure.
6. Unlock and carefully open the lid. Stir in the nutritional yeast, spinach, vegan butter, and black pepper.
7. Stir until very well combined. If the dish is still liquidly, just let it sit for a few minutes – it will thicken as it cools.

Edamame Risotto

(Prep + Cook Time: 30 minutes | Servings: 6)

Ingredients:
- 1 tablespoon butter
- 1 tbsp olive oil
- 1 onion, medium-sized, finely minced
- 2 cups rice, short-grain (Carnaroli or Arborio are traditional)
- 1 cup edamame, shelled, thawed if frozen (run water over them for a few minutes to thaw)
- ½ cup dry white wine
- ½ tsp kosher salt
- 2 tbsp butter, cut into rough ½-inch cubes
- 2 tsp kosher salt (if using homemade stock)
- 4 cups chicken stock (preferably homemade)

Directions:
1. Set the Instant Pot to SAUTE. Put the oil and 1 tablespoon butter in the pot and let melt.
2. Add the onion and season with 1/2 teaspoon salt. Sauté for about 5 minutes or until softened.
3. Stir in the rice until well coated with the butter and oil. Cook for about 4 minutes, occasionally stirring, until the rice color is pearly white.
4. Add the wine and stir. Cook until the rice absorbs the wine.
5. Stir in the broth and 1 teaspoon kosher salt. Close and lock the lid. Press PRESSURE, set to HIGH, and set the time to 8 minutes.
6. When the timer beeps, quick release the pressure. Carefully open the lid.
7. Add the 2 tablespoons butter and stir until well mixed with the rice. Stir in the edamame.
8. Cover the pot and let stand for 5 minutes or until the edamame is heated through. Serve.

Notes: If you want a traditional flavored risotto, use shredded parmesan cheese instead of the batter and use thawed frozen peas instead of edamame.

Vegetable Cajun Rice (V)

(Prep + Cook Time: 30 minutes | Servings: 2)

Ingredients:
- 1½ heaped cups frozen vegetables
- 1 cup white basmati rice, washed in a sieve with cold running water
- 1 tsp olive oil
- ½ onion, finely diced
- ½ tsp ground cumin
- ½ tsp smoked paprika
- 1/3 tsp dried oregano
- 1/3 tsp dried thyme
- ¼-½ tsp chili powder, less or more to taste
- 2 tbsp tomato purée, dissolve in 1 cup just boiled water

Final seasonings:
- 1 squeeze lime
- 1 tbsp fresh coriander, chopped
- Salt and black pepper to taste

Directions:
1. Press the SAUTE key of the Instant Pot. Put the oil in the pot and add the onion; sauté until the edges of the onion is starting to brown and softened – this will add flavor to the dish.
2. Stir in the rice and add all the spices, stirring and mixing until well combined.
3. Add your preferred frozen veggies and the tomato puree dissolved in water.
4. Press CANCEL to stop SAUTÉ. Cover and lock the lid. Select MANUAL and cook at HIGH pressure for 4 minutes.
5. When the Instant Pot timer beeps, press the CANCEL key. Use a quick release. Unlock and carefully open the lid.
6. Using a fork, fluff the rice and then season well with black pepper and salt, 1 squeeze lime juice, and as much coriander as you desire.
7. You can leave out the coriander, but definitely season and squeeze with lime juice. Serve immediately.

Notes: Use small-sized frozen veggies in this dish, such as chopped onions and peppers, shelled soya beans or edamame, chopped green beans, sweet corn, and peas.

Rice Pilaf (V)

(Prep + Cook Time: 30 minutes | Servings: 4)

Ingredients:

- 2½ rice cups vegetable broth OR water
- 2-3 cups kale, chopped with stem
- 2 waxy potatoes, cubed
- 2 tbsp soy sauce
- 2 rice cups raw short-grain white rice
- 2 carrots, chopped
- 1 pound white mushrooms, halved
- 1 pound green beans, chopped (1/3-inch)
- 1 cup fried tofu
- 1 tbsp vegetable oil
- 1 tbsp rice wine (OR Japanese sake)
- 1 tbsp mushroom sauce
- Green onions, chopped, for garnish, optional

Directions:

1. Rinse the rice with tap water for about 2-3 times. Transfer in a strainer to drain excess water.
2. Meanwhile, prepare and chop the vegetables. Combine the rice with the broth, vegetable oil, and rice wine in the Instant Pot, preferably a 6-quart.
3. Top the rice mix with the tofu, carrot, potato, green beans, mushrooms, and kale.
4. Pour the soy sauce over the top – do not stir. Cover and lock the lid. Press MANUAL and cook at HIGH pressure for 8 minutes.
5. When the timer beeps, release the pressure naturally or do a quick release. Carefully open the lid.
6. Gently mix the cooked ingredients in the pot. Add the mushroom sauce and green onions in the pot. Gently mix again. If necessary, add more sauce to adjust the seasoning.
7. If not serving immediately, let the pot sit covered. Serve warm as a main dish.

Notes: The cup used to measure the ingredients for this dish is the one that comes with the Instant Pot, which is a standard 180 mL Asian rice cup. If using American cups, measure 1 1/2 cups of rice instead. For the vegetable broth, measure 2 cups minus 2 tablespoons. The soy sauce will char the bottom layer of the rice. If there too much soy sauce, the rice may burn.

Mexican Casserole (V, E&S)

(Prep + Cook Time: 35 minutes | Servings: 4)

Ingredients:
- 5 cups water
- 2 cups uncooked brown rice
- 1 cup soaked black beans
- 6 oz tomato paste
- 2 tsp chili powder
- 2 tsp onion powder
- 1 tsp garlic
- 1 tsp salt

Directions:
1. A few hours before dinner, put your dry beans in a bowl with enough water to cover them.
2. Soak for at least two hours and drain.
3. Put everything in your Instant Pot. Close and seal the pressure cooker. Select MANUAL and cook at HIGH pressure for 28 minutes.
4. When time is up, hit CANCEL and use a quick release.
5. Taste and season more if necessary.

Sweet Coconut Rice (V, E&S)

(Prep + Cook Time: 30 minutes | Servings: 4)

Ingredients:
- 1½ cups water
- 1 cup Thai sweet rice
- ½ can full-fat coconut milk
- 2 tbsp sugar Dash of salt

Directions:
1. Mix rice and water in your Instant Pot.
2. Select MANUAL and cook for 3 minutes at HIGH pressure.
3. When time is up, hit CANCEL and wait 10 minutes for a natural release.
4. In the meanwhile, heat coconut milk, sugar, and salt in a saucepan.
5. When the sugar has melted, remove from the heat.
6. When the cooker has released its pressure, mix the coconut milk mixture into your rice and stir.
7. Put the lid back on and let it rest 5-10 minutes, without returning it to pressure.
8. Serve and enjoy!

Dried-Fruit Wild Rice (V)

(Prep + Cook Time: 55 minutes | Servings: 6)

Ingredients:
- 3½ cups water
- 1½ cups wild rice
- 1 cup dried, mixed fruit
- 2 peeled and chopped small apples
- 1 chopped pear
- ½ cup slivered almonds
- 2 tbsp apple juice
- 1 tbsp maple syrup
- 1 tsp veggie oil
- 1 tsp cinnamon
- ½ tsp ground nutmeg
- Salt and pepper to taste

Directions:
1. Pour water into your Instant Pot along the rice.
2. Close and seal the lid. Select MANUAL and cook for 30 minutes at HIGH pressure.
3. In the meanwhile, soak the dried fruit in just enough apple juice to cover everything.
4. After 30 minutes, drain the fruit. By now, the rice should be done, so hit CANCEL and let pressure release naturally for 10 minutes and then do quick pressure release. Drain the rice and move rice to a bowl.
5. Turn your pressure cooker to SAUTE and add veggie oil. Cook the apples, pears, and almonds for about 2 minutes.
6. Pour in two tablespoons apple juice and keep cooking for a few minutes more.
7. Add syrup, the cooked rice, soaked fruit, and seasonings. Keep stirring for 2-3 minutes. Serve.

Notes: You can eat this rice as-is, or for a full meal, you can fill a partially-baked butternut squash with the rice and bake for 30-45 minutes in a 350F oven.

Chipotle Styled Rice (V, E&S)

(Prep + Cook Time: 35 minutes | Servings: 4)

Ingredients:

- 2 cups brown rice, rinsed
- 1 lime, juiced
- 4 small bay leaves
- 1 tsp salt
- ½ cup chopped cilantro
- 1½ tbsp olive oil
- 2¾ cups water, hot

Directions:

1. In a 6-quarts Instant Pot place rice, then add bay leaves and water.
2. Plug in and switch on the pot, select RICE option and secure pot with lid. Then position pressure indicator and let cook on default time.
3. When the timer beeps, switch off the Instant Pot and let pressure release naturally for 10 minutes and then do quick pressure release.
4. Uncover the pot, add salt, oil, lime juice and cilantro and mix until combined. Serve immediately.

Green Rice

(Prep + Cook Time: 40 minutes | Servings: 6)

Ingredients:

- 2 cups rice basmati
- 1 cup spinach
- 1 cup dill
- 3 oz butter
- 1 tbsp salt
- 4 cups beef broth
- 1 tbsp minced garlic
- 1 tsp olive oil
- 1 tsp dried oregano

Directions:

1. Set the Instant Pot to SAUTE and preheat the pot.
2. Pour the olive oil into the Instant Pot. Add rice, butter, and minced garlic. Sauté the mixture for 5 minutes. Stir it frequently. Add beef broth.
3. Wash the spinach and dill carefully. Chop the greens.
4. Transfer the chopped greens in the blender and blend them well.
5. Then add the blended greens in the rice mixture.
6. Add butter, salt, and dried oregano.
7. Mix up the mixture carefully with the help of the wooden spoon. After this, close the lid and set the Instant Pot mode RICE. Cook the dish for 20 minutes.
8. When the time is over, do quick pressure release and transfer the green rice in the serving bowl. Enjoy!

Lentil and Wild Rice Pilaf (V)

(Prep + Cook Time: 20 minutes + 30 min. soaking | Servings: 6)

Ingredients:

For the lentils and rice (soak for 30 minutes before cooking):

- ¼ cup brown rice
- ¼ cup black/wild rice
- ½ cup black or green lentils

For the vegetables:

- 1 cup mushrooms, sliced
- 1 stalk celery, finely chopped
- ½ onion, medium-sized, finely chopped
- 3 cloves garlic, pressed/minced

For the spices:

- 1 bay leaf
- 1 tbsp Italian seasoning blend (no-salt added)
- 1 tsp dried coriander
- 1 tsp fennel seeds
- ½ tsp ground black pepper
- ¼ tsp red pepper flakes
- 2 cups vegetable broth

Directions:

1. Combine the rice and the lentils in a medium-sized bowl.
2. Let soak for 30 minutes. Drain and then rinse thoroughly.
3. Set the Instant Pot to SAUTE. Put the veggies in the inner pot and sauté for 3-5 minutes.
4. If needed, add a bit of water to prevent the veggies from burning.
5. Add the rice and lentils, vegetable broth, and spices into the pot. Close and lock the lid.
6. Press MANUAL and cook at HIGH pressure for 9 minutes.
7. When the timer beeps, let the pressure release naturally. Open the lid. Stir the pilaf.
8. If liquid remains, let sit for 5 minutes uncovered to allow the pilaf to absorb more liquid.
9. Serve this dish with steamed or fresh veggies.

Notes: If you don't like fennel seeds, then use 1 tablespoon of your preferred dried herbs, such as thyme, rosemary, parsley, basil, or oregano. If you don't have black or wild rice on hand, you can use all brown rice.

Rice-Stuffed Acorn Squash (V)

(Prep + Cook Time: 20 minutes | Servings: 4)

Ingredients:

- 3¾ cups veggie stock
- 2 medium-sized, halved acorn squash
- 1 cup white rice
- 1 cup diced onion
- ½ cup quinoa
- ½ cup vegan cheese
- 2 minced garlic cloves
- 1 tbsp Earth Balance spread (or any vegan butter)
- 1 tsp chopped rosemary
- 1 tsp chopped thyme
- 1 tsp chopped sage

Directions:

1. Turn your Instant Pot to SAUTE and melt the Earth Balance. Add onion and salt, and cook for two minutes.
2. Toss in the garlic and cook for another minute or so. Add rice, quinoa, herbs, and pour in the broth. Stir.
3. Put your de-seeded squash halves with the cut-side up in a steamer basket.
4. Put the trivet in the cooker, and place the basket on top. Close and seal the lid.
5. Hit MANUAL and cook for 6 minutes on HIGH pressure.
6. When the timer beeps, carefully quick-release the pressure after hitting CANCEL.
7. Take out the steamer basket and drain any liquid that's hanging around in the squash.
8. Add vegan cheese to the pot and stir. Wait 5 minutes or so for the stuffing to thicken.
9. Fill the squash and sprinkle on some extra cheese. Serve!

Sushi Rice

(Prep + Cook Time: 15 minutes | Servings: 18 sushi pieces)

Ingredients:
- 1 cup sushi rice
- 1½ cups water
- 3 tbsp rice wine vinegar or 1 tbsp apple cider vinegar and a pinch of sugar

Directions:
1. Rinse the sushi rice well, rubbing it around in the strainer as the water passes through. Rinse until the water runs clear (about 3 minutes). Measure the rice and cooking water carefully
2. To the inner pot, add the rinsed rice and water and mix to evenly distribute the rice. Close and lock the lid. Cook for 7 minutes at HIGH pressure.
3. When cooking time is up, count 5 minutes of natural pressure release. Then, quick release the rest of the pressure slowly using the valve. Even if all of the pressure is naturally released before the 5 minutes are up keep the lid closed the entire time. Otherwise, release any remaining pressure slowly using the valve.
4. Stir the rice-wine vinegar into the rice handling it delicately without over-working it.
5. Tumble the rice into a large wooden bowl or wooden cutting board and smooth-out into an even layer.
6. Let cool for about 10 minutes, and it's ready to be used to make sushi! Cool the cooked sushi rice by spreading in an even layer in a wooden bowl or cutting-board.

For making sushi: Slice fresh vegetables for filling into long thin, even strips – use avocado, fresh tomatoes, even peppers Layout nonlinear ingredients in a rectangular shape. Use cooked, smoked or pickled fish for filling – only experts should be purchasing and handling raw fish.

Egg Recipes

Hard-Boiled Eggs (E&S)
(Prep + Cook Time: 15 minutes | Servings: 6)

Ingredients:
- 5-15 eggs
- 1 cup water

Directions:
- Pour the water into the Instant Pot, and place the eggs in a steamer basket if you have one. If you don't, just use the rack that came with your pot.
- Close the lid, select MANUAL and cook at HIGH pressure for 5 minutes.
- It will take the cooker approximately 5 minutes to build to pressure and then 5 minutes to cook.
- Let the pressure naturally reduce for an additional 5 minutes after the cooking cycle completed, and then did a quick pressure release.
- Place the hot eggs into cool water to halt the cooking process.
- You can peel immediately, or wait-- it's up to you

Soft-Boiled Egg (E&S)
(Prep + Cook Time: 6 minutes | Servings: 2)

Ingredients:
- 4 eggs
- 1 cup of water
- Two toasted English muffins
- Salt and pepper to taste

Directions:
1. Pour 1 cup of water into the Instant Pot and insert the steamer basket.
2. Put four canning lids into the basket before placing the eggs on top of them, so they stay separated. Secure the lid.
3. Press the STEAM setting and choose 4 minutes.
4. When ready, quick-release the steam valve.
5. Take out the eggs using tongs and dunk them into a bowl of cold water. Wait 1-2 minutes.
6. Peel and serve with one egg per half of a toasted English muffin. Season with salt and pepper.

Delightful Soft Eggs (E&S)

(Prep + Cook Time: 10 minutes | Servings: 4)

Ingredients:
- 3 eggs
- 6 oz ham
- 1 tsp salt
- ½ tsp white pepper
- 1 tsp paprika
- ¼ tsp ground ginger
- 2 tbsp chives

Directions:
1. Take the small ramekins and beat the eggs in them.
2. Sprinkle the eggs with the salt, ground black pepper, and paprika.
3. Transfer the ramekins to the Instant Pot and set the mode STEAM. Close the lid and cook the dish for 4 minutes.
4. Meanwhile, chop the ham and chives and combine the ingredients together.
5. Add ground ginger and stir the mixture carefully.
6. Transfer the mixture to the serving plates.
7. When the time is up, remove the eggs from the Instant Pot and put them over the ham mixture. Serve the dish immediately.

Scrambled Eggs

(Prep + Cook Time: 15 minutes | Servings: 4)

Ingredients:
- 7 eggs
- ½ cup milk
- 1 tbsp butter
- 1 tsp basil
- ¼ cup fresh parsley
- 1 tsp salt
- 1 tsp paprika
- 4 oz bacon
- 1 tbsp cilantro

Directions:
1. Beat the eggs in the mixing bowl and whisk them well.
2. Then add milk, basil, salt, paprika, and cilantro. Stir the mixture. Chop the bacon and parsley.
3. Set the Instant Pot mode SAUTE and transfer the chopped bacon. Cook it for 3 minutes.
4. Then add whisked egg mixture and cook the dish for 5 minutes more.
5. After this, mix up the eggs carefully with the help of the wooden spoon.
6. Then sprinkle the dish with the chopped parsley and cook it for 4 minutes more.
7. When the eggs are cooked – remove them from the Instant Pot. Serve the dish immediately. Enjoy!

Poached Tomato Eggs

(Prep + Cook Time: 15 minutes | Servings: 4)

Ingredients:

- 1 cup water
- 4 eggs
- 3 medium tomatoes
- 1 red onion
- 1 tsp salt
- 1 tbsp olive oil
- ½ tsp white pepper
- ½ tsp paprika
- 1 tbsp fresh dill

Directions:

1. Place the trivet in the bottom of the Instant Pot liner and pour in 1 cup of water.
2. Spray the ramekins with the olive oil inside.
3. Beat the eggs in every ramekin.
4. Combine the paprika, white pepper, fresh dill, and salt together in the mixing bowl. Stir the mixture.
5. After this, chop the red onion.
6. Chop the tomatoes into the tiny pieces and combine them with the onion. Stir the mixture.
7. Then sprinkle the eggs with the tomato mixture.
8. Add spice mixture and transfer the eggs to the Instant Pot.
9. Close the lid and set the Instant Pot mode STEAM. Cook the dish for 5 minutes. Then remove the dish from the Instant Pot and chill it little.
10. Serve the dish immediately. Enjoy!

Notes: The steam has condensed on the lid and will drip onto your eggs. Twist the lid to unlock, then tilt to keep the water on the edge of the lid until you can position it over the edge of the liner or move it straight to the sink.

Cheesy Sausage Frittata

(Prep + Cook Time: 45 minutes | Servings: 4)

Ingredients:
- 1½ cups water
- 4 beaten eggs
- ½ cup cooked ground sausage
- ¼ cup grated sharp cheddar
- 2 tbsp sour cream
- 1 tbsp butter
- Salt to taste
- Black pepper to taste

Directions:
1. Pour water into the Instant Pot and lower in the steamer rack.
2. Grease a 6-7 inch soufflé dish.
3. In a bowl, whisk the eggs and sour cream together.
4. Add cheese, sausage, salt, and pepper. Stir.
5. Pour into the dish and wrap tightly with foil all over.
6. Lower into the steam rack and close the pot lid.
7. Press MANUAL and cook for 17 minutes on LOW pressure.
8. Quick-release the pressure. Serve hot!

Easy Cheesy Hash Brown Bake

(Prep + Cook Time: 10 minutes | Servings: 8)

Ingredients:
- 8 eggs
- 6 slices chopped bacon
- 2 cups frozen hash browns
- 1 cup shredded cheddar cheese
- ¼ cup milk
- 1 tsp salt
- ½ tsp black pepper

Directions:
1. Turn your Instant Pot to SAUTE and cook the bacon until it becomes crispy.
2. Add hash browns and stir for 2 minutes, or until they start to thaw.
3. In a bowl, whisk eggs, milk, cheese, and seasonings.
4. Pour over the hash browns in the pot, and lock and seal lid.
5. Press MANUAL, set the pressure to HIGH and adjust time to 5 minutes.
6. When time is up, press CANCEL and quick-release the pressure. Serve in slices.

Bacon and Cheese Egg Muffins

(Prep + Cook Time: 25 minutes | Servings: 8)

Ingredients:

- 4 eggs
- 4 slices bacon, cooked and crumbled
- 4 tbsp cheddar or pepper jack cheese, shredded
- 1 green onion, diced
- ¼ tsp lemon pepper seasoning
- 1½ cup water, for the pot

Directions:

1. Pour the water into the Instant Pot container and then put a steamer basket into the pot. In a large-sized measuring bowl with a pour pout, break the eggs.
2. Add the lemon pepper and beat well. Divide the bacon, cheese, and green onion between 4 silicone muffin cups.
3. Pour the egg mix into each muffin cups; with a fork, stir using a fork to combine. Put the muffin cups onto the steamer basket, cover and lock the pot lid.
4. Set to MANUAL mode, the pressure to HIGH, and the timer to 8 minutes.
5. When the timer beeps, turn off the pot, wait for 2 minutes, and then turn the steam valve to quick release the pressure. Carefully open the pot lid, lift the steamer basket out from the container, and then remove the muffin cups.
6. Serve immediately.

Notes: These muffins can be stored in the refrigerator for more than 1 week. When ready to serve, just microwave for 30 seconds on HIGH to reheat.

Eggs, Bacon and Sausage Omelet

(Prep + Cook Time: 50 minutes | Servings: 6)

Ingredients:

- 6-12 eggs
- ½ cup milk
- 6 slices bacon, cooked
- 6 sausages links, sliced
- 1 onion, diced Garlic powder
- 16 ounces water
- Salt to taste
- Pepper to taste
- Olive oil cooking spray

Equipment:

1½ quart ceramic baking dish or Pyrex

Directions:

1. Crack the eggs into a large measuring cup. Add ½ cup milk into the egg.
2. With a hand mixer, whisk the eggs and the milk until well combined.
3. Add the sausages and add the onion. Season with garlic powder, salt, and pepper to taste Spray a Pyrex glass bowl with cooking spray; use a deep one that will fit your Instant Pot. Pour the egg mix into the Pyrex; cover tightly with foil.
4. Add 16 ounces water into the Instant Pot. Put the bowl into a handy rack and put into the Instant Pot.
5. Press MANUAL, the pressure to HIGH, and the timer to 25 minutes. When cooked, let the pressure release naturally. Remove the foil. The egg may pop-out of the bowl; just push it back.
6. Layer the cooked bacon on top of the omelet and then cover with shredded cheese.
7. Set the timer for another 5 minutes on MANUAL. Take out from the Instant Pot.
8. Sprinkle with a bit of dried oregano. Slice into servings and enjoy.

Eggs En Cocotte

(Prep + Cook Time: 15 minutes | Servings: 4)

Ingredients:

- 3 eggs, pasture raised, fresh
- 3 tbsp cream
- 1 tbsp chives
- 1 cup water, for the pot
- Butter, at room temperature
- Sea salt and freshly ground pepper

Directions:

1. With a paper towel, wipe the bottoms and sides of 3 pieces 4-5 ounces ramekins with butter.
2. Pour 1 tablespoon cream into each ramekin.
3. Carefully crack 1 egg into each, making sure not to break the yolks, and then sprinkle with chives.
4. Pour the water into the bottom of the Instant Pot and then put a rack with handle or a trivet into the bottom of the pot.
5. Put the ramekins onto the rack. Close the lid and make sure the valve is closed.
6. Plug the pot, set to MANUAL, the pressure to LOW, and the timer to 2 minutes for runny yolks or 4 minutes for firm yolks.
7. When the timer beeps, turn the steam valve to quick release the pressure and let the steam dissipate.
8. Carefully open the lid and with a kitchen towel or a hot pad, carefully remove the rack with the handle or, if using trivet, the ramekins.
9. Season the eggs en cocotte with salt and pepper. Enjoy as is or on toasts.

Notes: If you are cooking less than 3 eggs, fill the remaining ramekins with water, and put in the pot as well. Otherwise, the eggs will cook too fast.

Spinach Tomato Crustless Quiche

(Prep + Cook Time: 40 minutes | Servings: 6)

Ingredients:

- 12 large eggs
- ¼ tsp fresh ground black pepper
- 3 cups fresh baby spinach, roughly chopped
- ¼ cup Parmesan cheese, shredded
- 3 large green onions, sliced
- ½ tsp salt
- 4 tomato slices, for topping the quiche
- ½ cup milk
- 1 cup tomato, seeded, diced
- 1½ cups water, for the pot

Directions:

1. Pour the water into the Instant Pot container. In a large-sized bowl, whisk the eggs with the milk, pepper, and salt.
2. Add the tomato, spinach, and the green onions into a 1 1/2 quart-sized baking dish; mix well to combine.
3. Pour the egg mix over the vegetables; stir until combined. Put the tomato slices gently on top.
4. Sprinkle with the shredded parmesan cheese. Put the baking dish into the rack with a handle.
5. Put the rack into the Instant Pot and then lock the lid. Set the pressure to HIGH and the timer to 20 minutes.
6. When the timer beeps, wait for 10 minutes, then turn the steamer valve to Venting to release remaining pressure. Open the pot lid carefully.
7. Hold the rack handles and lift the dish out from the pot.
8. Serve and enjoy.

Notes: You can cover the baking dish with foil to prevent moisture from gathering on the quiche top. You can cook uncovered; just soak the moisture using a paper towel.

Spinach-Feta Egg Cups

(Prep + Cook Time: 10 minutes | Servings: 4)

Ingredients:

- 6 eggs
- 1 cup water
- 1 cup chopped baby spinach
- 1 chopped tomato
- ½ cup mozzarella cheese
- ¼ cup feta cheese
- 1 tsp black pepper
- ½ tsp salt

Directions:

1. Pour water into the Instant Pot and lower in trivet.
2. Layer silicone ramekins with spinach.
3. In a bowl, mix the rest of the ingredients and pour into cups, leaving ¼-inch of head room.
4. Put in pressure cooker (you may have to cook in batches) and adjust time to 8 minutes on HIGH pressure.
5. When time is up, turn off the cooker and quick-release.
6. Serve and enjoy!

Eggs De Provence

(Prep + Cook Time 40 minutes | Servings: 6)

Ingredients:

- 1 cup kale leaves, fresh, chopped
- 1 cup cheddar cheese
- ½ cup heavy cream
- 1 onion, small, chopped
- 6 eggs, large
- 1 tsp Herbes de Provence
- ⅛ tsp sea salt and pepper
- 1 cup bacon or ham, cooked
- 1 cup water

Directions:

1. Whisk the eggs together with the heavy cream in a large bowl.
2. Add in the remaining ingredients; mix well.
3. Transfer the mixture into a dish, preferably heat proof & then cover.
4. Add a cup of water into the bottom of your Instant Pot. Place the steamer basket or trivet inside.
5. Tightly close the lid and close the vent valve. Select MANUAL and cook at HIGH pressure for 20 minutes.
6. Once you are done with the cooking process, let the pressure release naturally. Serve immediately.

Meat Lover's Crustless Quiche

(Prep + Cook Time: 45 minutes | Servings: 4)

Ingredients:

- 6 large eggs, well beaten
- ½ cup milk
- ¼ tsp salt
- 1/8 tsp ground black pepper
- 4 slices bacon, cooked and then crumbled
- 1 cup ground sausage, cooked
- ½ cup ham, diced
- 2 large green onions, chopped
- 1 cup cheese, shredded
- 1½ cups water, for the pot

Directions:

1. Pour the water into the Instant Pot container and put a stainless steel rack with handle into the bottom of the pot.
2. In a large-sized bowl, whisk the eggs with the milk, salt, and pepper.
3. Add the sausage, bacon, ham, cheese, and green onions into a 1-quart soufflé dish; mix well.
4. Pour the egg mix over the meat; stir well to combine.
5. With an aluminum foil, loosely cover the dish. Put onto the rack. Lock the pot lid.
6. Set the PRESSURE to HIGH and the timer to 30 minutes.
7. When the timer beeps, turn the pot off, let the pressure release naturally for 10 minutes, and then turn the valve to release remaining pressure. Carefully open the pot lid. Lift out the rack with the dish.
8. Remove the foil covering and, if desired, sprinkle the top of the quiche with additional cheese and broil in the oven until melted and slightly browned.
9. Serve immediately.

Aromatic Egg Side Dish
(Prep + Cook Time 20 minutes | Servings: 6)

Ingredients:
- 1 tbsp mustard
- ¼ cup cream
- 1 tsp salt
- 8 eggs
- 1 tsp mayo sauce
- ¼ cup dill
- 1 tsp ground white pepper
- 1 tsp minced garlic
- 1 cup water

Directions:
1. In the Instant Pot pour down about 1 cup of water into the bowl.
2. Place stainless steamer basket inside the pot.
3. Place the eggs in the steamer basket.
4. Cook the eggs at the HIGH pressure for 5 minutes.
5. Then remove the eggs from the Instant Pot and chill in cold water.
6. Peel the eggs and cut them into 2 parts.
7. Discard the egg yolks and mash them.
8. Then add the mustard, cream, salt, mayo sauce, ground white pepper, and minced garlic in the mashed egg yolks.
9. Chop the dill and sprinkle the egg yolk mixture with the chopped dill.
10. Mix up it carefully until you get smooth and homogenous mass.
11. Then transfer the egg yolk mixture to the pastry bag.
12. Fill the egg whites with the yolk mixture.
13. Serve the dish immediately. Enjoy!

Slow Cook Maple French Toast Casserole
(Prep + Cook Time: 1 hour 40 minutes | Servings: 8)

Ingredients:
- Cooking Spray
- 12 slices sandwich bread cut into 1 inch pieces, can use gluten free bread
- 4 eggs lightly beaten
- ½ cup maple syrup
- 1 tsp cinnamon
- ½ tsp salt
- ¼ tsp nutmeg grated
- 1/8 tsp cloves ground
- 2 cups milk reduced fat 2%
- 1 tsp powdered sugar

Directions:
1. Coat the inner pot of the Instant Pot with cooking spray.
2. Place cubed bread in the pot
3. Combine eggs, maple syrup, cinnamon, salt, cloves and nutmeg in a large bowl.
4. Add milk, stirring with a whisk until blended. Pour milk mixture over bread in the pot, pressing gently with a spoon to coat all bread pieces.
5. Tear off a 10½ inch long piece of aluminum foil; lay foil on top of inner pot, gently smoothing it down the side of the pot. trim pointed corners even with rest of the foil, and tightly tuck it under the rim
6. Cut 2 (1¼ inch long) slit in the foil about one inch from the edge with a thin sharp knife. Cut a second slit parallel to and about 1 inch to the inside of the first. Repeat this procedure 3 times, creating 2 concentric slits in foil at intervals of 12, 3, 6, and 9 o'clock.
7. Set inner pot inside cooker. Close and lock the lid of the Instant Pot. Turn steam release handle to Venting. Select the SLOW Cook function and adjust time to 90 minutes cooking time.
8. Serve warm sprinkled with powdered sugar. Enjoy!

Shrimp and Pork Dumplings (Shumai)
(Prep + Cook Time: 55 minutes | Servings: 4-8)

Ingredients:
- ½ pound tiger prawns finely chopped, or shrimps
- 1 tsp cornstarch
- ¼ tsp salt
- ¼ - ½ tsp oil, optional
- ½ pound ground pork
- 2 tbsp chicken stock unsalted
- 1 tbsp cornstarch
- 1 tbsp Shaoxing wine
- 2 tsp light soy sauce
- 1 tsp fish sauce
- 1 tsp sesame oil
- ½ tsp white pepper ground
- ½ tsp sugar
- ¾ stalk green onions finely chopped
- 2 slices Ginger grated
- 1-2 shiitake mushrooms dried, re-hydrated and finely chopped (see tips)
- 20-24 wonton wrappers round

Directions:
1. Dry the shrimps with paper towels. Place the chopped shrimps in a medium mixing bowl. Add in 1 teaspoon of cornstarch and 1/4 teaspoon of salt.
2. Place the ground pork in a large mixing bowl. Pour 1 tablespoon of cornstarch, white pepper, sugar, Shaoxing wine, soy sauce, fish sauce, sesame oil, and chicken stock.
3. Squeeze and mix the seasoned ground pork with your hands, then throw it against the mixing bowl until it resembles a paste-like consistency. Wash your hands and do the same with the seasoned shrimps. Put the pastes into the fridge and prepare the remaining ingredients.
4. Finely chop green onions and re-hydrated shiitake mushrooms. Grate the ginger slices.
5. Remove the pork and shrimp pastes from the fridge. Pour all the ingredients into the ground pork paste mixing bowl. Squeeze and mix the ingredients with your hands until blended. Remember to throw the paste against the mixing bowl.
6. Place a wonton wrapper on one hand. Scoop roughly 3/4 - 1 tablespoon of mixed paste on the wonton wrapper with a butter

knife or the dull end of a spoon. Then, wrap it into a cylinder shape with an open top.

7. Place a parchment liner into the bamboo steamer, then place the Shumai on the liner. Close the bamboo steamer lid.

8. Place a steamer rack and pour one cup of water into the Instant Pot. Place the bamboo steamer filled with Shumai into the pressure cooker. Close lid and cook on MANUAL at HIGH Pressure for 3 minutes. Wait for another 5 minutes and do a quick release.

9. Remove the bamboo steamer from the pot and enjoy them immediately!

Savory Blue Cheese Appetizer Cheesecake

(Prep + Cook Time: 1 hour 50 minutes | Servings: 8-12)

Ingredients:

- Nonstick cooking spray
- 1 cup buttery crackers finely crushed
- ½ cup pecans finely chopped
- 3 tbsp butter melted
- 16 ounces cream cheese softened
- 4 ounces blue cheese crumbled
- ¼ cup heavy cream
- 1 tsp dried basil
- ½ tsp garlic powder
- ¼ tsp ground white pepper
- 3 eggs room temperature
- ¼ cup green onions diced
- 2 cups water
- Crackers or crostini, for serving
- Pear and/or apple slices, for serving

Directions:

1. Lightly spray a 6-or 7-inch springform pan with cooking spray. Cut a piece of parchment paper to fit the bottom of the pan. Place in the pan and spray again; set aside.
2. Combine crackers, pecans, and butter; mix well. Press into bottom and about 1½-inches up the sides of the springform pan.
3. Beat cream cheese, blue cheese, and cream in a large bowl until smooth and creamy. Beat in basil, garlic powder, and white pepper.
4. Add eggs, one at a time, beating just until egg is combined. Fold in green onions.
5. Pour into prepared crust. (Pan will be full.) Tent with foil. Place trivet in the bottom of the pot. Pour the water into the Instant Pot.
6. Cut a piece of foil the same size as a paper towel. Place the foil under the paper towel and place the pan on top of the paper towel.

7. Wrap the bottom of the pan in the foil with the paper towel as a barrier.Fold an 18-inch-long piece of foil into thirds lengthwise. Place under the pan and use the two sides as a sling to place cheesecake on the trivet in the pot.
8. Secure the lid on the pot. Close the pressure-release valve.
9. Select MANUAL and cook at HIGH pressure for 40 minutes. When cooking is complete, use a natural release.
10. Remove the cheesecake from the pot using the sling. Cool on the rack for 1 hour and refrigerate for at least 4 hours.
11. Carefully remove pan sides.
12. Serve cheesecake with crackers or crostini and pear and/or apple slices.

Macaroni and Cheese
(Prep + Cook Time: 20 minutes | Servings: 8)

Ingredients:
- 1 pound elbow macaroni
- 4 cups chicken broth or vegetable broth, low sodium
- 3 tbsp unsalted butter
- 12 ounces sharp Cheddar cheese shredded, 3 cups tightly packed
- ½ cup Parmesan cheese shredded, about 2 ounces
- ½ cup sour cream
- 1½ tsp yellow mustard
- 1/8 tsp cayenne pepper

Directions:
1. Combine the macaroni, broth, and butter in the Instant Pot.
2. Secure the lid and set the steam release to Sealing. Select the MANUAL setting and set the cooking time for 6 minutes at HIGH pressure.
3. Perform a quick release by moving the steam release to Venting.
4. Open the pot and stir in the cheeses, sour cream, mustard, and cayenne pepper. Let sit for 5 minutes to thicken, then stir again and serve.
   Optional:
   If you like, finish the macaroni and cheese under the broiler for a crispy topping.
5. Transfer to a 3-quart flameproof baking dish, sprinkle evenly with 1 cup panko bread crumbs, and then broil for just a few minutes, until the bread crumbs are golden brown.

Rigatoni with Meat Sauce

(Prep + Cook Time: 45 minutes | Servings: 4-6)

Ingredients:

- 2 tbsp olive oil
- 2-3 cloves garlic
- 3,5 oz white mushrooms, finely chopped (pulse in food processor or chop by hand)
- 1 onion finely chopped
- 1 tbsp tomato paste
- 2 tsp basil dried
- 2 tsp oregano dried
- Kosher salt to taste
- Black pepper to taste
- 1 lb italian sausage a combo of sweet and hot tastes delicious
- 1 can tomatoes 28-ounce can
- 1 can tomato puree 14.5-ounce can
- 3½ cups water
- 1 pound rigatoni dried

Directions:

1. Heat the oil in your Instant Pot on SAUTÉ mode. When display reads "Hot" add in and sauté the onions, mushrooms, garlic and a pinch of kosher salt and a few grinds of black pepper until softened, at least five minutes.
2. Stir in the oregano, basil and tomato paste and cook another minute, stirring constantly with a wooden spoon.
3. Add in the sausage meat that you have removed from the casings and brown, breaking it up with your spoon, until no pink remains.
4. Pour in the water, the tomato puree and, using your hand, squish the tomatoes in to break them up and then pour in all of the liquid from the can.
5. Give the pot a good stir to make sure you get up all of the fond on the bottom of the pot and then add in the dry rigatoni.
6. Give it one more good stir, close and lock the lid. Select MANUAL and cook at HIGH pressure for 6 minutes.
7. When the time is up, quick release the pressure and open the lid.
8. Let it sit for another minute or two, giving it a couple of stirs, to thicken up a bit. If the sauce seems too thin, you can turn the SAUTÉ feature back on and simmer it for a couple of minutes as well.
9. Serve in big bowls with freshly grated parmesan. Enjoy!

Chicken Alfredo Pasta (E&S)

(Prep + Cook Time: 5 minutes | Servings: 3)

Ingredients:
- 8-ounces fettuccine
- One 15-ounce jar of Alfredo sauce
- 2 cups water
- 1 cup cooked + diced chicken
- 2 tsp chicken seasoning

Directions:
1. Break your pasta in half so it fits in the cooker.
2. Add pasta, water, and chicken seasoning to Instant Pot.
3. Seal the lid. Select MANUAL and cook at HIGH pressure for 3 minutes.
4. When the timer beeps, press CANCEL and use a quick release.
5. Drain the pasta and add to serving bowl.
6. Mix in Alfredo sauce and chicken. Serve!

Pepper Jack Mac'n Cheese (E&S)

(Prep + Cook Time: 10 minutes | Servings: 4)

Ingredients:
- 2 ½ cups elbow macaroni
- 2 cups chicken stock
- 1 ½ cups shredded pepper jack cheese
- 1 ½ cups mozzarella cheese
- 1 cup heavy cream
- ½ cup whole milk
- 1 tbsp butter
- 1 tsp salt
- 1 tsp black pepper

Directions:
1. Pour chicken stock and cream into the Instant Pot. Add macaroni, salt, and pepper. Seal and close the lid.
2. Select MANUAL and cook at HIGH pressure for 7 minutes.
3. When time is up, press CANCEL and use a quick release.
4. Mix in butter, milk, and cheese.
5. Stir well and serve!

Slow Cook Spinach and Goat Cheese Lasagna
(Prep + Cook Time: 2 hours 20 minutes | Servings: 8)

Ingredients:
- 1 tsp extra-virgin olive oil
- 1¾ cups onion, chopped
- 1 cup zucchini, diced
- ½ cup carrot, shredded
- 2 cloves garlic, chopped
- ½ tsp salt
- ½ tsp black pepper freshly ground
- 1 can tomatoes crushed, undrained, 28-ounce can
- Cooking Spray
- 1 cup basil fresh, chopped
- ¾ cup part-skim ricotta cheese
- 20 ounces spinach frozen and chopped, thawed, drained, and squeezed dry
- 2 ounces goats cheese roughly 1/4-cup
- 8 gluten free lasagna noodles
- 1 ounce Parmesan cheese, shredded fresh, about 1/4-cup
- Basil leaves, optional

Directions:
1. Heat a 4-quart saucepan over medium heat. Add oil to the pan; swirl to coat.
2. Add onion, zucchini, and carrot; cook, stirring constantly for 5 minutes.
3. Add garlic; cook, stirring constantly for 1 minute. Stir in the salt, pepper and tomatoes; bring to a simmer, and cook for 5 minutes, stirring occasionally.
4. Coat the inner pot of a 6 quart Instant Pot with cooking spray.
5. Combine basil, ricotta, spinach and goat cheese in a medium bowl.
6. Spread 1/2 cup spinach mixture in the cooker, Arrange 1/3 of the lasagna noodles over spinach mixture in the pot, breaking noodles as necessary to fit in the pot; top with half of the remaining spinach mixture and 1 cup tomato mixture. Repeat procedure once, ending with noodles.
7. Pour the remaining tomato mixture over noodles, being careful to cover noodles completely.
8. Close and lock the lid of the Instant Pot. Turn the steam release handle to Venting position. Press SLOW COOK

function and adjust to select Less mode. Adjust time to 2 hours cooking.
9. When time is up, uncover and sprinkle with Parmesan cheese; cover and let stand 15 minutes before serving. Garnish with basil leaves, if desired.

Couscous and Vegetable Medley (V)

(Prep + Cook Time: 30 minutes | Servings: 3)

Ingredients:
- 1 tbsp olive oil
- 2 bay leaves or Tej Patta
- ½ large onion chopped
- 1 large red bell pepper chopped
- 1 cup carrot grated
- 1¾ cup couscous Isreali
- 1¾ cup water
- 2 tsp salt or to taste
- ½ tsp garam masala
- 1 tbsp lemon juice
- Cilantro to garnish

Directions:
1. Heat the Instant Pot in SAUTÉ mode and add olive oil to it. Add the bay leaves and onions. Sauté for 2 minutes.
2. Add the bell peppers and carrots. Sauté for one more minute.
3. Add the couscous, water, garam masala and salt. Stir well.
4. Change the Instant Pot setting to MANUAL and cook at HIGH pressure for 2 minutes. When the Instant Pot beeps, do 10 minutes natural pressure release.
5. Fluff the couscous, it is fully cooked. Mix in the lemon juice. Garnish with cilantro and serve hot.

Notes: Prepare with vegetables of your choice. I used bell peppers, carrots and onions, which I had at home. Other options are cauliflower, broccoli, edamame and green peas.
If you like, you can add more spices.

Instant Pot Carbonara

(Prep + Cook Time: 25 minutes | Servings: 4)

Ingredients:

- 1 pound pasta dry, rigatoni, penne or cavatappi are great
- 4 cups water
- Pinch kosher salt
- 4 large eggs
- 8 ounces bacon pancetta or guanciale
- 1 cup Pecorino Romano finely grated, can also use parmesan
- Black pepper as much as you like

Directions:

1. Put the pasta and the water, with a pinch of kosher salt, in the Instant Pot and program it to cook on MANUAL for 5 minutes at HIGH pressure.
2. While the cooker heats up, crack the eggs in a bowl, add in the cheese and the black pepper, whisk it until it's all mixed together and put aside until you need it.
3. Cook the bacon (pancetta or, if you can find it, the guanciale), in a frying pan over medium heat for a few minutes until it's crispy and has rendered lots of fat and then remove the pan from the heat.
4. When the cooking time on the Instant Pot is up, do a controlled quick release. Pasta can foam up so release with small spurts until you are sure it's not going to spew all over the place and then release it all at once.
5. Put the pan with the bacon/pancetta back on the heat and dump in the pasta and any liquid left in the pot, wait for the water to come to a fierce bubbling up and cook for about 30 seconds until there is just a bit of water left. You want to see some liquid but you don't it to be all soupy.
6. Now, remove the pan from the heat again so that you can add in the eggs/cheese and quickly stir it all together until the eggs thicken into a sauce.
7. If you like it super peppery, season with a bit more, more grated cheese if you like and serve right away. Enjoy!

Vegetarian Rigatoni Bolognese

(Prep + Cook Time: 30 minutes | Servings: 6)

Ingredients:
- 3 tbsp olive oil
- ½ cup onion, chopped fine
- ½ cup celery, chopped fine
- ½ cup carrots, chopped fine
- ½ cup bell peppers, chopped fine
- 1 tbsp garlic, minced
- 2 cups mushrooms, chopped
- 1 cup water
- 1 ounce dried porcini mushrooms, chopped
- 1 can crushed tomatoes 28-ounce can
- ½ tsp black pepper
- 1 tsp salt or to taste
- ¼ tsp dried thyme
- 1 tsp dried oregano
- 1 tsp dried basil
- 1 tsp sugar
- 1 tbsp balsamic vinegar
- 1 tbsp tomato paste
- ½ tsp crushed red pepper flakes or to taste
- 12 ounces rigatoni pasta
- 1 cup whole milk
- 1 cup red wine
- 4 ounces Mascarpone cheese
- ¼ cup Parmesan cheese finely grated
- 3 tbsp parsley fresh, chopped

Directions:
1. Press SAUTÉ and add olive oil to inner pot of Instant Pot. Add onions, celery, carrots, bell peppers and garlic and sauté for 3 minutes, stirring frequently.
2. Add fresh mushrooms and sauté for 2 minutes. Turn off Instant Pot by pressing CANCEL.
3. If there's food stuck to the bottom, deglaze pot with 2 tablespoons of water.

4. Add in dried porcini mushrooms, crushed tomatoes, black pepper, salt, thyme, oregano, basil, sugar, balsamic vinegar, tomato paste, crushed red pepper, pasta, milk, wine and water. Stir to combine.
5. Close Instant Pot lid, and make sure steam release handle is in the Sealing position. Select MANUAL and cook at HIGH pressure for 7 minutes. Use a quick release.
6. There might seem to be more liquid than you'd like, but don't worry, the liquid will get absorbed by the pasta.
7. Stir in mascarpone cheese. Let the pasta rest for a few minutes and it will thicken up.
8. Sprinkle each serving with Parmesan and fresh parsley.

Red White and Green Brussels Sprouts
(Prep + Cook Time: 20 minutes | Servings: 4)

Ingredients:
- 1 pound Brussels Sprouts
- ¼ cup pine nuts toasted
- 1 Pomegranate
- 1 tbsp extra-virgin olive oil
- ½ tsp salt
- 1 grate pepper

Directions:
1. Remove the outer leaves and trim the stems of the washed Brussels Sprouts. Cut the largest ones in half to get them to a uniform size for even cooking.
2. Prepare the Instant Pot by pouring in one cup of water, and adding the steamer basket. Put the sprouts in the basket.
3. Close the lid and set the valve to pressure cooking position. Cook for 3 minutes on MANUAL at HIGH pressure.
4. When time is up, quick release the pressure.
5. Move the sprouts to a serving dish and dress in olive oil, salt and pepper prior to sprinkling with toasted pine nuts and pomegranate seeds.
6. Serve warm or room temperature. Enjoy!

Candied Cajun Trail Mix

(Prep + Cook Time: 25 minutes | Servings: 5)

Ingredients:

- 1 ½ cups raw pecan halves
- 1 cup raw almonds
- 1 cup chickpeas drained, or more if preferred, omit for paleo friendly
- 1/3 - ½ cup cashews
- ¼ cup raw sunflower seeds
- 2-3 tbsp vegan butter or regular butter
- 1 tbsp water optional
- ½ cup pure maple syrup
- ½ -1 tbsp spicy cajun seasoning or mix, you can also use use 1/4 to ½ tsp each of cayenne, garlic, onion powder, paprika, and pepper
- 1 pinch ground ginger
- 1 pinch sea salt
- 6 oz dried mango or spicy chili dried mango, add after

Directions:

1. Heat the Instant Pot in SAUTÉ mode.
2. Place all ingredients into the Instant Pot. Mix thoroughly.
3. Sauté with plastic spatula until butter is melted and nuts/ chickpeas are coated with the seasoning and maple syrup. If batter seems too sticky/thick once sautéing, add the 1 tablespoon of water.
4. Close and lock the lid. Select MANUAL and cook at HIGH pressure for 10 minutes. Use a quick release.
5. Remove from pot and spread the nut mix onto a lined cooking sheet.
6. Bake on 375F for 7-10 minutes in the oven; turning nuts/seeds half way. Any longer might burn the nuts. The chickpeas will be a little less cooked but still tasty! See notes for other options.
7. Remove from oven and Let Cajun trail mix completely cool.
8. Lastly, dice you mango into small pieces. Then add to your candied Cajun trail mix and stir all together. It's easiest to this in large zip lock or air tight container. If you are using plain dried mango, feel free to add more spices to the mix to coat.
9. Store in air tight container. Makes 5 cups or so.

Notes: If want crispier chickpeas, try adding in roasted chickpeas snacks after cooking, instead of cooking the canned.

The Whole Chicken

(Prep + Cook Time: 30 minutes | Servings: 8)

Ingredients:

- 1 medium-sized, whole chicken
- 1 minced green onion
- 2 tbsp sugar
- 2-3 cups water or chicken broth
- 1 tbsp cooking wine
- 1 minced piece of ginger
- 2 tsp soy sauce
- 2 tsp salt

Directions:

1. Season the chicken thoroughly with salt and sugar.
2. Sprinkle 1 teaspoon of salt into the bottom of the Instant Pot.
3. Pour the wine, water or broth and soy sauce into the cooker, and add the chicken.
4. Choose POULTRY and cook on HIGH pressure for 15 minutes.
5. When time is up, flip the chicken, and push POULTRY again.
6. Let the pressure come down naturally before opening the cooker.
7. Serve chicken pieces with green onion on top and any side dishes you'd like.

Salsa Verde Chicken (E&S)

(Prep + Cook Time: 25 minutes | Servings: 6)

Ingredients:

2 ½ pounds of boneless chicken breasts
16 ounces of salsa verde
1 tsp smoked paprika
1 tsp cumin
1 tsp salt

Directions:

1. Throw everything into your Instant Pot pressure cooker.
2. Select MANUAL and cook at HIGH pressure for 25 minutes.
3. When the timer goes off, quick-release the pressure.
4. Carefully open the cooker and shred the chicken.
5. Serve and enjoy.

Buttery Chicken
(Prep + Cook Time: 30 minutes | Servings: 4)

Ingredients:
- 1 ½ pounds chicken thighs, skinless, cut into bite-sized pieces
- 1 can (15 ounce) tomato sauce
- 1 green bell pepper, chopped in large pieces
- 1 onion, diced
- 1 tsp coriander powder
- 1 tsp garam masala
- 1 tsp paprika
- 1 tsp salt
- 1 tsp turmeric
- ¼ tsp black pepper
- ¼ tsp cayenne
- ¼ tsp cumin
- 1-inch ginger, minced
- 2 tbs butter, grass-fed OR ghee, OR your choice of fat
- 5 garlic cloves, minced

After cooking:
- 1 cup coconut cream
- Pinch dried fenugreek leaves (kasoori methi)
- Cilantro, for garnish, optional

Directions:
1. Press the SAUTE key of the Instant Pot. Put the ghee and onion in the pot. Stir-fry the onion for about 8 to 10 minutes or until starting to brown.
2. Add the ginger and garlic; stir-fry for 30 seconds. Stir in the spices.
3. Add the chicken and mix well until combined. Continue stirring for about 4 to 5 minutes or until the chicken is seared.
4. Add the green bell pepper and tomato sauce. Cover and lock the lid. Turn the steam valve to Sealing.
5. Press the POULTRY key – this will automatically set the time for 15 minutes.

6. When the Instant Pot timer beeps, turn the steam valve to quick release the pressure or let the pressure release naturally. Unlock and carefully open the lid. Stir in the coconut cream and dried fenugreek leaves.
7. If desired, garnish with cilantro. Serve.

Balsamic Chicken Thighs
(Prep + Cook Time: 25 minutes | Servings: 2)

Ingredients:
- 1 pound boneless, skinless chicken thighs
- ½ cup balsamic vinegar
- ⅓ cup cream sherry wine
- 2 tbsp chopped cilantro
- 2 tbsp olive oil
- 2 tbsp minced green onion
- 1½ tsp minced garlic
- 1 tsp dried basil
- 1 tsp garlic powder
- 1 tsp Worcestershire sauce
- ½ tsp black pepper

Directions:
1. Mix basil, salt, garlic, pepper, sherry, Worcestershire sauce, onion, and vinegar in a plastic bag.
2. Add chicken and squish around, so the chicken becomes completely coated. Turn your Instant Pot on and select SAUTE.
3. Pour in the olive oil and cook the minced garlic, stirring, until fragrant.
4. Pour the chicken and sauce. Secure the lid.
5. Select POULTRY. The POULTRY setting defaults to 15 minutes, which is the correct length of time for this recipe.
6. When it beeps, quick-release the pressure.
7. Serve with chopped cilantro and a side dish like rice or veggies.

Creamy Chicken and Mushroom
(Prep + Cook Time: 35 minutes | Servings: 4)

Ingredients:
- 2 pounds chicken thighs
- 16 ounces baby portabella mushrooms, sliced
- 1 can coconut cream
- Chicken broth, enough to fill the can of coconut cream after the coconut water is poured out
- 1 tsp dried thyme
- 1 tsp garlic powder
- 1 tsp onion powder
- 1 tsp salt
- 1 tbsp water
- 2 tbsp tapioca starch

Directions:
1. The night before cooking, chill the coconut cream can in the refrigerator overnight.
2. Before cooking, take the can out from the fridge and, without shaking the can, turn it upside down. Open the can. The coconut cream and water should be separated with the coconut water on top. Scoop or pour out the coconut water from the can.
3. Add chicken broth to replace the coconut water, filling the can to the top. Pour the broth and coconut cream into a medium-sized bowl.
4. Add the spices in the bowl. Whisk until well combined. Put the chicken in the Instant Pot.
5. Add the mushrooms on top of the chicken, covering the meat. Pour the coconut cream mix over the chicken and mushrooms. Cover and lock the lid. Press the MANUAL key, set the pressure to HIGH, and set the timer for 10 minutes.
6. When the Instant Pot timer beeps, let the pressure release naturally. Turn the steam valve to Venting to release remaining pressure. Unlock and carefully open the lid.
7. With a slotted spoon, remove the mushroom and chicken from the pot, leaving the cooking liquid in the pot. Set aside the chicken and mushroom.

8. Discard ½ of the cooking liquid. Press the SAUTE key and bring to cooking liquid in the pot to a boil. In a small-sized bowl, combine the tapioca starch and water, whisking until smooth.
9. When the cooking liquid is boiling, whisk in the starch mixture until smooth and the liquid is thick as gravy. Turn off the Instant Pot.
10. Place the chicken and mushroom, ladle the gravy over, and serve.

Sticky Sesame Chicken (E&S)
(Prep + Cook Time: 30 minutes | Servings: 4)

Ingredients:
- 6 boneless chicken thigh fillets
- 4 peeled and crushed garlic cloves
- 5 tbsp hoisin sauce
- 5 tbsp sweet chili sauce
- ½ cup chicken stock
- 1 chunk of peeled, grated fresh ginger
- 1 ½ tbsp sesame seeds
- 1 tbsp rice vinegar
- 1 tbsp soy sauce

Directions:
1. Spread chicken thigh fillets and place them into the Instant Pot.
2. Whisk garlic, ginger, chili sauce, hoisin, vinegar, sesame seeds, broth, and soy sauce into a sauce.
3. Pour over chicken and stir.
4. Select MANUAL and cook for 15 minutes at HIGH pressure.
5. When time is up, hit CANCEL and wait for a natural pressure release.
6. When all the pressure is gone, open up the cooker and serve the chicken with rice.

Autumn Chicken and Vegetables

(Prep + Cook Time: 30 minutes | Servings: 4-6)

Ingredients:

- 3-4 pounds chicken thighs bone in
- ½ tsp salt
- ½ tsp black pepper
- ½ cup all-purpose flour gluten free, if celiac
- 2 tbsp olive oil
- ½ cup apple cider or juice
- ¼ cup chicken broth
- 1 tsp dried thyme
- 1 small butternut squash cut into ¾-inch pieces, 3-4 cups
- 1 bulb fennel thinly sliced
- ½ cup walnuts optional
- ¼ cup basil leaves fresh, very thinly sliced, optional

Directions:

1. Season chicken with salt and pepper; coat lightly with flour. Press SAUTÉ; heat oil in the Instant Pot, Add chicken in batches; cook about 8 minutes or until browned on both sides. Remove to plate.
2. Stir in cider, broth and thyme; cook 1 minute, scraping up browned bits from bottom of pot. Return chicken to pot, pressing into liquid.
3. Secure lid and move pressure release valve to Sealing position. Press MANUAL and cook at HIGH pressure for 6 minutes.
4. When cooking is complete, press CANCEL and use quick release.
5. Add squash and fennel to pot. Secure the lid. Select MANUAL and cook at HIGH pressure for 3 minutes.
6. When cooking is complete, press CANCEL and use quick release. Remove chicken and vegetables to platter; cover loosely to keep warm.
7. Press SAUTÉ; cook sauce about 5 minutes or until slightly thickened and reduced by one third.
8. Serve sauce with chicken and vegetables; sprinkle with walnuts and basil, if desired.

Chicken Thighs with Cranberries and Pears

(Prep + Cook Time: 25 minutes | Servings: 6)

Ingredients:

- 2 pounds boneless, skinless chicken thighs
- 2 big, firm peeled and sliced Bosc pears
- 1 chopped shallot
- ⅔ cup chicken broth
- ¼ cup dried cranberries
- 2 tbsp balsamic vinegar
- 2 tbsp butter
- ½ tsp dried dill
- ½ tsp salt
- ½ tsp pepper

Directions:

1. Press SAUTE and melt the butter in your Instant Pot.
2. Season your chicken with salt and pepper.
3. In batches, brown the thighs on both sides in your pot until golden, turning once.
4. When the thighs are all browned and in a bowl, add pears and shallot to the pot.
5. Stir until the shallot is soft. Add vinegar, cranberries, and dried dill.
6. When the pot is bubbling, pour in broth and stir. Add chicken and lock and seal the lid.
7. Select MANUAL and cook at HIGH pressure for 15 minutes.
8. When time is up, Press CANCEL and quick-release the pressure.
9. Stir and serve!

Hot Buffalo Wings

(Prep + Cook Time: 20 minutes | Servings: 6)

Ingredients:

- 4 pounds chicken wings, sectioned, frozen or fresh
- 1-2 tbsp sugar, light brown
- ½ tsp kosher salt
- ½ cup cayenne pepper hot sauce (I used frank's red hot)
- ½ cup butter
- 1 tbsp Worcestershire sauce
- 1½ cups water

Directions:

For the sauce:

In a microwavable container, mix the hot sauce with the Worcestershire sauce, butter, salt, and brown sugar; microwave for 15 seconds or until the butter is melted.

For the wings:

1. Pour the water into the Instant Pot. Set a trivet in the bottom of the pot.
2. Put the chicken wings on the trivet. Cover and lock the lid. Press the MANUAL key, set the pressure to HIGH, and set the timer for 5 minutes.
3. When the Instant Pot timer beeps, release the pressure naturally for 5 minutes, then turn the steam valve to quick release the pressure. Unlock and carefully open the lid.
4. Put the oven rack in the center of the oven. Turn the oven to the broil.
5. Carefully transfer the chicken wings from the pot into a cookie sheet. Brush the tops of the chicken wings with the sauce.
6. Place the cookie sheet in the oven and broil for 5 minutes.
7. Turn the chicken wings and brush the other side with the remaining sauce.
8. Serve with celery sticks and blue cheese dressing.

Notes: If you want a hotter sauce, use more hot sauce. If you want a milder sauce, use more butter.

Easy Spicy Chicken Wings (E&S)

(Prep + Cook Time: 20 minutes | Servings: 4)

Ingredients:

- 3 pounds chicken wings
- 1½ cup chicken broth or water
- ¼ cup light brown sugar
- 2 tbsp olive oil
- ½ tsp garlic powder
- ½ tsp paprika
- ½ tsp cayenne pepper
- ½ tsp salt
- ½ tsp black pepper

Directions:

1. Rinse and dry the chicken wings with a paper towel. Tumble into a mixing bowl.
2. In a separate bowl, mix the seasonings. You want about 3 tablespoons total of the mixed spice rub, so feel free to add more of whatever spice you like.
3. More sugar will make it sweeter, more pepper will make it spicier.
4. Add olive oil and your spice rub to the chicken wings, and rub.
5. Pour chicken broth in your cooker and add wings. Close and seal the lid.
6. Select MANUAL and cook at HIGH pressure for 9 minutes.
7. When time is up, press CANCEL and use a quick release.
8. Optional: For really crispy skin, broil for 5-6 minutes, flipping halfway through.
9. Serve with hot sauce on the side!

Chicken and Corn Stew

(Prep + Cook Time: 35 minutes | Servings: 4)

Ingredients:

- 8 chicken drumsticks, skinless (28 ounces total)
- 2 corn on the cob, husked and halved
- 1 can (8 ounces) tomato sauce
- 3 scallions, chopped
- 2 cups water
- 1/4 cup cilantro, chopped PLUS
- 1 tbsp, chopped, for garnish
- ½ tsp kosher salt
- ½ tsp garlic powder
- ½ tsp cumin
- ½ onion, medium-sized, chopped
- 1 tsp olive oil
- 1 tbsp chicken bouillon (I used Chicken Better than Bouillon)
- 1 plum tomato, diced
- 1 garlic, crushed

Directions:

1. Season the chicken drumsticks with garlic powder and salt.
2. Press the SAUTÉ key of the Instant Pot.
3. When the pot is hot, add the olive oil.
4. Add the garlic, scallions, onions, and tomato. Sauté for about 2-3 minutes or until softened.
5. Add 1/4 cup of the cilantro and sauté, stirring, for 1 minute.
6. Add the water, tomato sauce, cumin, bouillon, and stir to combine. Put the chicken in the sauce.
7. Top the chicken with the corn. Cover and lock the lid.
8. Press the MANUAL key, set the pressure to HIGH, and set the timer for 20 minutes. When the Instant Pot timer beeps, turn the steam valve to Venting to quick release the pressure.
9. Unlock and carefully open the lid.
10. Garnish with the cilantro and serve.

Chicken, Mushroom, and Jasmine Rice in One Pot
(Prep + Cook Time: 15 minutes | Servings: 4)

Ingredients:

- 8 ounces cremini mushrooms (or your preferred kind)
- 3 pounds chicken legs and/ or thighs, skinless, boneless, any fat removed, cut into large chunks
- 3 cups Jasmine rice (18 ounces), washed until the water runs clear
- 2½ cups (about 24 ounces) chicken broth OR water

For the marinade:

- 1 tsp rice wine vinegar
- ¼ tsp Chinese five spice
- 2 tsp ginger, grated
- 3 tbsp black soy sauce
- 3 tbsp soy sauce (low sodium)
- Scallions, to garnish

Directions:

1. Put the chicken chunks into large-sized bowl.
2. Add the mushrooms. In another bowl, whisk together all of the marinade ingredients until well combined.
3. Pour the marinade over the chicken and mushroom. Toss to coat and marinate in the fridge for at least 30 minutes or overnight.
4. Put the rice, broth, and chicken and mushroom mixture in the Instant Pot. Cover and lock the lid.
5. Press the MANUAL key, set the pressure to HIGH, and set the timer for 10 minutes.
6. When the Instant Pot timer beeps, let the pressure release naturally for 10 minutes.

Notes: The cup I used to measure the rice is a "rice cup". If you want less rice for your dish, use 2 "rice cups" of Jasmine rice and 1½ cups broth or water. You can use chicken breast for this dish – just cut it into large chunks. If you reduce this recipe tin half, reduce the cooking time to 3 minutes and release the pressure naturally.

Honey Garlic Chicken Wings

(Prep + Cook Time: 25 minutes | Servings: 2-4)

Ingredients:
- 1½ pounds chicken wings
- 4 cloves garlic roughly minced
- ½ shallot roughly minced
- 1-2 star anise
- 1 tbsp Ginger sliced
- 1 tbsp honey
- ½ cup water warm
- 1 tbsp peanut oil
- 1 ½ tbsp cornstarch
- 2 tbsp light soy sauce
- 1 tbsp dark soy sauce
- 1 tbsp Shaoxing wine
- 1 tsp sugar
- ¼ tsp salt

Directions:
1. Make the Marinade by mixing together light soy sauce, dark soy sauce, Shaoxing wine, sugar, and salt. Marinate the chicken wings with the Chicken Wing Marinade for 20 minutes.
2. Heat up the Instant Pot by pressing SAUTÉ button and click the adjust button to go to Sauté More function. Wait until the indicator says "Hot".
3. Add the tablespoon of peanut oil into the pot. Ensure to coat the oil over the whole bottom of the pot. Add the marinated chicken wings into the pot (do not discard the chicken wing marinade).
4. Then, brown the chicken wings for roughly 30 seconds on each side. Flip a few times as you brown them as the soy sauce and sugar can be burnt easily. Remove and set aside.
5. Reduce the heat to medium by pressing Cancel button, then press SAUTÉ button. Add the minced shallot, star anise and sliced ginger, then stir for roughly a minute.

6. Add the minced garlic and stir until fragrant (roughly 30 seconds).
7. Mix 1 tablespoon of honey with 1/2 cup of warm water, then add it into the pot and deglaze the bottom of the pot with a wooden spoon.
8. Place all the chicken wings with all the meat juice and the leftover chicken wing marinade into the pot. Close lid and cook on MANUAL at HIGH pressure for 5 minutes.
9. When time is up fully natural release (roughly 10 minutes).
10. Open the lid carefully and taste one of the honey soy chicken wings and the honey soy sauce. Season with more salt or honey if desired.
11. Remove all the chicken wings from the pot and set aside.
12. Press SAUTÉ button. Mix 1½ tablespoons of cornstarch with 1 tablespoon of cold running tap water. Keep mixing and add it into the honey soy sauce one third at a time until desired thickness.
13. Turn off the heat and add the chicken wings back into the pot. Coat well with the honey soy sauce and serve immediately.
14. Enjoy!

Indian-Style Apricot Chicken

(Prep + Cook Time: 35 minutes | Servings: 4-6)

Ingredients:

- 2 ½ pounds chicken thighs bone-in skinless
- ½ tsp salt
- ¼ tsp black pepper
- 1 tbsp vegetable oil
- 1 large onion chopped
- ½ cup chicken broth divided
- 1 tbsp Ginger grated fresh
- 2 cloves garlic minced
- ½ tsp ground cinnamon
- 1/8 tsp ground allspice
- 1 can diced tomatoes 14-ounce can
- 1 package dried apricots 8-ounce can
- 1 pinch saffron threads optional
- Italian parsley chopped fresh, optional

Directions:

1. Season both sides of chicken with 1/2 teaspoon salt and 1⁄4 teaspoon pepper. Press SAUTÉ; heat oil in Instant Pot. Add chicken in batches; cook about 8 minutes or until browned on both sides. Remove to plate.
2. Add onion and 2 tablespoons broth to pot; cook and stir 5 minutes or until onion is translucent, scraping up browned bits from bottom of pot.
3. Add ginger, garlic, cinnamon and allspice; cook and stir 30 seconds or until fragrant.
4. Stir in tomatoes, apricots, remaining broth and saffron, if desired; mix well. Return chicken to pot, pressing into liquid.
5. Secure lid and move pressure release valve to Sealing position. Press MANUAL and cook at HIGH pressure for 11 minutes.
6. When cooking is complete, press CANCEL and use a quick release. Season with additional salt and pepper.
7. Garnish with parsley and serve.

Indian Chicken Curry

(Prep + Cook Time: 55 minutes | Servings: 6)

Ingredients:
- 3 tbsp butter or ghee
- 1 large bay leaf
- 2 inch cinnamon stick
- ½ tsp cumin seeds
- 2 cups onions chopped fine
- 1 tbsp garlic minced
- 1 tbsp Ginger minced
- 2 tbsp tomato paste
- 1½ tbsp coriander powder
- ¾ tsp turmeric powder
- ¾ tsp ground black pepper
- ¾ tsp Indian chili powder or cayenne, or to taste
- 1½ tsp salt or to taste
- 3 pounds chicken thighs or drumsticks, bone-in
- 2 cups potato cut into 1½ inch cubes
- ½ cup water or chicken broth
- 1½ tsp garam masala
- 2 tbsp cashew paste
- ¼ cup cilantro chopped

Directions:
1. In SAUTÉ mode, melt butter. Add cinnamon, cumin seeds and bay leaf and stir till fragrant, being careful not to burn.
2. Add onions, garlic and ginger, and sauté till golden brown, about 7 minutes.
3. Add tomato paste mixed with 2 tablespoons water and stir.
4. Sauté until tomato paste is cooked, about 3 minutes. If it sticks to the bottom, add another tablespoon or two of water.
5. Turn off Instant Pot, otherwise spices can burn when you add them. Add coriander, turmeric, black pepper, cayenne, salt and stir till fragrant.
6. In SAUTÉ mode, add chicken pieces and stir to coat with spice mixture.
7. Add 1/2 cup water or chicken broth and cook in POULTRY mode for 15 minutes. When time is up, do a quick release.
8. Add cubed potatoes and garam masala to chicken and stir gently. Select MANUAL and cook at HIGH pressure for 6 minutes. When time is up, do a quick release.

9. To make cashew paste, blend 1/4 to 1/3 cup cashews with water to make a thick (like peanut butter) paste. Substitute cashew paste with cashew butter or heavy cream or coconut cream. You can also thicken the curry by cooking down the liquid at the end, in SAUTE mode. If you prefer a thin curry, you can omit the thickener altogether
10. Add cashew paste, stir the chicken curry and heat through in SAUTÉ mode.
11. Turn off Instant Pot, sprinkle chicken curry with cilantro and serve with Instant Pot basmati rice, bread or naan.

Curry In a Hurry (E&S)
(Prep + Cook Time: 25 minutes | Servings: 6)

Ingredients:
- 2 pounds chicken breast or thighs
- 2 tbsp curry powder
- 3 tbsp honey
- 6 ounces can tomato paste
- 2 cloves garlic, minced
- 16 ounces canned tomato sauce
- 16 ounces canned coconut milk
- 1 tsp salt
- 1 cup onion, chopped OR
- ¼ cup dry minced onion

Directions:
1. Except for the chicken, put all of the ingredients into the Instant Pot.
2. Stir to combine and then add the chicken. Cover and lock the lid.
3. Press the MANUAL key, set the pressure to HIGH, and set the timer for 15 minutes.
4. When the Instant Pot timer beeps, press the CANCEL key and unplug the Instant Pot.
5. Let the pressure release naturally for 10-15 minutes or until the valve drops. Turn the steam valve to release remaining pressure.
6. Unlock and carefully open the lid. Serve with rice and/ or peas.

Italian Chicken

(Prep + Cook Time: 25 minutes | Servings: 6)

Ingredients:

- 8 boneless, skinless chicken thighs
- 2 medium-sized, chopped carrots
- ½ pound stemmed and quartered cremini mushrooms
- 2 cups cherry tomatoes
- 3 smashed garlic cloves
- ½ cup pitted green olives
- ½ cup thinly-sliced fresh basil
- ¼ cup chopped fresh Italian parsley
- 1 chopped onion
- 1 tbsp olive oil
- 1 tbsp tomato paste
- ½ tsp black pepper
- Salt to taste

Directions:

1. Season the chicken thighs with salt.
2. On your Instant Pot, hit SAUTE and pour in the olive oil.
3. When shiny, toss in the carrots, mushrooms, onions, and a little salt.
4. Cook for about 3-5 minutes until soft.
5. Add the smashed garlic and tomato paste and cook for another 30 seconds.
6. Last, add the cherry tomatoes, chicken thighs, and olives.
7. Turn off SAUTE before locking the pressure cooker.
8. Select MANUAL and cook at HIGH pressure for 10 minutes.
9. When the beeper goes off, quick-release the pressure right away.
10. Take off the lid and season. Serve.

Italian Chicken Liver Pate' Spread

(Prep + Cook Time: 15 minutes | Servings: 8-12)

Ingredients:

- ¾ pound chicken livers
- 1 onion roughly chopped
- 1 bay leaf
- ¼ cup red wine
- 2 Anchovies in oil
- 1 tbsp Capers
- 1 tbsp butter
- 1 tsp Rum or Whiskey
- ½ tsp salt
- ¼ tsp pepper

Directions:

1. Heat up your pressure cooker using the SAUTÉ mode, put a little olive oil in your Instant Pot and begin to soften the onion with a little salt and pepper.
2. Add the chicken livers and bay leaf and swish everything around for about 2 minutes until the outside of the livers are seared.
3. Add the red wine and, with a wooden spoon, quickly rub (deglaze) any brown bits stuck to the bottom or sides of the pan and incorporate them into the wine.
4. Close the lid and set the valve to pressure cooking position. Cook for 5 minutes on MANUAL at HIGH pressure.
5. When time is up, open the Instant Pot by quick releasing pressure through the valve.
6. Remove and discard the Bay Leaf and add the Anchovies and Capers. Puree' the contents of the cooker with an immersion blender.
7. Taste to check if the seasoning is correct and fold in the butter, which will melt with the residual heat, and Rum. Mix well.
8. Transfer to serving container and sprinkle with fresh herbs to garnish. Chill before serving.
9. Serve with crostini or lightly toasted french bread slices. Enjoy!

Chinese Simmered Chicken

(Prep + Cook Time: 25 minutes | Servings: 4-6)

Ingredients:

- 4 pounds chicken white and/or dark meat, boneless or bone in, skin removed
- 1 tbsp extra-virgin olive oil

Sauce:

- 1/3 cup soy sauce low sodium
- 1/3 cup brown sugar
- ¼ cup water
- ¼ cup dry Sherry or apple juice
- 1 tbsp ketchup
- ¼-½ tsp red pepper flakes crushed
- 1 clove garlic minced
- 1 scallion sliced

Other:

- 2 tbsp potato starch or cornstarch
- 2 tsp sesame seeds toasted (optional)
- Rice already cooked,

Directions:

1. Remove skin and fat from chicken.
2. Combine Sauce ingredients and whisk together well.
3. Select SAUTÉ on your Instant Pot and allow to fully heat. Add 1 tablespoon of oil to the cooking pot and lightly sear chicken pieces, doing the dark meat first.
4. Deglaze the cooking pot with the Sherry and then add the sauce and mix through.
5. If making this a One Pot Meal, add the prepared rice now.
6. Close and Lock the lid of the Instant Pot and set the valve to Sealing. Cook at HIGH Pressure for 6 minutes. When beep sounds, allow a 15 minute natural pressure release.
7. Turn off the Instant Pot and then select SAUTÉ function again.
8. Remove rice and trivet and cover rice. Remove white meat chicken to a platter.
9. Remove 1/2 cup of sauce, add potato starch and whisk until smooth. Add the slurry to the cooking pot and incorporate.
10. Remove dark meat chicken to the platter. Continue whisking until sauce is sticky and thick.
11. Pour sauce over chicken and garnish with toasted sesame seeds.

Butter Chicken Murgh Makhani

(Prep + Cook Time: 30 minutes | Servings: 4)

Ingredients:
- 1 can tomatoes diced, 14 ounce can
- 5-6 cloves garlic minced
- 1-2 tsp Ginger chopped
- 1 tsp turmeric
- ½ tsp cayenne pepper
- 1 tsp paprika
- 1 tsp salt
- 1 tsp garam masala
- 1 tsp cumin powder
- 1 pound chicken thighs boneless, skinless (or use breast, bone-in, or whatever works for you. If frozen, add 1-2 minutes to total time)

To finish:
- 4 ounces butter cut into cubes, use coconut oil if dairy free
- 4 ounces heavy cream use full-fat coconut milk if dairy free
- 1 tsp garam masala
- ¼ - ½ cup cilantro chopped

Directions:
1. Place all ingredients in the Instant Pot in the order listed, excluding the butter, cream, cilantro and 1 teaspoon of the garam masala, mixing the sauce well.
2. Place the chicken on top of the sauce. If it's frozen, push it into the sauce a bit so it defrosts better.
3. Close and lock the lid. Select MANUAL and cook at HIGH pressure for 10 minutes. When time is up, allow for natural pressure release.
4. Remove the chicken carefully from the Instant Pot and set aside. Blend together all the ingredients, preferably using an immersion blender.
5. Add the cut up butter, cream, cilantro, and garam masala and stir until well incorporated. It's best to let the sauce cool just a little before adding the butter and the cream.
6. Adding it into the boiling sauce will make your sauce very thin. If that happens, just put it in the fridge for a little and let it

thicken up. It should be thick enough to coat the back of a spoon.

7. Take out half the sauce and freeze for later or store in the fridge for 2-3 days.
8. Add the chicken back and heat through. Break it up into smaller pieces if you need but don't shred it.
9. Serve over rice, or zucchini noodles. Enjoy!

Chicken, Shrimp and Broccoli Alfredo
(Prep + Cook Time: 30 minutes | Servings: 4)

Ingredients:
- 8 ounces shrimp, small-sized
- 6 ounces Parmesan cheese, fresh grated
- 4 pieces (4 ounces each) chicken breast, cubed
- 4 leaves fresh basil, chopped
- 4 cloves garlic, minced
- 2 cups heavy cream
- 2 cups broccoli
- ¼ cup fresh parsley, chopped
- 1 stick butter
- 1 bar (8 ounces) cream cheese

Directions:
1. Press the SAUTÉ key of the Instant Pot. Put the stick of butter and melt.
2. Add the cream cheese and whisk until the mixture is creamy. Slowly add the heavy cream.
3. Add the freshly grated Parmesan cheese. Add the rest of the ingredients. Cover and lock the lid.
4. Press MANUAL, set the pressure to HIGH, and set the time for 15 minutes.
5. When the timer beeps, turn the steam valve to Venting to quick release the pressure.
6. Carefully open the lid. Serve.

Chicken Parmesan Pasta (E&S)

(Prep + Cook Time: 30 minutes | Servings: 6)

Ingredients:
- 1 cup water
- 1 box linguine noodles
- 4 skinless, boneless, frozen chicken breasts
- 1 jar of spaghetti sauce
- 5 chopped garlic cloves
- 1 large onion
- 30 halved cherry tomatoes
- 1 cup Italian breadcrumbs
- ½ cup chopped parsley
- 1 tbsp butter
- Salt and crushed red pepper to taste
- ½ tsp Italian seasoning
- Parmesan cheese

Directions:
1. Put water, chicken, and noodles in your Instant Pot.
2. You'll probably have to break the noodles in half.
3. Pour in jar of sauce. Mix. Add everything else except the butter, cheese, and breadcrumbs.
4. Stir again before closing and sealing the lid.
5. Select MANUAL and cook at HIGH pressure for 20 minutes.
6. When time is up, turn off the cooker and quick-release.
7. Toast the bread crumbs in melted butter.
8. Sprinkle on top of pasta with Parmesan cheese. Serve!

Chicken Piccata

(Prep + Cook Time: 40 minutes | Servings: 4)

Ingredients:
- 4 chicken breasts skinless, boneless, 1½ to 1¾ pounds
- ½ tsp salt
- ¼ tsp black pepper
- 1 tbsp olive oil
- 1 cup chicken broth
- ¼ cup fresh lemon juice
- 2 tbsp butter
- 2 tbsp brined capers drained
- 2 tbsp flat-leaf parsley chopped fresh
- Hot cooked pasta or rice
- Lemon slices

Directions:
1. Season the chicken with salt and pepper. Select SAUTÉ mode and adjust to normal. Heat oil in the Instant Pot; add chicken and cook for 2 to 3 minutes per side until browned.
2. Add broth. Press CANCEL. Secure the lid on the pot.
3. Close the pressure-release valve. Select MANUAL and cook at HIGH pressure for 3 minutes. When cooking is complete, use a quick release pressure.
4. Use tongs to remove chicken to a serving platter; cover to keep warm.
5. Add lemon juice to cooking liquid in pot. Select SAUTÉ and adjust to normal. Bring to a simmer and cook for 5 minutes to reduce. Press CANCEL.
6. Whisk butter into sauce; add capers and parsley.
7. Pour sauce over chicken. Serve over pasta or rice.
8. Serve with lemon slices.

Chicken Nachos
(Prep + Cook Time: 35 minutes | Servings: 6)

Ingredients:
- 1½ pounds chicken thighs, boneless, skinless
- 1 package (1 ounce) taco seasoning mix
- ½ cup Herdez salsa Verde (mild)
- ½ cup mild red salsa

Directions:
1. Press the SAUTE key of the Instant Pot and select the MORE option for high heat.
2. Put the oil in the pot and heat. When the oil is hot, add the chicken thighs and cook until the chicken begins to brown nicely.
3. In a bowl, combine the taco seasoning and salsa and stir to combine. Pour the salsa mixture in the pot. Stir to combine.
4. Press the CANCEL key to stop the sauté function. Cover and lock the lid.
5. Press the POULTRY key and set the timer for 15 minutes.
6. When the Instant Pot timer beeps, press the CANCEL key. Let the pressure release naturally for 10-15 minutes. Turn the steam valve to release remaining pressure.
7. Unlock and carefully open the lid. Shred the chicken and serve with tortilla chips.
8. Optional: Top each serving with shredded cheese, sour cream, diced green onions, black beans, and chopped cilantro to taste.

Chicken Tostadas

(Prep + Cook Time: 35 minutes | Servings: 6-8)

Ingredients:

- 2 pounds chicken breast boneless skinless, fresh or frozen
- 1 cup water
- 1 tbsp chili powder
- 1 tsp cumin
- 1 tsp salt
- ½ tsp pepper
- 1 tsp paprika
- 1 tsp garlic powder
- 1 tsp onion powder
- ¼ tsp cayenne powder
- 1 cup salsa

Directions:

1. Place fresh or frozen chicken breasts in the Instant Pot and cover with 1 cup of water.
2. Set to MANUAL mode on HIGH pressure, adjusting the time to 9 minutes for fresh and 12 minutes for frozen. Lock the lid, making sure the valve is in the Sealing position.
3. When finished, allow the pressure to release naturally for 5 minutes, then do a quick pressure release by switching the valve to venting.
4. Remove the chicken and allow to cool for a few minutes. Drain the liquid from the Instant Pot.
5. Shred the chicken. Return shredded chicken into the Instant Pot.
6. Set the pot to SAUTÉ. Stir 1 cup of jarred salsa, and all of the spices and seasoning into the shredded chicken. Allow to cook for about 3 minutes to combine all of the flavors.
7. Serve as tostadas, tacos, or bowls. Top with your favorites like avocado, Queso Fresco, cilantro, onion, and lime juice.

Chicken Congee (E&S)

(Prep + Cook Time: 65 minutes | Servings: 7)

Ingredients:

- 6 chicken drumsticks
- 7 cups water
- 1 cup Jasmine rice
- 1 tbsp fresh ginger
- Salt to taste

Directions:

1. Rinse rice under cool water for a few minutes.
2. Pour rice, water, ginger, and drumsticks into Instant Pot. Seal the lid.
3. Select MANUAL and cook at HIGH pressure for 30 minutes.
4. When time is up, press CANCEL and wait for a natural pressure release.
5. When safe, open the lid and press SAUTE.
6. Keep stirring while the congee thickens.
7. Season with salt.
8. Pull off the chicken with tongs, and throw away the bones.
9. Serve right away!

Honey-Sriracha Chicken

(Prep + Cook Time: 15 minutes | Servings: 4)

Ingredients:

- 4 diced chicken breasts
- ¼ cup sugar
- 5 tbsp soy sauce
- 2-3 tbsp sriracha
- 2-3 tbsp honey
- 2 tbsp cornstarch
- 2 tbsp water + 2 tbsp cold water
- 1 tbsp minced garlic

Directions:

1. Mix soy sauce, honey, sriracha, sugar, 2 tablespoons of water, and garlic in your Instant Pot.
2. Add chicken and mix to coat in the sauce. Close and seal the lid. Select MANUAL and cook for 9 minutes at HIGH pressure.
3. When time is up, quick-release the pressure after turning the cooker off. In a cup, mix 2 tablespoons of cold water with cornstarch.
4. Turn the pot to SAUTE and pour in the cornstarch mixture.
5. Stir constantly until the pot boils and the sauce begins to thicken.
6. Serve over rice.

Chicken Korma

(Prep + Cook Time: 25 minutes | Servings: 6)

Ingredients:

- 1 pound chicken breasts and/or legs, boneless and skinless or with bones, as you prefer

For the Sauce:

- 1 ounce cashews raw, or substitute with almonds if you prefer
- 1 small onion chopped
- ½ cup tomatoes diced
- ½ green Serrano pepper Jalapeño, or Thai chili pepper
- 5 cloves garlic
- 1 tsp Ginger minced
- 1 tsp turmeric
- 1 tsp salt
- 1 tsp garam masala
- 1 tsp cumin-coriander powder
- ½ tsp cayenne pepper adjust to your preference
- ½ cup water (use this to slosh about in the blender jar and then pour it into the pressure cooker)

For Finishing:

- 1 tsp garam masala
- ½ cup coconut milk full fat, add more if you'd like
- ¼ cup cilantro chopped

Directions:

1. Blend together all ingredients listed under "For the Sauce" (all ingredients excluding chicken, garam masala, coconut milk and cilantro).
2. Pour the sauce into the Instant Pot. Place the chicken on top. If your chicken is frozen, just push it down into the sauce a little
3. Cook at HIGH pressure for 10 minutes. When time is up, wait 15 minutes for a natural pressure release.
4. Open the lid and carefully take out the chicken and cut into bite size pieces. Add coconut milk and garam masala into the pot and stir.
5. Put the chicken back in, serve and garnish with cilantro if you'd like. Enjoy!

Chicken Rogan Josh Curry

(Prep + Cook Time: 60 minutes | Servings: 8)

Ingredients:

- 5-pounds boneless, skinless chicken thighs
- 1/3 pound curry paste
- 1½ cups Greek Yogurt
- 1 tbsp vegetable oil
- 1 onion – cut into wedges
- 2 coarsely chopped large tomatoes
- 4 ounces baby spinach leaves
- 4 ounces coriander leaves

Directions:

1. First, combine the yogurt and the curry paste in a large bowl.
2. Add the chicken and pour over with the mixture.
3. The chicken should be completely coated in the yogurt and curry mixture.
4. Leave the chicken in the bowl and cover with plastic wrap. Place the bowl in your refrigerator for about 30 minutes.
5. Press SAUTE mode and heat the vegetable oil in your Instant Pot.
6. Add the onion and cook until it is golden brown. This should take about 8 to 10 minutes.
7. Add the onion and the diced tomatoes to the marinated chicken.
8. Combine the ingredients and then pour into the Instant Pot.
9. Close the lid. Press the MANUAL key, set the pressure to HIGH, and set the timer for 15 minutes.
10. When the Instant Pot timer beeps. Allow the pressure to release naturally and then serve over rice or steamed vegetables.

Chicken BBQ

(Prep + Cook Time: 30 minutes | Servings: 6)

Ingredients:
- 4-5 pound chicken thighs, bone-in or boneless, skinless, fat trimmed off
- 2 garlic cloves, chopped
- 1/8 tsp pepper, or more to taste
- ¼ tsp salt, or more to taste
- ½ cup PLUS 1½ tbsp water, divided
- ½ cup barbecue sauce (use your favorite)
- 1 tbsp olive oil
- 1 onion, medium-sized, chopped
- 1½ tbsp cornstarch

Directions:
1. Press the SAUTE key of the Instant Pot. Add the oil and heat.
2. Add the garlic and onion and sauté for about 1 to 2 minutes or until soft. Add the 1/2 cup of water and barbecue sauce.
3. With the meaty side faced up, add the chicken in the pot. Press the CANCEL key to stop the SAUTÉ function. Cover and lock the lid.
4. Select MANUAL and cook at HIGH pressure for 10 minutes.
5. When the Instant Pot timer beeps, let the pressure release naturally. Turn the steam valve to release remaining pressure.
6. Unlock and carefully open the lid. Preheat the broiler. Grease a broiler pan and transfer the chicken into the greased pan.
7. Generously season both sides with salt and pepper. Arrange the chicken in the pan with the meaty side faced down. Set aside.
8. Press the SAUTE key of the Instant Pot. Bring the cooking liquid in pot to a boil. In a small-sized bowl, combine the cornstarch with 1 ½ tablespoon of water until smooth.
9. When the cooking liquid is boiling, add about ½ of the cornstarch mix into the pot, stir until the sauce is thick.
10. Add more cornstarch mix, if needed. Simmer the sauce until thick. Taste the sauce and, if needed, season with salt and pepper to taste.
11. Turn off the Instant Pot. Brush the top of the chicken with the sauce.
12. Turn the oven setting to broil, and preheat the broiler 10 to 15 minutes before cooking.
13. Place the pan 6 inches from the heat source and broil for about 2-3 minutes or until the chicken is glazed.

14. Remove the pan from the oven, flip the chicken, and brush the other side with the sauce.
15. Return the pan to the oven and broil for 2-3 minutes more or until the other side is glazed. Serve the chicken barbecue while it's still hot.
16. Serve the remaining sauce on the side.

Chicken Drumsticks BBQ
(Prep + Cook Time: 35 minutes | Servings: 4-6)

Ingredients:
- 4-10 chicken drumsticks
- ¾ cup water
- ¼ cup sweet paprika
- 4½ tsp black pepper freshly ground
- 1 tbsp salt
- 1½ tsp celery salt
- 1½ tsp cayenne pepper
- 1½ tsp garlic powder
- 1½ tsp dry mustard
- 1½ tsp ground cumin

Directions:
1. Add 3/4 cup of water in the Instant Pot. Place the trivet inside.
2. Place the chicken drumsticks on the trivet. Close the lid tightly and close the vent.
3. Press POULTRY function on the Instant Pot and set the time to 20 minutes.
4. Preheat the oven to Broil. Line a cookie sheet with parchment paper.
5. When the timer goes off, release pressure naturally. Open the lid and take out the drumsticks.
6. Coat the drumsticks with the BBQ rub evenly.
7. Place the drumsticks on the lined cookie sheet (or tinfoil). Broil the drumsticks for 2 minutes per side or until the skin is browned. Be careful not to burn them.
8. Serve immediately. Enjoy!

Chicken Pina Colada

(Prep + Cook Time: 35 minutes | Servings: 4)

Ingredients:
- 1 cup pineapple chunks, frozen or fresh
- 2 pounds chicken thighs, organic, cut into 1-inch chunks
- 1/8 tsp salt
- ½ cup green onion, chopped, for garnish
- ½ cup coconut cream, full fat
- 1 tsp cinnamon
- 2 tbsp coconut aminos (or soy sauce)

Optional:
- 1 tsp arrowroot starch
- 1 tbsp water

Directions:
1. Except for the green onions, put all of the ingredients in the Instant Pot. Cover and lock the lid.
2. Press the POULTRY key and cook on preset HIGH pressure and 15 minutes cooking time.
3. When the Instant Pot timer beeps, press the CANCEL key and turn off the Instant Pot.
4. Let the pressure release naturally for 10-15 minutes or until the valve drops.
5. Turn the steam valve to Venting to release remaining pressure. Unlock and carefully open the lid. Stir to mix.
6. If you want a thick sauce, stir in 1 teaspoon arrowroot starch with 1 tablespoon water.
7. Press the SAUTÉ key of the Instant Pot.
8. Add the arrowroot starch mixture into the pot and cook until thick to preferred thickness.
9. Turn the Instant Pot off.
10. Serve garnished with green onions.

Notes: To make your own coconut cream, simply place a can of full fat coconut milk in the fridge overnight. When ready to use, open can from bottom and drain out coconut water (you can drink it or discard it). You will be left with pure coconut cream in the can.

Chicken with Cherries & Pumpkin Seed Wild Rice
(Prep + Cook Time: 55 minutes | Servings: 4-8)

Ingredients:
- 1 cup balsamic vinegar
- ½ cup evaporated palm sugar
- 1 tbsp molasses
- ¼ cup butter melted
- 1 orange peeled and quartered
- 1 onion julienned
- 12 chicken thighs
- ¼ tsp sea salt
- 4 sprigs rosemary
- 2 cups Bing Cherries pitted and halved fresh
- 4 cups vegetable stock low sodium
- 1 1/3 cups wild rice rinsed
- ¼ cup butter
- 1 onion minced
- 2 plum tomatoes diced
- ½ cup pumpkin seeds toasted
- Sea salt to taste

Directions:
1. In the inner pot of the Instant Pot add the balsamic vinegar, evaporated palm sugar, molasses, butter, orange and onion. Mix well.
2. Add the chicken, salt and rosemary. Stir to coat.
3. Add 1½ cups of cherries. Place the lid on the pressure cooker and lock into place. Press the MEAT/STEW button; adjust pressure cooking time to 25 minutes.
4. When done and pressure has naturally released, remove the lid.
5. While the chicken is cooking: Bring veggie stock to boil in a medium saucepan on the stove top. Add rinsed wild rice. Cover and simmer for 50 minutes.
6. In a large sauté pan, heat the butter. Sauté onion until caramelized.
7. Add tomato and sauté for 3 to 4 minutes. Add onions and tomato to the rice.
8. Add 1/2 cup of cherries to the sauté pan and sauté for 3 to 4 minutes until soft and juicy.

9. Add cherries and toasted pumpkin seeds to the rice. Stir to incorporate. Add salt if needed.
10. Place wild rice on a serving platter and top with chicken. Pour juices from the chicken over the entire platter and garnish with rosemary. Enjoy!

Cola Chicken Wings
(Prep + Cook Time: 35 minutes | Servings: 2-4)

Ingredients:
- 1 ½ pounds chicken wings
- 4 cloves garlic crushed
- 1 stalk green onion cut 2 inches long
- 1 tbsp Ginger sliced
- 200 mL coca cola
- 2 tbsp light soy sauce
- 1 tbsp dark soy sauce
- 1 tbsp Chinese rice wine
- 1 tbsp peanut oil

Directions:
1. Heat up your Instant pot using the SAUTÉ function Make sure your pot is as hot as it can be by waiting until indicator says "Hot"
2. Pour in 1 tablespoon of peanut oil into the pressure cooker. Ensure to coat the oil over the whole bottom of the pot. Add the crushed garlic, sliced ginger and green onions into the pot, then stir for roughly a minute until fragrant.
3. Add the chicken wings into the pot and stir fry them together with the garlic, ginger slices and green onions for roughly one to two minutes.
4. When the edges of the chicken skin starts to brown, pour in the coca cola and fully deglaze the bottom of the pot with a wooden spoon. Add in 2 tablespoons of light soy sauce, 1 tablespoon of dark soy sauce, and 1 tablespoon of Chinese rice wine. Mix well.
5. Close and lock the lid. Select SUATE and cook at HIGH pressure for 5 minutes. Use a natural release (roughly and minutes).
6. Open the lid carefully and taste one of the chicke and the cola sauce (It shouldn't taste like coca cola y season the sauce with more salt if desired.
7. Serve immediately with rice or other side

One Pot Chinese Chicken and Rice

(Prep + Cook Time: 60 minutes | Servings: 4)

Ingredients:

- 6 shiitake mushrooms dried, marinated
- 6 - 8 chicken drumsticks, marinated
- 3 cups jasmine rice rinsed
- 1 tsp salt
- 1½ cups water
- Ginger shredded, for garnish
- Green onions sliced, for garnish

Marinade:

- 1 tbsp light soy sauce
- 1 tsp dark soy sauce
- ½ tsp sugar
- ½ tsp corn starch
- 1 tsp Shaoxing rice wine
- Dash white pepper powder
- 1 tbsp Ginger shredded
- 1 tsp five spice powder

Directions:

1. Place the dried shiitake mushrooms in a small bowl. Rehydrate them with cold water for 20 minutes.
2. Chop the drumsticks into 2 pieces. Then, marinate the chicken and mushrooms with the marinade sauce for 20 minutes.
3. Rinse rice under cold water by gently scrubbing the rice with your fingertips in a circling motion. Pour out the milky water, and continue to rinse until the water is clear. Then, drain the water.
4. Add the rice, 1 teaspoon of salt, marinated chicken and mushrooms, and 1½ cups of water in the Instant Pot. Close the lid. Select MANUAL and cook at HIGH pressure for ꞈ minutes.
   ꞈen time is up, use natural pressure release for 15 minutes.
   ꞈ immediately.

Filipino Chicken Adobo

(Prep + Cook Time: 55 minutes | Servings: 4)

Ingredients:
- 6 chicken drumsticks or two pounds of chicken
- 1 tbsp oil
- Green onions chopped for garnish

Sauce:
- ¼ cup Filipino soy sauce
- ½ cup light soy sauce
- ¼ cup Filipino vinegar
- 1 tbsp fish sauce
- 1 tbsp sugar

Spice:
- 10 cloves garlic crushed
- 1 small onion minced
- 1 tsp black peppercorn ground
- 1 red chili dried
- 4 bay leaves dried
- 1 tsp cornstarch mixed with 1 tbsp water, optional

Directions:
1. Combine Filipino soy sauce, light soy sauce, Filipino vinegar, fish sauce and sugar in a medium mixing bowl.
2. Press the SAUTÉ function. Add oil to the Instant Pot and brown the chicken for 1 to 2 minutes with the skin side down first. Then, remove the chicken from the pot.
3. Sauté garlic and onion in the pot until fragrant and golden in color. Then, add ground black peppercorn, red chili, and bay leaves to the pot and sauté for 30 seconds.
4. Add the Sauce mixture and deglaze the pot.
5. Cook at HIGH pressure for 9 minutes, then use a natural release.
6. Optional: remove the chicken from the pot. Simmer the sauce using the Sauté function and add cornstarch mixture until the sauce is reduced.
7. Optional: Brown the chicken underneath a broiler with the skin side up for 5 minutes.
8. Place the chicken on serving plate, pour in the Sauce mixture, add chopped green onions for garnish.
9. Serve and enjoy!

Cordon Blue Chicken Casserole

(Prep + Cook Time: 50 minutes | Servings: 8)

Ingredients:

- 1 cup panko bread crumbs
- 1 pound chicken breast, boneless, skinless, sliced into thin strips
- 1 pound ham, cubed
- 1 tbsp spicy mustard
- 16 ounces Rotini pasta
- 16 ounces Swiss cheese
- 2 cups chicken broth
- 2 tbsp butter
- 8 ounces Gouda cheese
- 8 ounces heavy cream

Directions:

1. Put the uncooked pasta in the Instant Pot. Cover the pasta with 2 cups of chicken broth.
2. Put the chicken strips and ham cubes on top. Cover and lock the lid.
3. Press the MANUAL key, set the pressure to HIGH, and set the timer for 25 minutes.
4. When the Instant Pot timer beeps, press the CANCEL key and unplug the Instant Pot. Turn the steam valve to quick release the pressure. Unlock and carefully open the lid.
5. Pour the mustard and heavy cream in the pot. Add both the cheeses in the pot and stir until smooth and creamy. In a small-sized pan, add the butter and melt.
6. When the butter is melted, add the bread crumbs and stir for about 2 to 3 minutes or until golden and toasty.
7. Serve the pasta mixture sprinkled with the toasted bread on top.

Salt Baked Chicken

(Prep + Cook Time: 50 minutes | Servings: 8)

Ingredients:

- 2 tsp sand ginger dried, Kaempferia Galanga or Zeodary Powder
- 1¼ tsp kosher salt
- ¼ tsp five spice powder
- Dash white pepper optional, ground

Directions:

1. Season the chicken legs by placing the chicken legs in a large mixing bowl. Pour in 2 teaspoons of dried sand ginger, 1¼ teaspoon of kosher salt, and 1/4 teaspoon of five spice powder. Mix well.
2. Place the seasoned chicken legs on a large piece of parchment paper (Do NOT use aluminum foil). Wrap it up tightly and place it on a shallow dish with the opening side facing upwards. Do not stack more than 2 levels of chicken legs.
3. Place a steamer rack in the pressure cooker and pour in 1 cup of water. Carefully place the chicken legs dish onto the rack. Close the lid and cook at HIGH Pressure for 18 – 26 minutes, then natural release for 20 minutes (turn off the heat and do NOT touch it). Open the lid carefully. Remove the dish from the pressure cooker and unwrap the parchment paper carefully
4. Optional Step: Pour out all the juice on a small bowl (don't throw it away!), then place the chicken legs on a wire rack on top of an oven tray. Put it under the broiler until the skin is browned but not dried out.
5. Serve immediately. The remaining meat juice can be used as a dipping sauce for the chicken. Taste and add more dried sand ginger to your liking. Enjoy!

Crack Chicken

(Prep + Cook Time: 40 minutes | Servings: 4)

Ingredients:
- 8 ounces cream cheese
- 6-8 bacon slices, cooked
- 4 ounces cheddar cheese
- 3 tbsp cornstarch
- 2 pounds chicken breast, boneless
- 1 packet ranch seasoning
- 1 cup water

Directions:
1. Put the chicken breasts and cream cheese in the Instant Pot. Sprinkle the top of the chicken and cream cheese with the ranch seasoning.
2. Pour in 1 cup of water. Cover and lock the lid.
3. Press the MANUAL key, set the pressure to HIGH, and set the timer for 25 minutes.
4. When the Instant Pot timer beeps, turn the steam valve to Venting to quick release the pressure.
5. Carefully open the lid. Transfer the chicken into a large plate and shred the meat.
6. Press the SAUTÉ key of the Instant Pot and select LESS. Whisk in the cornstarch.
7. Add the cheese and the shredded chicken into the pot. Stir in the bacon. Serve.

Shredded Chicken Breast (E&S)

(Prep + Cook Time: 30 minutes | Servings: 4)

Ingredients:
- 1,5-2 lbs boneless chicken breasts
- ½ tsp salt
- ½ tsp garlic salt
- ⅛ tsp pepper
- ½ cup chicken broth

Directions:
1. Place chicken in your Instant Pot. Season both sides of chicken with garlic salt and pepper. Pour the chicken broth.
2. Seal Instant Pot, making sure your valve is set to sealing. Press POULTRY button. Once done, wait for Instant Pot to depressurize on it's own, known as natural release.
3. **Note:** If you are wanting to use the quick release method, I suggest adding 5 extra minutes to the Instant Pot cooking timer.
4. Place chicken on a cutting board and shred with 2 forks, OR slice chicken breast.

Lemon and Garlic Chicken

(Prep + Cook Time: 25 minutes | Servings: 4)

Ingredients:

- 1 lemon, large-sized, juiced, or more to taste
- 1 onion, diced
- 1 tbsp avocado oil, OR ghee, OR lard
- 1 tsp dried parsley
- 1 tsp sea salt
- ½ cup chicken broth, organic or homemade
- ¼ cup white cooking wine
- ¼ tsp paprika
- 1-2 pounds chicken, thighs or breasts
- 3-4 tsp arrowroot flour, or more
- 5 garlic cloves, minced

Directions:

1. Press the SAUTE key of the Instant Pot. Put the cooking fat and the diced onion into the pot.
2. Cook for about 5 minutes or until the onions are softened, or you can cook until they begin to brown.
3. Except for the arrowroot flour, add the rest of the ingredients into the pot. Cover and lock the lid.
4. Press the POULTRY key let cook on preset cooking time.
5. When the Instant Pot timer beeps, press the CANCEL key and unplug the Instant Pot.
6. Turn the steam valve to quick release the pressure. Unlock and carefully open the lid.
7. If you want a thick sauce, remove about 1/4 cup of the sauce, add the arrowroot flour in the cup and stir to make slurry.
8. Pour the slurry back into the pot. Stir until thicken. Serve immediately.

Honey Garlic Chicken Lettuce Wraps

(Prep + Cook Time: 70 minutes | Servings: 4)

Ingredients:
- 1/8 cup honey garlic sauce store bought or recipe below
- 2 tbsp coconut aminos (or soy sauce)
- ¼ tsp chilies
- 1 tbsp onion minced
- ½ tsp salt
- 1 tsp black pepper
- 8-10 chicken thighs boneless, skinless
- 1 jalapeno thinly sliced (optional)
- 1 head lettuce
- 1 medium carrot grated
- ½ bell pepper, thinly sliced
- 1 green onion diced
- 1 avocado thinly sliced
- 1/8 cup cashews crushed or chopped

Fermented Honey Garlic Sauce (Optional):
- 1 Fido Jar or a jar with cover
- Cloves garlic peeled
- Raw honey enough to cover the amount of garlic cloves being used

Instructions:
1. Combine coconut aminos, onions, chilies, salt, pepper and honey garlic sauce (if using the recipe below, crush the garlic cloves and include some of the honey) in a bowl.
2. Put boneless skinless chicken thighs into the mixture and let marinate for 20 to 40 minutes.
3. Put chicken and sauce into the Instant Pot. Close and lock the lid. Select MANUAL and cook at HIGH pressure for 6 minutes.
4. While you are waiting for the chicken to cook (likely 10 minutes to reach pressure, 6 minutes cooking time and a 6-8 minute natural pressure release). Prepare the remaining vegetables, chopping and dicing as needed.
5. Prepare the washed lettuce into full leaves. You can use whatever type of lettuce you prefer.
6. Once the natural pressure release time readout reaches 6 minutes open up the valve and release any remaining pressure. The chicken should shred easily with a fork. Leave the shredded chicken marinating in the sauce until you are ready to assemble wraps.

7. Lay chicken, grated carrot, pepper slices, chopped cashews, green onion, and avocado, in slices inside the lettuce, drizzling sauce over top of the chicken and veggies before rolling the lettuce around ingredients. Serve and Enjoy!

Making the Honey Garlic Sauce
1. In a clean dry jar, place the garlic cloves, you want to leave a little room at the top.
2. Pour the honey into the jar coving the cloves but again making sure there is some space at the top. As the garlic ferments in the honey, it can bubble up.
3. Make sure the garlic cloves stay covered with honey, and that you regularly "burp" the lid of the fido jar or covering.
4. Let sit for 4 weeks, or 28 days. The garlic will darken, and the honey slightly more liquid, and then you know it is ready!

8-Ingredient Chicken Dinner (E&S)
(Prep + Cook Time: 45 minutes | Servings: 4)

Ingredients:
- 2 pounds boneless chicken thighs
- ¼ cup coconut oil
- ¼ cup coconut aminos (or soy sauce)
- ¼ cup honey
- 3 tbsp organic ketchup
- 2 tsp garlic powder
- 1 ½ tsp sea salt
- ½ tsp black pepper

Directions:
1. Put everything in your Instant Pot. Stir, so the chicken becomes completely coated. Close and seal the lid.
2. Press MANUAL and adjust time to 18 minutes. For frozen chicken, 40 minutes.
3. When time is up, hit CANCEL and quick-release.
4. Take out the chicken and hit SAUTE.
5. Simmer for 5 minutes until the sauce has thickened nicely.
6. Serve with a vegetable side dish!

Chipotle Chicken, Rice, and Black Beans (E&S)

(Prep + Cook Time: 30 minutes | Servings: 6)

Ingredients:

- 1 onion, small-sized, chopped
- 1 can black beans, organic, drained and rinsed
- 1 cup Jasmine Rice, uncooked
- 1 pound chicken thighs or breasts, boneless, skinless, cut into bite sized pieces
- 1 tbsp chipotle peppers, in adobo sauce
- ½ cup water, filtered
- ½ lime, juiced
- ½ tsp black pepper, finely ground
- 2 tbsp butter, ghee, or coconut oil
- 2 tsp real salt, OR sea salt
- 4 cups diced tomatoes in juice

Directions:

1. Put the chicken, butter, pepper, salt, rice, lime juice, water, chipotle peppers, tomatoes with its juices, and onion in the Instant Pot, stir and combine. Cover and lock the lid.
2. Press the MANUAL key, set the pressure to HIGH, and set the timer for 6 minutes.
3. When the Instant Pot timer beeps, press the CANCEL key and unplug the Instant Pot. Turn the steam valve to quick release the pressure.
4. Unlock and carefully open the lid.
5. Add the black beans into the pot and stir to combine.
6. Taste and, if needed, season with pepper and salt to taste.
7. Divide between serving bowls and garnish each serving with sour cream, shredded cheese, and guacamole.

Fall Off The Bone Chicken Half An Hour

(Prep + Cook Time: 45 minutes | Servings: 10)

Ingredients:

- 1 whole chicken, about
- 4 pounds, preferably organic
- 1½ cups chicken bone broth
- 1 tbsp coconut oil, organic virgin
- 1 tsp dried thyme
- 1 tsp paprika
- ½ tsp sea salt
- ¼ tsp black pepper, fresh ground
- 2 tbsp fresh squeezed lemon juice
- 6 cloves garlic, peeled

Directions:

1. In a small-sized bowl, combine the pepper, salt, thyme, and paprika. Rub the outside of the chicken with the spice mix.
2. Press the SAUTÉ key of the Instant Pot. Put the oil in the pot and heat until shimmering.
3. With the breast side faced down, put the chicken in the pot and cook for 6-7 minutes. Rotate the chicken.
4. Add the broth, garlic cloves, and lemon juice. Cover and lock the lid.
5. Press the MANUAL key, set the pressure to HIGH, and set the timer for 25 minutes.
6. When the timer beeps, let the pressure release naturally. Turn the steam valve to Venting to release any remaining pressure. Carefully open the lid.
7. Transfer the chicken into a large plate and let stand for 5 minutes. Carve and serve.

Cacciatore

(Prep + Cook Time: 40 minutes | Servings: 8)

Ingredients:
- 1 can pitted black olives
- 1 green bell pepper, seeded and diced
- 1 package (8-10 ounces) mushrooms, sliced
- ½ cup chicken broth, OR vegetable broth
- 2 cans crushed tomatoes, organic
- 2 tbsp organic tomato paste
- 3 shallots, chopped
- 4 garlic cloves, crushed
- 5-6 chicken breasts, boneless, skinless
- Extra-virgin olive oil
- Fresh parsley
- Red pepper, to taste
- Sea salt and black pepper, to taste

Directions:
1. Put the oil in a 4-quart or larger Instant Pot. Press the SAUTE key and heat the oil. When the oil is hot, add the bell pepper and shallots into the pot and cook for about 2 minutes, frequently stirring, until the shallots are slightly softened.
2. Stir in the broth and let simmer for about 2-3 minutes, scraping up any browned off from the bottom of the pot. Stir in the garlic and mushrooms.
3. Put the chicken on top and cover the chicken layer with the chopped tomatoes –do not stir. Put the tomato paste on top of the crushed tomatoes.
4. Press the CANCEL key to stop the sauté function. Cover and lock the lid. Turn the steam valve to Sealing.
5. Press the MANUAL key, set the pressure to HIGH, and set the timer for 8 minutes.
6. When the Instant Pot timer beeps, press the CANCEL key and unplug the Instant Pot.
7. Let the pressure release naturally for 10-15 minutes or until the valve drops. Turn the steam valve to release remaining pressure.
8. Unlock and carefully open the lid. Stir in the olives, red pepper flakes, pepper, and salt.
9. Divide the cacciatore between serving bowls. If desired, serve heaping over shredded cabbage.

Garlic-Ginger Drumsticks

(Prep + Cook Time: 45 minutes | Servings: 4)

Ingredients:

- 6-8 chicken drumsticks, skin on

For the sauce:

- 2 tbsp rice wine vinegar
- 2 tbsp honey
- 2 tbsp brown sugar
- 2 cloves garlic, minced
- ¼ cup water
- ½ onion, chopped
- ½ cup soy sauce
- 1 tsp fresh ginger, minced

Directions:

1. In a bowl, mix all of the sauce ingredients until well combined. Pour the sauce in the Instant Pot.
2. Add the chicken in the pot and push them down to submerge them in the sauce – they do not have to be covered completely with sauce. Cover and lock the lid.
3. Press the MANUAL key, set the pressure to HIGH, and set the timer for 15 minutes.
4. When the Instant Pot timer beeps, let the pressure release naturally for 15 minutes. Turn the steam valve to release remaining pressure. Unlock and carefully open the lid.
5. Press the SAUTE key and boil until the sauce is reduced.
6. Remove the drumsticks and transfer them into a parchment paper lined cookie sheet.
7. Turn the oven setting to broil, and preheat the broiler 10 to 15 minutes before cooking. Broil each side of the chicken for 2 minutes.
8. Meanwhile, let the sauce cook in the Instant Pot until reduced more.
9. Remove the chicken from the oven and put on a serving platter.
10. Pour the sauce over the chicken. Serve and enjoy!

Braised Chicken with Capers and Parsley

(Prep + Cook Time: 45 minutes | Servings: 4)

Ingredients:
- 4 chicken breasts, skinless, bone-in
- 1 can (14.5 ounces) chicken broth
- 1 onion, large-sized, minced
- 1 tbsp cornstarch
- 1 tbsp water
- ½ cup flat-leaf parsley, minced, plus more for garnish
- 1/3 cup salted capers, soaked well in several changes of water
- 1/3 cup white wine vinegar
- 2 tbsp olive oil, divided
- Freshly ground black pepper
- Salt to taste

Directions:
1. Season the chicken with salt and pepper generously.
2. Press the SAUTE key of the Instant Pot. Put 1 tablespoon olive oil in the pot and heat.
3. Cooking in 2 batches, cook the chicken in the pot until both sides are browned. Transfer the browned chicken onto a platter.
4. Put the remaining 1 tablespoon olive oil in the pot.
5. When hot, add the onion; cook, stirring, for about 5 minutes or until soft.
6. Add the capers and parsley and cook for 1 minute. Stir in the broth.
7. Add the vinegar. Return the chicken, along with any accumulated juices, into the pot. Cover and lock the lid.
8. Press the MANUAL key, set the pressure to HIGH, and set the timer for 13 minutes.
9. When the Instant Pot timer beeps, use a quick release. Unlock and carefully open the lid.
10. Transfer the chicken onto a platter using tongs. Cover the platter with foil to keep warm. In a small-sized bowl, mix the cornstarch with the water.
11. Press the SAUTÉ key. Bring the broth in the pot to a boil.
12. Add the cornstarch mix, constantly stirring until the sauce is thick. Turn off the Instant Pot.
13. Season the salt and pepper to taste. Spoon the sauce over the cooked chicken.
14. Garnish with parsley and serve.

Melted Mozzarella Marinara Chicken

(Prep + Cook Time: 35 minutes | Servings: 4)

Ingredients:

- 4 large chicken breasts, boneless, skinless
- 1 can (14 ounces) crushed tomatoes in puree
- 1 cup low-fat Mozzarella, grated
- 1 cup water
- 1 tbsp olive oil
- 1 tsp dried basil
- ¼ tsp red pepper flakes
- ¼ tsp salt
- 2 cloves garlic, crushed or pressed

Directions:

1. Season the chicken breast with salt and pepper.
2. Add the oil into the Instant Pot, press the SAUTÉ key, and heat the oil.
3. Cooking in 2 batches, cook the chicken breast until browned. Transfer onto a plate. If needed, add more oil in the pot.
4. Add the garlic; sauté for 1 minute. Add the water, tomatoes, red pepper flakes, basil, or salt. Stir until combined.
5. Return the chicken into the Instant Pot. Cover and lock the lid.
6. Press the MANUAL key, set the pressure to HIGH, and set the timer for 5 minutes.
7. When the Instant Pot timer beeps, turn the steam valve to Venting to quick release the pressure. Unlock and carefully open the lid.
8. Check the chicken to make sure the meat is cooked and the middle is no longer pink. Preheat the broiler.
9. Grease a small-sized glass casserole with nonstick cooking spray.
10. Put the chicken in the dish. Press the SAUTÉ key of the Instant Pot. Bring the sauce in the pot to a simmer and cook until thick to your preferred consistency.
11. Pour the thickened sauce over the chicken in the dish. Sprinkle grated mozzarella cheese over the chicken.
12. Put the dish in the broiler and broil until the cheese starts to brown lightly and melted.
13. Watch carefully because the cheese can brown quickly.

Asian Inspired Chicken
(Prep + Cook Time: 20 minutes | Servings: 6)

Ingredients:
- 6 chicken thighs, boneless, skinless
- 5 garlic cloves, minced
- 3 tbsp scallions, chopped
- 1/3 cup white wine
- ½ cup soy sauce
- 1 tsp sesame seeds
- 1 tbsp Sriracha Hot Chili Sauce
- 1 tbsp olive oil
- 1 ½ tsp fresh ginger, grated
- 1 ½ tbsp honey
- 1½ cups water

Directions:
1. Season both sides of the chicken thighs with garlic powder and pepper. Press the SAUTE key and select the More option. Add the olive oil and heat.
2. When the oil is hot, add the chicken and cook until both sides are browned – do not overcrowd the Instant Pot. You will need to cook in batches.
3. While the chicken is browning, mix the Sriracha with the water, honey, soy sauce, wine, ginger, and garlic in a bowl.
4. When the last batch of the chicken is browned, return all the browned chicken in the pot. Pour the Sriracha mixture in the pot.
5. Press the CANCEL key to stop the SAUTÉ function. Cover and lock the lid.
6. Press the MANUAL key, set the pressure to HIGH, and set the timer for 5 minutes.
7. When the Instant Pot timer beeps, turn the steam valve to quick release the pressure. Unlock and carefully open the lid.
8. Transfer the chicken into a serving platter and tent with foil to keep warm.
9. Press the SAUTÉ key and select the More option. Boil the sauce for 10 minutes. Pour the sauce over the chicken and top with scallions and sesame seeds.
10. Serve with broccoli and cauliflower rice.
11. You can pour some of the sauce over the broccoli and the cauliflower rice.

Slow Cook Chicken Paprikash

(Prep + Cook Time: 3 hours 25 minutes | Servings: 6)

Ingredients:

- 6 chicken thighs skinless and boneless, trimmed, about 1 3/4 pounds
- ½ tsp salt
- ½ tsp black pepper freshly ground
- 3 tbsp white rice flour
- 1 tbsp canola oil
- 2 cups onion chopped
- 1 cup red bell pepper chopped
- ½ cup carrots matchstick-cut
- 3 cloves garlic minced
- Cooking Spray
- 1 package mushrooms pre-sliced, 8 ounces
- 1¼ cups chicken broth fat-free, lower-sodium
- 2 tbsp Hungarian sweet paprika
- ½ cup sour cream reduced-fat
- 1 tbsp parsley chopped fresh

Directions:

1. Sprinkle chicken with 1/4 teaspoon of the salt and 1/4 teaspoon of the black pepper. Place flour in a shallow dish; dredge chicken in flour, reserving any remaining flour.
2. Heat a large well-seasoned cast-iron skillet over medium-high heat. Add oil to pan; swirl to coat. Add chicken to pan; cook 3 minutes on each side or until golden brown. Transfer chicken to a 6-quart Instant Pot.
3. Add onion, red bell pepper, carrots, and garlic to pan; coat vegetables with cooking spray. Cook, stirring constantly, 6 minutes or just until tender. Transfer onion mixture to cooker.
4. Coat mushrooms with cooking spray, and add to pan. Cook, stirring constantly, 5 minutes or until browned. Transfer mushrooms to cooker.
5. Combine reserved flour, remaining 1/4 teaspoon salt, remaining 1/4 teaspoon black pepper, broth, and paprika in a bowl; stir with a whisk.
6. Add broth mixture to cooker. Close and lock the lid. Press SLOW COOK, and adjust 3 hours cook time.
7. Remove chicken from cooker, and place on a serving platter. Skim fat from surface of cooking liquid.
8. Stir sour cream into cooking liquid. Serve sauce with chicken, and sprinkle with parsley.

Whole Turkey with Apricot Glaze (E&S)
(Prep + Cook Time: 55 minutes | Servings: 8)

Ingredients:

- 9 pound turkey
- 1¼ cup chicken stock
- 1 peeled and diced onion
- 1 diced carrot
- 5-ounces apricot jam
- 1 tsp salt
- 1 tsp black pepper
- ½ tsp cumin
- ½ tsp coriander
- ½ tsp turmeric

Directions:

1. Mix the jam, pepper, cumin, coriander, and turmeric together.
2. Rinse the bird and pat dry. Rub the glaze all over the turkey.
3. Pour broth and veggies into the pot, before putting the turkey on top. Close and seal the lid.
4. Select POULTRY and adjust time to 35 minutes.
5. When time is up, hit CANCEL and wait for a natural release.
6. Remove the turkey and serve!

Turkey Verde and Rice (E&S)
(Prep + Cook Time: 35 minutes | Servings: 4)

Ingredients:

- 2/3 cup chicken broth
- 1 ½ pounds turkey tenderloins (I used Jennie-O)
- 1 ¼ cup long grain brown rice
- 1 yellow onion, small-sized, sliced
- ½ cup salsa verde
- ½ tsp salt

Directions:

1. Put the rice in the Instant Pot. Pour in the broth.
2. Top the mix with the onion, turkey, and then the salsa. Sprinkle with the salt.
3. Cover and lock the lid. Press the MANUAL key, set the pressure to HIGH, and set the timer for 8 minutes.
4. When the Instant Pot timer beeps, let the pressure release naturally for 8 minutes. Turn the steam valve to release remaining pressure. Unlock and carefully open the lid.
5. Garnish each serving with fresh cilantro.

Turkey Legs with Gravy

(Prep + Cook Time: 45 minutes | Servings: 4)

Ingredients:

- 2 pieces turkey legs
- 1 cup chicken stock, homemade, unsalted
- 1 dash sherry wine
- 1 onion, small-sized, sliced
- 1 pinch rosemary
- 1 pinch thyme
- 1 stalk celery, chopped
- 1 tbsp light soy sauce
- 1 tbsp olive oil
- 2 bay leaves
- 3 cloves garlic, roughly minced
- Kosher salt and ground black pepper

Directions:

1. Generously season the turkey legs with salt and pepper. Press the SAUTÉ key of the Instant Pot and select the More option.
2. Wait for the indicator to show 'Hot'. When the pot is hot, put in the 1 tablespoon olive oil, making sure the bottom of the pot is coated. Add the turkey legs into the pot. Cook or about 2 to 3 minutes each side or until browned.
3. Transfer onto a plate. Set aside until ready to use. Press CANCEL to stop SAUTÉ and then press the SAUTE function again to set the heat Medium. Add the onion and stir.
4. Season with a pinch of salt and pepper and cook for 1 minute or until the onion is soft.
5. Add the garlic and sauté for about 30 seconds or until fragrant.
6. Add the celery and sauté for 1 minute. If desired, season with another pinch of salt and pepper.
7. Add the bay leaves. Slightly scrunch the thyme and the rosemary and then add them in the pot. Stir to combine.
8. Pour in 1 dash wine to deglaze the pot, scraping any browned bit off the bottom using a wooden spoon. Let cook until the alcohol is evaporated.
9. Add the stock. Stir in the soy sauce. Taste and, if needed, season to taste with salt and pepper. Press CANCEL to stop the SAUTÉ function. Cover and lock the lid.
10. Press the MANUAL key, set the pressure to HIGH, and set the timer for 18 or 20 minutes.
11. When the Instant Pot timer beeps, let the pressure release naturally for 10 minutes. Use a quick release. Remove the turkey legs. If desired, filter the turkey gravy.
12. If you want a thicker sauce, mix 3 tablespoons cornstarch with 1 tablespoon water. Pour about 1/3 of the mixture at a time into the pot until the sauce reaches your desired thickness.

Turkey Breast with Gravy

(Prep + Cook Time: 50 minutes | Servings: 4)

Ingredients:

- 6-pound bone-in, thawed turkey breast
- 4 cups chicken broth
- 3 smashed garlic cloves
- 2 halved celery stalks
- 1 halved onion
- 4 tbsp butter
- 1 tbsp chopped rosemary
- 1 tbsp sage
- 1 tbsp chopped parsley
- Salt and pepper to taste

Gravy:

- Leftover cooking liquid from turkey
- 2 tbsp flour
- 2 tbsp butter

Directions:

1. Pour broth in the cooker and lower in the steamer basket.
2. Put in the garlic, carrot, celery, and onion. In a bowl, mix rosemary and parsley.
3. Rinse and pat turkey dry. Season with salt and pepper.
4. Pull up the skin from the breast's top, and rub in chopped herbs. Put 4 pats of butter under the skin with a few sage leaves. Lower turkey into cooker. Close and seal lid.
5. Select MANUAL and cook for 30 minutes on HIGH pressure.
6. When time is up, hit CANCEL and wait for the pressure to come down.
7. Remove turkey and put under the broiler for a few minutes (on a baking sheet) to crisp up the skin.
8. Tent the bird in foil to rest. Throw out the veggies in the steamer basket, but save the liquid. In a saucepan, melt 2 tablespoons of butter and mix in flour.
9. Pour in 1 cup of the turkey liquid and whisk. You've just made a roux.
10. When incorporated, turn the cooker on to SAUTE and pour in roux.
11. Simmer until thickened. Serve turkey with this gravy.

Turkey Drumsticks

(Prep + Cook Time: 40 minutes | Servings: 5)

Ingredients:

- 6 turkey drumsticks
- 2 tsp brown sugar, packed tight
- ½ tsp garlic powder
- 1 cup water
- ½ cup soy sauce
- 1 tsp black pepper, fresh ground
- 1 tbsp kosher salt

Directions:

1. In a small-sized bowl, combine the garlic powder, pepper, brown sugar, and salt, breaking any clump of sugar.
2. Season the turkey drumsticks with the seasoning mix. Pour the water in the Instant Pot. Add the soy sauce.
3. Add the seasoned drumsticks with any remaining seasoning mix.
4. Cover and lock the lid. Press the MANUAL key, set the pressure to HIGH, and set the timer for 25 minutes.
5. When the Instant Pot timer beeps, let the pressure release naturally for 15 minutes. Turn the steam valve to release remaining pressure. Unlock and carefully open the lid.
6. Using tongs, carefully transfer the drumsticks into a serving plate – be very careful because the drumsticks are cooked to fall-off-the-bone tender.
7. If you have time, pour the cooking liquid into a fat strainer. Let the fat float to the top.
8. Pass the defatted cooking liquid at the table as a sauce.

Notes: If you want crispy turkey skin, brush the drumsticks with the cooking liquid and broil them until browned. This dish was cooked in a 6-quart Instant Pot. If the turkey legs are short, then you can stack them in the pot without any trouble. Longer turkey legs will take some working out. You may have to stack them like a jigsaw puzzle. Don't worry about the max fill line. You can stack them in the pot as long as you can close and lock the lid afterwards. The cooking liquid is also delicious with baked potatoes.

Cranberry Braised Turkey Wings

(Prep + Cook Time: 40 minutes | Servings: 6)

Ingredients:
- 2 tbsp butter
- 2 tbsp oil
- 4 turkey wings 2-3 pounds
- Salt to taste
- Pepper to taste
- 1 cup dried cranberries soaked in boiling water for 5 minutes, or 1 cup fresh cranberries or 1 rinsed canned cranberries
- 1 onion roughly sliced
- 1 cup walnuts
- 1 cup orange juice
- 1 cup vegetable stock
- 1 bunch thyme fresh

Instructions:
1. Press SAUTÉ function to pre-heat the Instant Pot. When "Hot" appears on the display, melt the butter and swirl the olive oil.
2. Place turkey wings in the Instant Pot and brown the wings on both sides, adding salt and pepper to taste. Make sure the skin is nicely coloured.
3. Remove the wings briefly from the cooker and add onion, followed by the wings again with the browned skin side facing up.
4. Add in the cranberries, walnuts, and the bunch of thyme. Pour the orange juice and stock over the contents of the pot.
5. Close and lock the lid. Press MANUAL and cook at HIGH pressure for 20 minutes. When time is up, open the pot using natural pressure release.
6. Remove the thyme and carefully move the wings to a serving dish. Place the wings under a broiler for about 5 minutes or until wings are sufficiently caramelized.
7. While wings caramelize, reduce the contents of the pot to about half by putting the Instant Pot in SAUTÉ mode.
8. Pour the reduced liquid over the wings and serve. Enjoy!

Notes: Turkey wings can be fully cooked in 20 minutes, while the legs require 30 minutes and boneless turkey breasts only need about 7 minutes. Use the same cut of turkey in this recipe to ensure even cooking!

Turkey Chili

(Prep + Cook Time: 30 minutes | Servings: 4)

Ingredients:

- 1 pound ground turkey (85% lean)
- 4-5 ounces water
- 15 ounces chickpeas (previously cooked in your Instant Pot, or your favorite white bean)
- 1 yellow bell pepper (diced, you can add another yellow bell pepper)
- 1 onion diced
- 2-3 cloves garlic (peeled and not chopped)
- 1½ tsp cumin
- 1/8 tsp cayenne
- 2 cans tomatoes with chilies, (10-ounce cans)
- 1 can tomato juice 5.5 ounces
- 12 ounces vegetable stock
- 2½ tbsp chili powder

Directions:

1. Add ground turkey and water into the Instant Pot. Select the MANUAL option, secure the pressure valve, set the pressure to HIGH and set the timer for 5 minutes.
2. When time is done allow to rest 5-10 minutes then quick release the pressure. Open the Instant Pot and break up the ground turkey.
3. Add the remaining ingredients and stir to combine. Select the MANUAL option and set cooking time for 5 minutes.
4. When time is up allow to rest for 10-15 minutes then release the pressure and open lid.
5. Stir and enjoy!

Hip Turkey Chili
(Prep + Cook Time: 60 minutes | Servings: 6-8)

Ingredients:
- 1 tbsp olive oil
- ½ turkey breast (roughly 1½ – 2 pounds, sliced 1-inch pieces)
- 1 red onion chopped
- 1 green bell pepper chopped
- 1 tsp cumin seeds
- ½ tsp hot red pepper flakes
- 2 sprigs thyme fresh
- 2 cups red kidney beans dry then soaked or quick-soaked
- 2 tbsp tomato paste
- 1 cup tomatoes chopped
- 2 cups bone broth or low sodium vegetable/chicken stock
- 1½ tsp salt
- ½ tsp white pepper
- 1 tsp cumin powder
- Parsley or coriander, fresh for garnish (optional)

Directions:
1. Press SAUTÉ and adjust to pre-heat the Instant Pot at the High setting. Then, add oil and brown the turkey pieces on two sides – working in batches if needed (about 5 to 10 minutes).
2. Remove the turkey pieces and set aside, in the empty pressure cooker add the onion and green pepper. Sauté, stirring infrequently until the onions have softened (about 3 minutes).
3. Toss in the cumin and red pepper flakes and sauté for another 30 seconds.
4. Add the thyme sprigs, beans, tomato paste, chopped tomatoes and stock and stir well.
5. Close and lock the lid of the pressure cooker. Choose the BEAN/CHILI program and use the Adjust button to choose Less mode to run for 25 minutes.
6. When time is up, use a natural release (10-15 minutes).
7. Press SAUTÉ and mix-in the salt, white pepper and cumin powder and simmer uncovered, stirring occasionally until the desired consistency is reached (about 5 minutes).
8. While the contents simmers, use the spoon/spatula to fish out the pieces of turkey and press them against the side of the cooker to break them up a little.
9. Portion and sprinkle with garnish before serving. Enjoy!

Turkey-Stuffed Bell Peppers

(Prep + Cook Time: 35 minutes | Servings: 4)

Ingredients:

- 1 pound ground turkey
- 4 big bell peppers (red or green)
- One 4 ½ -ounce can of mild green chilies
- 1 cup shredded sharp cheddar cheese
- 1 chopped yellow onion
- ½ cup corn kernels
- 2 tbsp butter
- 2 tsp minced garlic
- 1 tsp ground cumin
- 1 tsp dried oregano
- 1 cup water
- ¼ tsp salt
- ¼ tsp (or less) cayenne

Directions:

1. Melt the butter in your Instant Pot on the SAUTE setting.
2. Cook the onion until it becomes soft in about 3 minutes.
3. Add the ground turkey, breaking it up with a spatula, and cook for 3 minutes.
4. Add cayenne, garlic, oregano, cumin, and salt.
5. After half a minute of stirring, move everything to a large bowl to cool for 20 minutes.
6. Stir in the corn, cheese, and chilies into the turkey.
7. Prep your peppers by cutting off the tops and scraping out the seeds. Stuff the peppers with the turkey filling.
8. Wipe the inside of the cooker with a paper towel and lower in the steamer rack.
9. Pour 1 cup of water and arrange the peppers on top of the rack. Lock and seal the lid.
10. Select MANUAL and cook for 7 minutes at HIGH pressure.
11. When the timer beeps, turn off the cooker and quick-release. Serve!

Stuffed Turkey Tenderloin

(Prep + Cook Time: 30 minutes | Servings: 6)

Ingredients:

- 2 turkey breast tenderloins
- 2 cups white rice
- 2 bacon slices, diced
- 1-2 sprigs fresh rosemary, optional
- ½ cup dry white wine
- 1 tsp fresh rosemary, chopped
- 1 cup fresh cranberries
- 1 ½ cups butternut squash, diced, frozen or fresh
- 3 ½ cups chicken broth OR water

Directions:

1. Press the SAUTE key of the Instant Pot.
2. Add the bacon in the pot and sauté until some of the fat rendered and the edges start to crisp.
3. Add the squash and cranberries, along with the rosemary. Sauté until the edges of the squash are golden and the bacon is crisp. Turn the Instant Pot off.
4. Open the tenderloins like a butterfly by slicing them gently lengthwise, going almost all the way through the other edge, making sure to leave the other edge intact.
5. When the butternut mix is cooked, gently spoon the mix into the center of each butterflied turkey. Fold the tenderloin back.
6. Weave a rosemary sprig through the open edge of the tenderloin to seal. Alternatively, you can use a cooking twine. Press the SAUTÉ key of the Instant Pot.
7. When the pot is hot, cook the tenderloins for about 3 to 4 minutes per side or until both sides are golden.
8. Remove the browned tenderloins from the pot.
9. Add the rice in the pot and sauté for about 1 to 2 minutes or just until the rice begins to smell nutty.
10. Add the white wine in the pot to deglaze, stirring and scraping the browned bits off the bottom using a wooden spoon.
11. Add the broth and water in the pot. Place the stuffed tenderloin on top of the rice.
12. If desired, add the rosemary sprigs in the pot. Cover and lock the lid. Press the RICE key.
13. When the Instant Pot timer beeps, release the pressure naturally for 10 minutes.
14. Unlock and carefully open the lid. Remove the rosemary sprigs and then slice the tenderloin. Serve.

Turkey with Cranberries and Sauerkraut
(Prep + Cook Time: 40 minutes | Servings: 6)

Ingredients:
- 2 cups sauerkraut, drained
- ¼ cup raisins
- 3 cloves garlic, peeled, smashed, and roughly chopped
- 3 - 4 lbs (1.5 - 2kg) turkey wings or thighs
- 1½ cups fresh or frozen cranberries, divided
- 1 small preserved lemon, chopped and seeds removed
- 1 tsp ground cinnamon
- ½ tbsp dried parsley flakes
- 1 tsp dried thyme
- 1 tsp sea salt
- 1 cup apple cider (non-alcoholic hard cider)
- 1 tsp arrowroot flour
- 2 tsp water

Directions:
1. Place the sauerkraut at the bottom of the pot, then scatter the raisins and garlic over evenly
2. Place the turkey parts in the pot
3. Sprinkle 1 cup cranberries and preserved lemon over the turkey parts
4. In a bowl, combine the ground cinnamon, parsley flakes, thyme, sea salt and apple cider and pour into the pot
5. Seal the lid of the pressure cooker (set the valve to Sealing) and select POULTRY setting for 25- 30 minutes (depending on the size of the turkey parts used)
6. Once the cooking time is over, release the pressure naturally
7. Preheat the oven broiler in the meantime
8. Remove the turkey pieces from the pot and place them in an oven proof casserole, then broil for around 5 minutes until browned to your liking
9. Set the Instant Pot to SAUTE setting, then add in another ½ cup of cranberries
10. Prepare the arrowroot flour slurry by combining the arrowroot flour with water
11. Once the sauce begins to simmer, stir in the slurry, then allow the sauce to simmer until thickened
12. Turn off the Instant Pot and serve the cranberry and sauerkraut sauce with the browned turkey parts.

Marsala Turkey with Mushrooms

(Prep + Cook Time: 45 minutes | Servings: 4)

Ingredients:

- 1¼ pounds boneless, skinless turkey breasts
- 6 ounces sliced white mushrooms
- 3 tbsp chopped shallots
- 3 tbsp heavy cream
- 2 tbsp olive oil
- 1 minced garlic clove
- ⅔ cup chicken stock
- ⅓ cup dry Marsala wine
- 1 ½ tbsp cornstarch
- ½ tsp dried thyme
- Salt and pepper to taste

Directions:

1. Trim the turkey and cut away the sinews, which are silver-colored.
2. With string, tie the roasts crosswise every 2 inches. Season with salt and pepper.
3. In your cooker, heat 1 tablespoon of oil and when hot, brown the breasts on both sides for 3 minutes. Move to a plate.
4. Pour in the rest of the oil and cook shallots, thyme, garlic, and mushrooms.
5. When mushrooms are softening, add the turkey back into the cooker. Pour in wine and broth. Close and seal the lid.
6. Select MANUAL and cook on HIGH pressure for 15-20 minutes.
7. When time is up, turn off the cooker and quick-release.
8. Turkey should be 160-degrees F. If cooked through, tent with foil on a carving board.
9. Turn the cooker back on to SAUTE and bring to a boil. In a small bowl, mix cornstarch and heavy cream until smooth.
10. Pour into cooker and let the sauce thicken.
11. Season with more salt and pepper and move sauce to a serving bowl.
12. Cut the string off the roasts and slice into ½-inch pieces. Serve with sauce!

Mustard Beer Pulled Turkey

(Prep + Cook Time: 65 minutes | Servings: 4)

Ingredients:

- 2 pieces (1¼ to 1½ -pound each) turkey thighs, bone-in, skin removed
- 1 bottle (12-ounce) dark beer, preferably a porter
- 1 tbsp mustard, whole-grain
- 1 tbsp tomato paste, canned variety
- 1 tsp dry mustard
- 1 tsp ground black pepper
- 1 tsp salt
- ½ tsp garlic powder
- 2 tbsp apple cider vinegar
- 2 tbsp packed dark brown sugar
- 2 tsp ground coriander

Directions:

1. In a small-sized bowl, mix the coriander with the garlic powder, pepper, salt, and dry mustard.
2. Rub the seasoning mix all over the turkey thighs thoroughly and evenly coating them.
3. Pour the beer into the Instant Pot. Place the seasoned turkey thighs in the beer. Cover and lock the lid.
4. Press the MANUAL key, set the pressure to HIGH, and set the timer for 45 minutes.
5. When the Instant Pot timer beeps, turn the steam valve to quick release the pressure. Unlock and carefully open the lid.
6. Transfer the turkey onto a chopping board and let cool for a couple minutes.
7. Remove the bones and save to make bone broth. Chop the meat into small pieces. Press the SAUTE key of the Instant Pot.
8. Bring the liquid to a simmer and cook for about 4 minutes until reduced by half.
9. Stir in the tomato paste, mustard, vinegar, and brown sugar until the sauce is smooth, cooking for 1 minute and stirring all the time.
10. Add the turkey pieces into the pot and stir well to combine.
11. Turn off the Instant Pot and wait until the turkey is heated through.

Tomato Sauce Turkey Meatballs

(Prep + Cook Time: 40 minutes | Servings: 4)

Ingredients:

- 1 pound ground turkey, 93 % lean
- 1 jar (24-ounce) of your preferred pasta sauce
- 1 onion, medium-sized, diced
- 1 tsp Italian Seasoning (I used Penzey's Pasta Sprinkle)
- 1 tsp kosher salt
- ½ cup rice, long grain
- ½ cup water
- 2 tbsp fresh basil, chopped, optional
- 2 tbsp olive oil
- 2 zucchini, medium-sized, sliced
- 8 ounces cremini mushrooms, sliced

Directions:

1. Press the SAUTE key of the Instant Pot. Add the oil and onions; sauté for about 5 minutes or until the onions are soft.
2. Add the mushrooms and zucchini; sauté for about 3 minutes or until the mushrooms start to soften and release some of their liquid.
3. Add the water and pasta sauce in the pot. Stir well to combine.
4. While waiting for the sauce to simmer, form meatballs. In a medium-sized mixing bowl, combine the ground turkey with the rice, salt, and Italian herbs.
5. Combine well and then roll the mixture into 1 dozen meatballs that are just slightly larger than a golf ball.
6. Drop the meatballs gently into the simmering sauce into the Instant Pot. Spoon some sauce over the top of each meatball. Press the CANCEL key to stop the SAUTÉ function. Cover and lock the lid. Press the POULTRY key.
7. When the Instant Pot timer beeps, turn the steam valve to Venting to quick release the pressure. Unlock and carefully open the lid. Serve topped with fresh basil.
8. Serve over spaghetti squash.

Thanksgiving Turkey Casserole

(Prep + Cook Time: 45 minutes | Servings: 4)

Ingredients:

- 4 turkey breasts, boneless (about 2 pounds), or chicken breasts
- 2 small-sized cans cream of mushroom soup
- 1 stalk celery
- 1 onion, sliced
- 1 cup chicken broth
- 1 bag Pepperidge farms stuffing cubes
- 1 bag frozen mixed veggies

Directions:

1. Put the turkey breasts in the Instant Pot.
2. Add the broth, mixed vegetables, celery, and onion. Cover and lock the lid. Press the MANUAL key, set the pressure to HIGH, and set the timer for 25 minutes. Alternatively, you can press the POULTRY setting and adjust the timer for 25 minutes.
3. When the Instant Pot timer beeps, turn the steam valve to quick release the pressure. Unlock and carefully open the lid.
4. Add the stuffing cubes in the pot on top of the cooked mix. Pour in the cream of mushroom soup.
5. Press the SAUTE key and cook for 8 minutes.
6. Press CANCEL to stop the SAUTÉ function. Shred the turkey breast right in the pot. Serve.

Duck a L'Orange

(Prep + Cook Time: 1 hour 15 minutes | Servings: 4)

Ingredients:

- 2 halved duck breasts
- 2 halved duck legs
- 2 cups fresh orange juice
- 9 spring onions, green and white parts divided
- 3 tbsp fresh chopped ginger
- 2 tbsp fish sauce
- 2 tbsp white sugar
- 2 red chilies
- 1 whole star anise
- ½ tbsp dried lemongrass
- Black pepper to taste

Directions:

1. Turn your Instant Pot to SAUTE to heat up.
2. When hot, add duck skin-side down first and fry until the skin becomes crispy, and the fat has rendered out.
3. Skim out the fat, leaving a few tablespoons, and add garlic until it becomes fragrant.
4. Add the rest of the ingredients (minus spring onions). Put the duck back in the cooker. Close and seal the lid.
5. Select MANUAL and cook at HIGH pressure for 30 minutes. Press CANCEL when time is up, and let the pressure come down naturally.
6. Turn the cooker back to SAUTE. Add the white parts of the spring onion to the cooker and simmer until they've softened.
7. Take out the duck and skim out the layer of fat on the top.
8. Let the sauce keep simmering until it has become reduced and thick.
9. Serve duck with plenty of sauce and the green parts of the onion sprinkled on top.

Marinated Steak (E&S)

(Prep + Cook Time: 45 minutes | Servings: 4)

Ingredients:
- 2 pounds flank steak
- 2 tbsp onion soup mix, dried
- ¼ cups apple cider vinegar
- ½ cups olive oil
- 1 tbsp Worcestershire sauce

Directions:
1. Press the SAUTE key of the Instant Pot. Put the flank steak in the pot and cook each side until browned.
2. Add the Worcestershire sauce, vinegar, onion soup mix, and olive oil.
3. Press the CANCEL key to stop the SAUTÉ function. Cover and lock the lid.
4. Press the MEAT/ STEW key, and set the timer for 35 minutes.
5. When the Instant Pot timer beeps, turn the steam valve to quick release the pressure.
6. Unlock and carefully open the lid. Serve!

Shredded Pepper Steak (E&S)

(Prep + Cook Time: 1 hour 40 minutes | Servings: 6)

Ingredients:
- 3-4 pounds beef (cheap steak or roast cuts will all work)
- 1 16-oz jar Mild Pepper Rings (banana peppers or pepperoncini)
- ½ cup salted beef broth
- 1 tbsp garlic powder
- Red chili flakes to taste

Directions:
1. Season beef with garlic powder and red chili flakes before adding to cooker. Pour peppers (including juice) and broth into cooker, too. Seal the lid.
2. Select MANUAL and cook at HIGH pressure for 70 minutes.
3. When the timer beeps, press CANCEL. Use a natural release.
4. When safe, open the cooker and shred the meat. Serve!

Notes: The jarred peppers can typically be found in the "Italian" foods section of your grocery store.

Steak Fajitas

(Prep + Cook Time: 1 hour 45 minutes | Servings: 4)

Ingredients:

- 2 pounds Ribeye roast
- 1 tbs soy sauce
- 1 tbs worcestershire sauce
- ½ tsp lime juice
- 1 tbs olive oil more for sautéing
- 1 tsp cumin
- 1 tsp chili powder
- 1 tsp salt
- 1 tsp pepper
- 1 tsp minced garlic
- ½ red bell pepper
- ½ green pepper
- ½ yellow onion
- Tortillas and Mexican cheese for serving

Directions:

1. Make marinade out of liquids and seasoning and marinade meat for at least 1 hour, cube into 2-inch chunks
2. Turn Instant Pot to SAUTÉ and brown the meat on either side
3. Chop vegetables into strips, remove meat from Instant Pot and sauté vegetables for 3-5 minutes
4. Place meat on top of veggies and pour out remaining marinade over the meat
5. Press MEAT/STEW on Instant Pot and set timer for 35 minutes. Serve on tortillas with some cheese

Round Roast and Veggies (E&S)

(Prep + Cook Time: 40 minutes | Servings: 6)

Ingredients:

- 2-3 pound round roast (top or bottom)
- 1 large white onion, sliced or diced however you prefer
- 2-3 cups sliced mushrooms
- 1 pound potatoes, quartered or cubed
- 3 cups vegetable or beef broth
- 2 tbsp minced garlic
- 2 tbsp olive oil
- 1 tbsp thyme
- Generous pinch of salt and pepper

Directions:

1. Add all wet ingredients and spices to the Instant Pot and stir.
2. Add in meat and veggies, excluding potatoes.
3. Seal the lid and set the timer for 15 minutes on HIGH pressure. Do a quick release and add in the potatoes.
4. Cook for another 10 minutes on HIGH pressure.
5. Do another quick release. Remove and enjoy!

Beef Stroganoff

(Prep + Cook Time: 10 minutes | Servings: 4)

Ingredients:

- 1 pound steak, thin-cut
- 1 cup sour cream
- 1 onion, small-sized
- 16 ounces egg noodles
- 4 cups beef broth
- 4 tbsp butter
- 8 ounces mushrooms, sliced

Directions:

1. Dice the onion into small-sized pieces. Cut the steak into thin pieces. Press the SAUTÉ key of the Instant Pot.
2. Add the butter, onion, and steak and wait until the butter is melted.
3. Add the mushrooms, broth, and egg noodle.
4. Press the CANCEL key to stop the SAUTÉ function. Cover and lock the lid. Press the MANUAL key, set the pressure to HIGH, and set the timer for 4 minutes.
5. When the Instant Pot timer beeps, turn the steam valve to quick release the pressure. Unlock and carefully open the lid.
6. Stir in the sour cream and serve.

Beef and Broccoli

(Prep + Cook Time: 50 minutes | Servings: 4)

Ingredients:

- 1 pound stew beef meat, grass fed
- 1 bag (10-12 ounces) frozen broccoli, preferably organic
- 1 clove garlic, large-sized, pressed
- 1 onion, quartered
- 1 tsp ground ginger
- ½ cup beef or bone broth
- ½ tsp salt
- ¼ cup coconut aminos (or soy sauce)
- 2 tbsp fish sauce

Directions:

1. Except for the broccoli, put the rest of the ingredients in the Instant Pot. Cover and lock the lid.
2. Press the MEAT/STEW key, and cook on pre-set time.
3. When the Instant Pot timer beeps, press the CANCEL key and turn the steam valve to quick release the pressure. Unlock and carefully open the lid.
4. Add the broccoli, loosely cover with the lid, and let sit for 15 minutes. Serve!

Garlic Teriyaki Beef (E&S)
(Prep + Cook Time: 55 minutes | Servings: 4)

Ingredients:
- 1 piece (2 pounds) flank steak
- 2 cloves garlic, finely chopped

For the teriyaki sauce:
- 2 tbsp fish sauce
- ¼ cup maple syrup, preferably organic grade B or higher
- ¼ cup coconut aminos OR soy sauce instead
- 1 tbsp raw honey
- 1 ½ tsp ground or fresh ginger, optional

Directions:
1. Slice the flank steak into 1/2-inch strips.
2. In a bowl, put all of the teriyaki sauce and mix until combined.
3. Put the steak strips and the sauce in the Instant Pot – there is no need to brown the meat. Add garlic. Cover and lock the lid.
4. Press the MANUAL key, set the pressure to HIGH, and set the timer for 40 minutes.
5. When the Instant Pot timer beeps, turn the steam valve to quick release the pressure. Unlock and carefully open the lid.
6. Serve and enjoy!

Beef Roast with Potatoes and Carrots
(Prep + Cook Time: 60 minutes | Servings: 6)

Ingredients:
- 2-4 pound beef roast no longer than the width of the pressure cooker
- 1½ cups chicken stock
- 1 tbsp olive oil
- 2 pounds potatoes roughly cubed
- 1 pound carrots peeled
- 1 bunch parsley chopped
- 1 cup red wine
- 4 tbsp butter unsalted
- 2 tbsp thyme fresh
- 4 tbsp pistachio chopped

Optional Crust:
- 4 ounces pistachio nuts crushed, shelled and salted
- 1 tbsp black pepper
- 2 tbs fresh thyme

Directions:

1. Optional crusting: Start by making the rub. Crush the nuts well, and mix the pistachio powder with the black pepper and thyme. Reserve a quarter of the rub to garnish the roast after cooking. Press as much of the crust on the roast - some may fall off during cooking - but you will add another layer when the roast is finished. Reserve half of the rub to garnish the roast after cooking.

2. Preheat the Instant Pot by using the SAUTÉ function. When "Hot" appears on the display, add a swirl of olive oil and sear the roast well on all sides. Deglaze the pot with the stock.

3. Close and lock the lid. Select MANUAL and cook at HIGH pressure for 45-50 minutes (depending on the thickness of your roast).

4. When time is up, open the Instant Pot using a quick release method.

5. Add the potatoes and place the whole carrots on top of the roast - do this quickly.

6. Close and lock the lid. Select MANUAL and cook at HIGH pressure for 10 minutes.

7. When time is up, open the Instant Pot using quick release.

8. Remove the carrots and transfer them to a serving plate, slicing them. Remove the potatoes with a slotted spoon and transfer to the serving plate.

9. Take out the roast and set it on a plate tented with aluminum foil to rest. While the roast is resting, make the au jus sauce.

10. Filter the cooking liquid through a fine sieve and put it back in the Instant Pot. Add the wine and butter and reduce the liquid in the pressure cooker at high heat, without the pressure cooking lid, to about half. Add salt and pepper to taste. On the SAUTÉ function, reduce the cooking liquid to about half its volume.

11. Slice up the roast and serve on a platter with the carrots and potatoes. Drizzle with the reduced cooking liquid and sprinkle with fresh thyme and nuts. Enjoy!

Korean Beef

(Prep + Cook Time: 75 minutes | Servings: 6)

Ingredients:

- 4 pounds bottom roast, cut into cubes
- 1 apple, Granny Smith or pear, peeled and then chopped
- 2 tablespoons olive oil
- ½ cup soy sauce
- 1 tablespoon ginger, fresh grated
- 1 large orange OR
- 2 small orange, juice only
- 1 cup beef broth
- 5 cloves garlic, minced
- Salt and pepper

Directions:

1. Season the roast cubes generously with pepper and salt. Press the SAUTE key of the Instant Pot.
2. When the pot is hot, coat with the olive oil. In batches, cook the meat until all sides are browned –transfer the browned meat into a plate while cooking.
3. When all the meat is browned, pour the beef broth in the pot and deglaze the pot – scrape the browned bits off from the bottom of the pot.
4. Pour the soy sauce in the pot and stir to mix. Return all the browned meat into the pot.
5. Add the ginger, garlic, and pear /apple on top of the meat. Lightly stir to combine slightly.
6. Add the orange juice.
7. Press the CANCEL key to stop the SAUTÉ function. Cover and lock the lid. Press the MANUAL key, set the pressure to HIGH, and set the timer for 45 minutes.
8. When the Instant Pot timer beeps, turn the steam valve to Venting to quick release the pressure. Unlock and carefully open the lid.
9. Serve over rice or cauliflower rice.

Mongolian Beef

(Prep + Cook Time: 25 minutes | Servings: 4)

Ingredients:

- 1½ pound Flank steak
- 1 carrot, shredded
- 1 garlic clove, minced
- 1 green onion, sliced, for garnish
- 1 tbsp olive oil
- ½ cup brown sugar
- ½ tsp fresh ginger, minced
- ¼ cup water
- ¾ cup soy sauce

To thicken the sauce:

- 3 tbsp water
- 3 tbsp cornstarch

Directions:

1. Slice the flank into the strips. In a bowl, combine the soy sauce with the oil, garlic, ginger, sugar, and water.
2. Pour the sauce in the Instant Pot.
3. Add the shredded carrot and beef strips, and mix until the beef is coated with the sauce. Cover and lock the lid.
4. Press the MANUAL key, set the pressure to HIGH, and set the timer for 8 minutes.
5. When the Instant Pot timer beeps, press the CANCEL key and unplug the Instant Pot.
6. Let the pressure release naturally for 10-15 minutes or until the valve drops. Turn the steam valve to release remaining pressure. Unlock and carefully open the lid.
7. In a small-sized bowl, combine the cornstarch with the water until there are no more lumps.
8. Press the SAUTÉ key and pour cornstarch mixture into the pot. Boil for about 1 to 2 minutes or until the sauce is thick.
9. Serve on a platter and garnish with chopped green onions.

Italian Beef
(Prep + Cook Time: 50 minutes | Servings: 8)

Ingredients:
- 5-6 lbs chuck roast
- 1 tbsp canola oil
- 1 pkt Italian dressing seasoning mix
- 16 oz jar sliced pepperoncini peppers
- ½ yellow onion, thinly sliced
- 1 cup water

Directions:
1. Set the SAUTE mode on your Instant Pot and add in oil
2. Once hot, brown roast on one side for 5-6 minutes then turn over and brown the other side for another 5-6 minutes.
3. Add in onions, half of the jar of pepperoncini pepper, ¼ cup pepperoncini brine, Italian seasoning mix and water.
4. Cover and lock the lid. Press MANUAL mode, set the pressure to HIGH, and set time to 55 minutes.
5. Give the lid a quick release and remove lid.
6. Shred roast with 2 forks and add in the remaining pepperoncini peppers that have been drained. Serve.

Herbs and Meatloaf
(Prep + Cook Time: 55 minutes | Servings: 2)

Ingredients:
- 2 pound of ground beef
- 2 pieces of eggs
- 1 cup of almond flour
- 1 tsp of thyme
- 1 tsp of rosemary
- 1 tsp of garlic powder
- 3 tbsp of olive oil

Directions:
1. Take a large sized mixing bowl and toss in your eggs, beef and flour alongside the seasoning.
2. Take a wooden spoon and mix them very gently.
3. Open up the lid of your Instant Pot and grease up the inner pot with olive oil.
4. Gently place the meatloaf mixture in your greased up Instant Pot and firmly pack it up with your hand to make sure it's even.
5. Set the Instant Pot to MEAT mode and let it cook for about 40 minutes.
6. Once done, wait for about 10 minutes and manually release the pressure of your Instant Pot.
7. Open it up and serve the meal with salad and mashed potatoes.

Beef Pitas with Red Onion & Tzatziki
(Prep + Cook Time: 50 minutes | Servings: 8)

Ingredients:
- 1½ pound beef chuck boneless, thinly sliced
- 1 tbsp kosher salt
- Pepper freshly ground
- 1 yellow onion thinly sliced
- 3 tbsp olive oil
- Juice of 1 lemon
- 2 tsp dried oregano
- 1 tbsp garlic powder

For the Tzatziki:
- 1 cup plain greek yogurt
- ½ cucumber finely diced
- 1 clove garlic minced
- 2 tbsp fresh dill finely chopped
- Juice of 1 lemon
- Kosher salt to taste
- Pepper freshly ground

For Serving:
- 8 pita breads
- Small lettuce leaves
- Tomatoes sliced
- Red onion thinly sliced
- Dill chopped

Directions:
1. Season the beef on both sides with the salt and pepper. Put the beef and onion into the Instant Pot.
2. In a small bowl, whisk together the water, oil, lemon juice, oregano, and garlic powder, then add to the pot.
3. Lock the lid and turn the valve to Sealing. Press the MANUAL button. Set the cook time for 30 minutes at HIGH pressure.
4. While the beef cooks, make the Tzatziki: In a small bowl, whisk together yogurt, cucumber, garlic, dill, and lemon juice. Season to taste with salt and pepper. Set aside until ready to serve.
5. Let the steam release naturally for about 15 minutes, then turn the valve to Venting to release any residual steam. Remove the lid from the pot and, using a slotted spoon, transfer the beef and onion to a bowl.
6. To serve, spoon an equal amount of the beef mixture into each pita and top with lettuce, tomato, and onion. Sprinkle with chopped dill and finish with a dollop of Tzatziki.

Beef Short Ribs

(Prep + Cook Time: 60 minutes | Servings: 4-6)

Ingredients:

- 4 pounds beef short ribs
- 4-6 carrots, cut into bite sized pieces
- 3 cloves garlic, minced
- 2 tbsp olive oil
- 2 cups onions, diced
- 1 tbsp dried thyme
- 1½ cups beef broth
- Kosher salt and fresh cracked pepper

Directions:

1. Press the SAUTE key of the Instant Pot. Pat dry the short ribs and generously season with the pepper and salt.
2. Drizzle olive oil in the pot and, in one single layer at a time, put the ribs in the pot and cook for about 4-5 minutes each side or until all the sides are browned – do not crowd the pot, so brown the short ribs in batches.
3. Transfer the browned short ribs into a plate and set aside.
4. Put the garlic in the pot and sauté, constantly stirring, for about 1 minute. Add the onion, carrot, and thyme. Season to taste with more salt and pepper.
5. Cook for about 4 to 5, occasionally stirring, until the veggies are soft. Return the browned short ribs into the pot. Press the CANCEL key to stop the SAUTÉ function. Cover and lock the lid.
6. Press the MANUAL key, set the pressure to HIGH, and set the timer for 35 minutes.
7. When the Instant Pot timer beeps, release the pressure naturally for 10-15 minutes or until the valve drops.
8. Turn the steam valve to release remaining pressure.
9. Unlock and carefully open the lid. Serve hot.

Asian Sweet and Spicy Ribs

(Prep + Cook Time: 65 minutes | Servings: 4)

Ingredients:

- 1 ½ - 2 pounds Beef Country Style Ribs
- ½ cup water
- 1 cup mirin
- ½ cup sweet chili garlic sauce
- ¼ cup agave nectar or honey
- ¼ cup light brown sugar packed
- 1 tsp Ginger minced fresh
- Rice cooked, optional, for serving
- 1 tbsp lime juice
- 1 tbsp soy sauce reduced sodium

Directions:

1. Place beef ribs in the Instant Pot. Add 1/2 cup water.
2. Close and lock pressure cooker lid. Use MEAT/STEW function or MANUAL at HIGH pressure; set program to 60 minutes.
3. Meanwhile, combine mirin, chili garlic sauce, agave nectar, brown sugar, ginger, lime juice and soy sauce in large saucepan. Simmer 20 minutes.
4. When time is up for the ribs, use the quick release to release pressure; carefully remove the lid.
5. Return beef to cooking liquid; cook 1 to 2 minutes or until heated through, stirring occasionally.
6. Serve ribs with rice and remaining sauce, if desired. Enjoy!

Soy Braised Beef Ribs
(Prep + Cook Time: 1 hour 20 minutes | Servings: 4)

Ingredients:
- 4 pounds beef ribs (about 8), ask the butcher to saw or chop them in half
- 2/3 cup soy sauce
- 2/3 cup salt-free beef stock, homemade
- 2 tbsp cornstarch
- 2 cloves garlic, peeled and smashed
- 1-inch knob fresh ginger, peeled and finely chopped
- 1-2 tbsp water
- ¼ cup rice vinegar (or white balsamic vinegar)
- 1/3 cup raw sugar
- 1 tbsp sesame oil
- 1 pinch red pepper flakes

Directions:
1. Press the SAUTE key of the Instant Pot. Put in the sesame oil and heat. Add the ginger, garlic, and red pepper flakes; sauté for 1 minute.
2. Add the vinegar, soy sauce, sugar, and beef stock. Mix until well combined.
3. Add the ribs and stir to coat with the vinegar mix. Press the CANCEL key to stop the SAUTÉ function. Cover and lock the lid.
4. Press the MANUAL key, set the pressure to HIGH, and set the timer for 45-60 minutes.
5. When the Instant Pot timer beeps, turn off the Instant Pot and release the pressure naturally for 10-15 minutes or until the valve drops. Turn the steam valve to Venting to release remaining pressure. Unlock and carefully open the lid.
6. Preheat the oven to Broil.
7. Transfer the ribs into a cookie sheet and broil for about 5 minutes or until the color is rich dark brown.
8. Meanwhile, make a slurry of corn starch and water.
9. Turn on the Instant Pot and press the SAUTE key. Pour the cornstarch slurry in the pot and bring to a boil. Cook until the sauce is thick to desired consistency.
10. Pour over the broiled ribs. Serve with hot cooked rice.

Teriyaki Short Ribs

(Prep + Cook Time: 45 minutes | Servings: 4)

Ingredients:
- 4 big beef short ribs
- 1 cup water
- ¾ cup soy sauce
- 1 big, halved orange
- ½ cup brown sugar
- 1 full garlic bulb, peeled and crushed
- 1 large thumb of peeled and crushed fresh ginger
- ½ tbsp sesame oil
- Dried pepper flakes
- A bunch of chopped green onions

Directions:
1. In a Ziploc bag, mix water, sugar, and soy sauce.
2. Squish around until the sugar has dissolved.
3. Add the orange juice and stir, before adding the orange slices as well.
4. Lastly, throw in the garlic, ginger, onions, and dried pepper flakes. Stir before adding the ribs.
5. Stir one last time and marinate in the fridge for at least 4 hours.
6. When ready to cook the ribs, coat the bottom of the Instant Pot with olive oil and heat.
7. Remove the ribs from the bag (save the liquid!) with tongs and quickly sear for 2-3 minutes on both sides.
8. Pour in the marinade and close the lid.
9. Select the MEAT/STEW setting and select 30 minutes.
10. When time is up, press CANCEL and quick-release the pressure. Serve!

Beef and Noodles

(Prep + Cook Time: 1 hour 10 minutes | Servings: 4)

Ingredients:
- 3 pounds boneless beef chuck roast
- 8-ounces egg noodles
- 2 cups water
- 1 chopped onion
- 2 minced garlic cloves
- 2 tbsp veggie oil
- Salt and pepper to taste

Directions:
1. Cube roast into bite-sized pieces. Add oil to your Instant Pot, and turn to the SAUTE setting.
2. Brown meat before adding garlic, onion, salt, and pepper. Pour in water and seal the lid.
3. Select MANUAL and cook for 37 minutes at HIGH pressure.
4. When time is up, press CANCEL and wait for a natural pressure release.
5. Take out the meat. Pour another cup of water into the cooker and turn back to SAUTE. Bring liquid to a boil.
6. Add the noodles and cook, lowering the SAUTE heat if possible to thicken the liquid into gravy.
7. When noodles are done, add meat, and stir. Serve!

Pasta with Meat Sauce

(Prep + Cook Time: 15 minutes | Servings: 4)

Ingredients:
- 1 ½ pounds ground beef
- 8-ounces dried pasta
- 24-ounces pasta sauce
- 12-ounces water
- Italian seasoning to taste

Directions:
1. Turn your cooker to SAUTE.
2. Add ground beef to brown, breaking it up with a spatula as it cooks.
3. When browned, press CANCEL and pour in pasta, sauce, and water. You'll probably have to break the pasta in half.
4. Close and lock the lid. Select MANUAL and cook at HIGH pressure for 5 minutes.
5. When time is up, press CANCEL and use a quick release.
6. Season with Italian seasoning to taste and serve!

Beef Bourguignon

(Prep + Cook Time: 1 hour 15 minutes | Servings: 4)

Ingredients:

- 1 pound flank steak or stewing steak
- ½ pound bacon tips or rashers
- 5 carrots, medium-sized, cut into sticks
- 2 sweet potato, large white, peeled and cubed
- 1 cup red wine
- 1 red onion, large-sized, peeled and sliced
- 1 tbsp avocado oil or olive oil
- 1 tbsp maple syrup
- ½ cup beef broth or stock
- 2 cloves garlic, minced
- 2 tbsp parsley, dried or fresh
- 2 tbsp thyme, dried or fresh
- 2 tsp ground black pepper
- 2 tsp sea salt

Directions:

1. Press the SAUTE key of the Instant Pot. Put 1 tablespoon oil in the pot and heat.
2. Pat the beef dry and season with salt and pepper.
3. Working in batches, cook the beef in the pot until all sides are browned. Take out steak of the pot and set aside. Slice the bacon into strips and put into the pot.
4. Add the onions. Sauté until the onions are translucent and soft. Return the browned beef in the pot.
5. Add the remaining ingredients.
6. Press the CANCEL key to stop the SAUTÉ function. Cover and lock the lid. Press the MANUAL key, set the pressure to HIGH, and set the timer for 30 minutes.
7. When the Instant Pot timer beeps, turn the steam valve to Venting to quick release the pressure.
8. Unlock and carefully open the lid. Serve and Enjoy!

Beefy Lasagna

(Prep + Cook Time: 40 minutes | Servings: 6)

Ingredients:
- 1 lb ground beef
- 8 oz ricotta cheese
- 1 cup mozzarella cheese - divided in half
- 1 cup Parmesan cheese - divided in half - (or an Italian cheese blend - I use BelGioso Asiago, Fontonia, Parmesan, Provolone four cheese blend from Wegman's)
- 1 egg
- 1½ cups water
- Italian spices (I use oregano and Melting Pot's garlic and wine seasoning)
- Salt and pepper to taste
- No-boil lasagna noodles
- 1 jar pasta sauce

Directions:
1. Press the SAUTE key of the Instant Pot and brown 1lb ground beef.
2. In another bowl mix ricotta cheese, 1/2 cup mozzarella cheese, 1/2 cup Parmesan cheese, 1 egg, and spices.
3. Line bottom of 7" springform pan with no-boil lasagna noodles. Break into pieces to fit the pan.
4. Add layer of tomato sauce - enough to cover the noodles.
5. Add layer of half of ground beef.
6. Add layer of half of cheese mixture.
7. Repeat with another layer of noodles, tomato sauce, ground beef, and cheese.
8. Top with layer of noodles, and additional tomato sauce.
9. Add remaining mozzarella and Parmesan cheeses.
10. Place trivet (wire rack) into Instant Pot, and add 1 ½ cups of water.
11. Loosely cover pan of lasagna with foil to keep out water.
12. Place lasagna pan on the top of trivet.
13. Lock the lid and set valve to sealing.
14. Press MANUAL, 20 minutes (be sure pot is on HIGH pressure).
15. After cook finishes, allow to naturally release pressure - approximately 10 minutes.
16. Remove lasagna after pressure releases.
17. Broil on high for a few minutes to brown cheese.
18. Enjoy!

Beef Stew

(Prep + Cook Time: 1 hour 35 minutes | Servings: 4)

Ingredients:
- 1 ½ pound whole beef brisket
- 1 tbsp flour
- 2 bay leaves
- 2 carrots, chopped
- 2 onions, small-sized, finely chopped
- 2 stalks celery, chopped
- 2 tbsp olive oil, divided
- 3 cloves garlic, crushed and then chopped
- 3 russet potatoes, cubed (OR 3 Yukon gold potatoes)
- Couple pinches dried thyme
- Dash sherry wine
- Kosher salt and pepper

For the chicken stock mixture:
- 1 tbsp fish sauce
- 1 tbsp light soy sauce
- 1 tbsp Worcestershire sauce
- 2 cups chicken stock, homemade, unsalted OR chicken stock, low sodium
- 3 tbsp tomato paste

Directions:
1. In a medium-sized bowl, combine the tomato paste with the fish sauce, light soy sauce, Worcestershire sauce, and chicken stock.
2. Trim any excess fat off from the beef brisket and then generously season with salt and pepper.
3. Press the SAUTE key of the Instant Pot. Add 1 tablespoon oil.
4. Sear both sides of the beef for about 5 minutes each side. Transfer into a chopping board and let rest.
5. Add 1 tablespoon of olive oil in the Instant Pot. Add the onion, season with salt and pepper, and cook until tender and browned.
6. Add the garlic and stir until fragrant. Add the carrot, celery, season with pinch of salt and pepper, and cook for 2 minutes.
7. Add a dash of wine to deglaze the pot and cook until the wine is reduced. Add the chicken stock mix in the pot.
8. Cut the beef into 1 to 1½ -inch cube chunks.
9. Toss with the flour and then add into the pot, spreading them out so each chunk can soak the stock mix.

10. Do not stir. You don't want too much flour mix with the stock. Add the bay leaves.
11. Rub the dried thyme with your fingers and sprinkle in the pot.
12. Add the potato on top of the beef chunks.
13. Lock the lid and close the steam valve. Cook for 70 minutes on HIGH pressure.
14. When the timer beeps, let the pressure release naturally.
15. Carefully open the lid, taste, and adjust the salt and pepper to taste.
16. Serve immediately as is, or with rice or pasta.

Notes: If you want more texture in your stew, add parboiled potatoes, chopped celery and carrots in the stew, and cook until the veggies are tender.

Beef Curry
(Prep + Cook Time: 60 minutes | Servings: 4)

Ingredients:
- 1 ½ cups jarred tikka masala or madras curry sauce
- 1 ½ pounds of beef chuck steak (trimmed to ¼" fat), cut into cubes
- 1 cup beef broth
- ½ cup coconut milk
- Salt and pepper, to taste

Optional toppings:
- Sliced green chilies
- Chopped coriander or basil leaves

Directions:
1. Season the beef with salt and pepper.
2. Press the SAUTE button and add the beef.
3. Cook until evenly browned on all sides. Stir in the remaining ingredients and mix until well combined.
4. Press the CANCEL button.
5. Close the lid completely and press the MANUAL button and set the pressure cooking time to 25 minutes.
6. When the pressure cooking cycle is completed quick release the pressure. Open the lid when the float valve has dropped down.
7. Serve over rice with any additional toppings you desire.

Homemade Pastrami

(Prep + Cook Time: 30 minutes | Servings: 8)

Ingredients:

- 3-4 pounds corned beef
- 2 cups water
- 3 tbsp black pepper
- 2 tbsp ground coriander
- 1 tbsp kosher salt
- 1 tbsp onion powder
- 1 tbsp garlic powder
- 1 tbsp brown sugar
- 2 tsp paprika
- ¼ tsp cloves
- ¼ tsp ground allspice
- Vegetable oil

Directions:

1. Take out the beef and rinse. Pour 2 cups of water in your cooker and lower in the trivet.
2. Put the meat, fatty side up, on the trivet and close and seal the lid.
3. Select MANUAL and cook for 45 minutes at HIGH pressure.
4. When time is up, press CANCEL and wait for a natural pressure release.
5. When that's done, take off the lid and wait another 20 minutes.
6. When cool, take out the meat and throw out the water. Pat dry and coat with veggie oil.
7. In a bowl, mix the spices and press on the meat. Store in a fridge wrapped in plastic wrap at least for the night, or as long as a few days.

Corned Beef and Cabbage

(Prep + Cook Time: 1 hour 45 minutes | Servings: 4-6)

Ingredients:
- 4-5 garlic cloves
- 4 cups water
- 2.5-3 lb. corned beef brisket, including spice packet or DIY spice packet
- 2 lbs petite red potatoes, quartered
- 3 cups baby carrots
- 1 head green cabbage, cut into large wedges

Directions:
1. Place corned beef brisket, spice packet, garlic and 4 cups of water into the Instant Pot. I used the rack to keep the brisket off the bottom of the pot.
2. Cook on 90 minutes using the MEAT/STEW setting or HIGH pressure for 90 minutes. Once time is up, quick release pressure. Remove corned beef to a platter and cover with foil. Let rest while cooking the vegetables.
3. Without discarding liquid, add potatoes, carrots, and cabbage to pressure cooker, you may remove the rack if desired.
4. Cook at HIGH pressure for 5-6 minutes. Use a quick release.
5. Serve corned beef with vegetables.

Mississippi Pot Roast

(Prep + Cook Time: 1 hour 55 minutes | Servings: 6)

Ingredients:
- 5-6 pounds beef, chuck roast
- ½ cup beef broth
- ½ cup pepperoncini juice
- 1 envelope ranch dressing mix
- 1 envelope au jus gravy mix (or brown gravy mix)
- ¼ cup butter
- 6-8 pepperoncini

Directions:
1. Pour the pepperoncini juice and the broth in the pot.
2. Add the roast beef. Sprinkle the gravy and the dressing mix over the roast, and then top with the butter and pepperoncini. Cover and lock the lid.
3. Press the MANUAL key, set the pressure to HIGH, and set the timer for 90 minutes.

4. When the Instant Pot timer beeps, turn off the pot, release the pressure naturally for 10-15 minutes or until the valve drops.
5. Turn the steam valve to release remaining pressure.
6. Unlock and carefully open the lid.
7. Set aside the Mississippi roast on a serving plate.
8. Serve and enjoy!

Instant Pot Beef Roast

(Prep + Cook Time: 70 minutes | Servings: 8)

Ingredients:

- 4 pounds beef chuck roast, cut into cubes (2 inches)
- 1 cup beef broth
- 5 minced garlic cloves
- 1 peeled and chopped Granny Smith apple
- 1 thumb of grated ginger
- ½ cup soy sauce
- Juice of one big orange
- 2 tbsp olive oil
- Salt and pepper to taste

Directions:

1. Season the roast with salt and pepper. Turn on your Instant Pot to SAUTE.
2. When hot, pour in the olive oil and brown the roast all over.
3. Move the meat to a plate.
4. Pour in the beef broth and scrape any stuck bits of meat.
5. Pour in soy sauce and stir.
6. Put the roast back into the pot.
7. Arrange the cut apple, garlic, and ginger on top.
8. Pour in the orange juice. Close the pressure cooker lid.
9. Select MANUAL and cook for 45 minutes at HIGH pressure.
10. Press CANCEL and quick-release the pressure when the timer beeps. Serve!

The Ultimate Pot Roast

(Prep + Cook Time: 50 minutes | Servings: 6)

Ingredients:

- 2-3 pounds beef, chuck roast
- 4 potatoes, large-sized, cut into large cubes
- 4 carrots, chopped
- 3 tbsp steak sauce, optional
- 3 cloves garlic
- 2 tbsp olive oil
- 2 tbsp Italian Seasonings
- 2 stalks celery, chopped
- 1 onion
- 1 cups beef broth
- 1 cup red wine

Directions:

1. Press the SAUTE key of your Instant Pot.
2. Pour in the olive oil. Add the roast beef and cook each side for about 1 to 2 minutes or until browned.
3. Transfer the browned beef into a plate.
4. Put the celery, carrots, and potatoes in the pot. Top with the garlic and onion.
5. Pour the beef broth and the wine in the pot. Put the roast on top of the vegetables.
6. Spread the seasonings over the top of the roast and then spread with the steak sauce.
7. Press the CANCEL key to stop the SAUTÉ function. Cover and lock the lid. Turn the steam valve to Sealing.
8. Press the MANUAL key, set the pressure to HIGH, and set the timer for 35 minutes.
9. When the Instant Pot timer beeps, release the pressure naturally for 10-15 minutes or until the valve drops.
10. Turn the steam valve to Venting to release remaining pressure. Unlock and carefully open the lid. Serve!

Balsamic Maple Beef

(Prep + Cook Time: 55 minutes | Servings: 6)

Ingredients:

- 3 pounds chuck steak, boneless, fat trimmed, sliced into ½-inch strips
- 2 tbsp avocado oil OR olive oil
- ½ cup balsamic vinegar
- 1 tsp ground ginger
- 1 tsp garlic, finely chopped
- 1 cup maple syrup
- 1 cup bone broth
- 1 ½ tsp salt

Directions:

1. Trim the fat off from the joint the beef and slice the meat into 1/2-inch thin strips. In a bowl, mix the ground ginger with the salt. Season the meat with the ginger mix.
2. Press the SAUTE key of the Instant Pot. Put the oil in the pot and heat.
3. When the oil is hot and shimmery, but not smoking, add the beef and cook until all sides are browned – you will have to cook in batches.
4. Transfer the browned beef into a plate and set aside. Put the garlic in the pot and sauté for about 1 minute.
5. Add the broth, maple syrup, and balsamic vinegar. Stir to mix. Return the browned beef into the pot.
6. Press the CANCEL key to stop the SAUTÉ function. Cover and lock the lid.
7. Press the MANUAL key, set the pressure to HIGH, and set the timer for 35 minutes.
8. When the Instant Pot timer beeps, turn the steam valve to Venting to quick release the pressure.
9. Unlock and carefully open the lid. If desired, you can thicken the sauce. Press the SAUTE key.
10. Mix 4 tablespoons arrowroot or tapioca starch with 4 tablespoons water until smooth and then add into the pot; cook for about 5 minutes or until the sauce is thick.
11. Serve!

Classic Corned Beef and Cabbage
(Prep + Cook Time: 1 hour 35 minutes | Servings: 6)

Ingredients:
- 3 pounds cabbage, cut into eight wedges
- 1 quartered onion
- 1 quartered celery stalk
- 1 corned beef spice packet
- 4 cups water
- 1 ½ pounds new potatoes, quartered
- 1 pound carrots, peeled and cut to 2.5 inches in length

Directions:
1. Rinse the beef. Put in the Instant Pot along with onion and celery.
2. Add in the spice packet and pour in water. Close and seal the lid.
3. Press MANUAL and cook for 90 minutes at HIGH pressure.
4. When time is up, press CANCEL and very carefully quick-release the pressure.
5. Plate beef and keep celery and onion in the pot.
6. Add potatoes, carrots and cabbage in the pot. Close and seal lid again.
7. Select MANUAL and cook for 5 minutes at HIGH pressure.
8. When time is up, turn off cooker and quick-release. Move veggies to plate with the corned beef.
9. Pour pot liquid through a gravy strainer.
10. Serve beef and veggies with a bit of broth on top, and the rest in a gravy boat.

Very Tender Pot Roast
(Prep + Cook Time: 50 minutes | Servings: 6)

Ingredients:
- 2-3 pounds beef, chuck roast
- 4 potatoes, large-sized, cut into large cubes
- 4 carrots, chopped
- 3 tbsp steak sauce, optional
- 3 cloves garlic
- 2 tbsp olive oil
- 2 tbsp Italian Seasonings
- 2 stalks celery, chopped
- 1 onion
- 1 cup beef broth
- 1 cup red wine

Directions:
1. Press the SAUTE key of your Instant Pot. Pour in the olive oil.
2. Add the roast beef and cook each side for about 1 to 2 minutes or until browned. Transfer the browned beef into a plate.
3. Put the celery, carrots, and potatoes in the pot. Top with the garlic and onion.
4. Pour the beef broth and the wine in the pot. Put the roast on top of the vegetables.
5. Spread the seasonings over the top of the roast and then spread with the steak sauce. Press the CANCEL key to stop the SAUTÉ function. Cover and lock the lid.
6. Press the MANUAL key, set the pressure to HIGH, and set the timer for 35 minutes.
7. When the Instant Pot timer beeps, release the pressure naturally for 10-15 minutes or until the valve drops.
8. Turn the steam valve to release remaining pressure. Unlock and carefully open the lid. Serve!

Cheesy Beef Pasta
(Prep + Cook Time: 30 minutes | Servings: 8)

Ingredients:
- 1 ¼ pounds ground beef
- 1 pound elbow macaroni
- 1 packet onion soup mix
- 3 ½ cups hot water
- 3 beef bouillon cubes
- 8 ounces sharp cheddar

Directions:
1. Press the SAUTE key of the Instant Pot. Add the beef and sauté until browned.
2. While the beef is cooking, combine the bouillon cubes with the hot water, and onion soup mix in a bowl and stir until well mixed.
3. When the beef browned, add the liquid mixture and the pasta in the pot and stir well to combine. Cover and lock the lid.
4. Press the MANUAL key, set the pressure to HIGH, and set the timer for 5 minutes.
5. When the Instant Pot timer beeps, press the CANCEL key. Turn the steam valve to quick release the pressure. Unlock and carefully open the lid.
6. Add the shredded cheese, press the SAUTE key, and sauté for about 1 to 2 minutes or until the cheese is melted. Serve immediately.

Stuffed Rigatoni

(Prep + Cook Time: 45 minutes | Servings: 6)

Ingredients:
- 1 pound rigatoni, cooked
- ½ pound ground beef
- ½ pound hot sausage
- 16 ounces mozzarella
- 16 ounces ricotta cheese
- 2 eggs
- 1 tbsp garlic powder
- 1 tbsp parsley
- 32 ounces of your favorite sauce

Equipment:
- Spring-form pan

Directions:
1. In a large-sized bowl, mix the ricotta cheese with the mozzarella cheese, 2 eggs, parsley, and garlic powder. Set aside.
2. Press the SAUTE key of the Instant Pot.
3. Brown the sausage and the ground beef in the pot, breaking up the sausages in the process.
4. Add into the bowl with the sauce and mix well. Turn off the pot for the time being.
5. Coat the bottom of the spring-form pan with the meat-sauce mix. In a standing up position, place the pasta in the pan.
6. Spoon the cheese mix into a plastic bag. Poke a hole in one corner of the plastic bag and squeeze the cheese mix inside each rigatoni. Top the sauce mix with additional mozzarella cheese.
7. Set a trivet in the Instant Pot and pour in 1 cup of water. Place the spring-form pan in the trivet. Cover and lock the lid.
8. Press the MANUAL key, set the pressure to HIGH, and set the timer for 20 minutes.
9. When the Instant Pot timer beeps, turn the steam valve to quick release the pressure.
10. Unlock and carefully open the lid. Let the pan sit in the pot for 10 minutes or until the dish settles. Serve!

Cheesy Taco Pasta

(Prep + Cook Time: 10 minutes | Servings: 8)

Ingredients:

- 1 pound ground beef
- 1 packet taco seasoning
- 16 ounces salsa
- 16 ounces pasta (I used ruffles)
- 16 ounces canned black beans
- 2 cups Doritos
- 16 ounces cheddar cheese
- 3 cups water
- Sour cream, for topping

Directions:

1. Press the SAUTE key of the Instant Pot.
2. Put the beef in the pot and add the taco seasoning. Sauté for about 1 to 2 minutes or until the beef is just crumbled.
3. Add the salsa, and black beans/ refried beans, uncooked pasta and water in the pot.
4. Press the CANCEL key to stop the SAUTÉ function. Cover and lock the lid.
5. Press the MANUAL key, set the pressure to HIGH, and set the timer for 4 minutes.
6. When the Instant Pot timer beeps, press the CANCEL key and unplug the Instant Pot. Turn the steam valve to quick release the pressure. Unlock and carefully open the lid.
7. Add 1/2 of the cheese and stir. Crumble the Doritos and line the bottom of the baking pan.
8. Pour the pasta over the Doritos, top with the rest of the cheddar cheese, and then with crumbled Doritos.
9. Bake in a preheated oven 350F for about 3-4 minutes or until the cheese is just melted.

Easy Teriyaki Beef

(Prep + Cook Time: 45 minutes | Servings: 4-6)

Ingredients:

- 1 cup water, plus 1 tbsp
- ¼ cup sodium-reduced soy sauce
- 2 tbsp brown sugar
- 3 cloves garlic, crushed
- 1 inch fresh ginger, grated
- ½ tsp pepper, plus more
- 1 tbsp extra virgin olive oil
- 1 small onion, sliced into sticks
- 1 small red pepper, sliced
- 1 small yellow pepper, sliced
- Salt to taste
- 1 lb stewing beef cubes
- 1 tbsp cornstarch
- 2 green onions, sliced

Directions:

1. Whisk together the 1 cup of water, the soy sauce, brown sugar, garlic, ginger and ½ teaspoon pepper (no salt); set aside.
2. Set your Instant Pot to SAUTÉ and add in the olive oil, when it's hot add the onion and peppers; season with salt and pepper.
3. Sauté for 2-3 minutes, just until the veggies start to soften and then set the veggies aside in a bowl.
4. Add the beef to the Instant Pot to brown (with the setting still on sauté) working in batches if needed; season with salt and pepper.
5. Give the soy mixture a quick mix and then add it to the pot, gently scraping the bottom of the pot to release any yummy bits.
6. Cover with the lid and lock it. Select MANUAL and cook at HIGH pressure for 45 minutes. Use a quick release.
7. Whisk together the 1 tbsp water and the cornstarch until completely smooth, it should look like white water.
8. Take the lid off the pot, set the pot back to SAUTÉ and when the liquid comes to a boil add in the cornstarch/water slurry; let it bubble until the sauce thickens.
9. Turn the pot off and add in the reserved peppers, onion and the green onion; mix well.
10. Taste and adjust seasoning before serving.
11. Serve on your favorite rice or noodles.

Notes: Use any combination of peppers you'd like. Feel free to add in more veggies of your choosing

Texas-Style Beef Chili

(Prep + Cook Time: 55 minutes | Servings: 4)

Ingredients:

- 1 pound beef, grass-fed, organic
- 1 onion, large-sized, diced
- 1 green bell pepper, seeds removed and diced
- 1 tbsp fresh parsley, chopped
- 1 tbsp Worcestershire sauce
- 1 tsp garlic powder
- 1 tsp onion powder
- 1 tsp paprika
- 1 tsp sea salt
- ½ tsp ground black pepper
- 26 ounces tomatoes, finely chopped
- 4 carrots, large-sized, chopped into small pieces
- 4 tsp chili powder
- Pinch cumin

For serving, optional:

- Jalapenos, sliced
- Onions, diced
- Sour cream, dairy-free

Directions:

1. Press the SAUTE key. Add the ground beef into the Instant Pot and cook until browned.
2. Add the remaining ingredients and mix well to combine. Lock the lid and close the steam valve.
3. Press CANCEL to stop the SAUTÉ function. Press MEAT/ STEW key. It will automatically be set for 35 minutes.
4. When the timer beeps, let the pressure release naturally. Enjoy!

Easy Seasoned Italian Beef

(Prep + Cook Time: 1 hour 55 minutes | Servings: 6)

Ingredients:

- 3 pounds of grass-fed chuck roast
- 6 garlic cloves
- 1 cup beef broth
- ¼ cup apple cider vinegar
- 2 tsp garlic powder
- 1 tsp oregano
- 1 tsp onion powder
- 1 tsp Himalayan pink salt
- 1 tsp marjoram
- 1 tsp basil
- ½ tsp ground ginger

Directions:

1. Cut a series of slits in the meat, and press the garlic cloves inside.
2. In a bowl, mix the onion powder, garlic powder, salt, ginger, basil, oregano, and marjoram.
3. Rub into the meat and put in your Instant Pot. Pour in the apple cider vinegar and broth.
4. Close and lock the lid. Press MANUAL and cook at HIGH pressure for 90 minutes.
5. When time is up, press CANCEL and wait for a natural release.
6. When all the pressure is gone, open the lid and shred the beef on a plate.
7. Serve over salad, cauliflower rice, cooked sweet potatoes, and so on.

Beef Tacos with Chili Sauce

(Prep + Cook Time: 1 hour 15 minutes | Servings: 6)

Ingredients:

- 3 pounds beef short ribs or beef chuck roast, boneless, cut into 1-inch strips
- 3 dried guajillo chilies, stemmed, seeded, and rinsed (or 2 more ancho chilies)
- 3 cloves garlic, peeled
- 2 dried ancho chilies, stemmed, seeded, and rinsed
- ½ cup beer (preferably Negra Modelo) OR water
- 1 tbsp Worcestershire sauce
- 1 tbsp soy sauce
- 1 onion, large-sized, sliced
- 1 dried chipotle chili, stemmed, seeded, and rinsed or
- 1 canned chipotle en adobo
- 1 ½ tsp kosher salt (I used Diamond Crystal)

Directions:

1. Season the short ribs with salt and stack them in the Instant Pot.
2. Top with the garlic, onions, and peppers.
3. Pour in the beer, Worcestershire sauce, and soy sauce. Cover and lock the lid.
4. Press the MANUAL key, set the pressure to HIGH, and set the timer for 40 minutes.
5. When the Instant Pot timer beeps, release the pressure naturally for 10-15 minutes or until the valve drops. Turn the steam valve to Venting to release remaining pressure. Unlock and carefully open the lid.
6. With a slotted spoon or with tongs, transfer the beef into a plate and set aside.
7. Pour the cooking liquid through a strainer set on a fat separator. Transfer the solids – garlic, onions, and pepper in blender.
8. When the fat surfaces, pour the de-fatted cooking liquid in the blender.
9. Starting from low power, blend the cooking liquid, slowly increasing to the highest speed, blending for 1 minute or until the sauce is very smooth.
10. Shred the beef and pour in the sauce.
11. Toss to coat the beef with the sauce.
12. Taste and adjust salt as needed.

Beef 'n Bean Pasta Casserole

(Prep + Cook Time: 20 minutes | Servings: 4)

Ingredients:

- 1 pound lean ground beef
- One 28-ounce can of diced tomatoes
- 2 cups corn kernels
- One 15-ounce can of drained and rinsed kidney beans
- One 12-ounce bottle brown ale
- 8-ounces pasta shells
- 1 chopped yellow onion
- 1 seeded and chopped green bell pepper
- 2 tbsp sweet paprika
- 1 tbsp olive oil
- 1 tbsp minced garlic
- 1 tsp dried oregano
- 1 tsp ground cumin
- ½ tsp chipotle pepper
- ½ tsp salt

Directions:

1. Heat your oil in the Instant Pot on the SAUTE setting.
2. When hot, add garlic, bell pepper, and onion. Stir until the onion becomes clear.
3. Add the ground beef, breaking it up with a spatula if necessary.
4. Keep stirring and browning, which should take about 4 minutes.
5. Add the corn, tomatoes, beans, and seasonings. Pour in the beer. Stir until the beer foam has gone down.
6. Add the pasta and stir so it becomes coated. Close and seal the lid.
7. Select MANUAL and cook at HIGH pressure for 8 minutes.
8. When time is up, hit CANCEL and carefully quick-release the pressure. Stir the casserole before serving.

Braised Beef Shank in Soybean Paste

(Prep + Cook Time: 60 minutes | Servings: 6-8)

Ingredients:

- 2 - 2½ pounds beef shank
- 2 tbsp olive oil
- 1 tbsp chili bean paste
- 1 tbsp sweet soybean paste
- 2 green onions chopped to 2-inch length
- 1 tsp Ginger sliced fresh
- 5-6 cloves garlic crushed
- 1 tsp Chinese cooking wine
- 1 tbsp light soy sauce
- 1 tbsp dark soy sauce
- 2 tsp sugar
- 1/3 tsp salt
- 3-4 tbsp water

Directions:

1. Soak beef in cold water for 30 minutes and then drain. Dice the beef into 1-inch pieces.
2. Heat 1 tablespoon of olive oil in the Instant Pot on the SAUTE setting and add beef.
3. Sauté for a few minutes until water evaporates and beef turns brown. Transfer beef in a bowl and set aside.
4. Add another 1 tablespoon of olive oil in the pot. Sauté chili bean paste and sweet soybean paste for about 30 seconds.
5. Add chopped green onion, ginger and garlic; continue to sauté for 30 seconds.
6. Put the beef back into the pot, and sauté for 1 minute, then add the cooking wine, both soy sauces, sugar, salt, and water.
7. Press the CANCEL key to stop SAUTE function.
8. Cover the lid and place the pressure valve in Sealing position. Select MANUAL and cook at HIGH pressure for 38 minutes. When the program is done, wait another 5 minutes.
9. Slowly release the pressure then open the lid. Select SAUTÉ and set temperature to More, stir occasionally until the sauce is reduced to 1/3 its volume.
10. Transfer the braised beef shank into to a serving bowl, serve immediately over rice. Enjoy!

Braised Pork Ribs with Garlic and Bamboo Shoots
(Prep + Cook Time: 55 minutes | Servings: 6)

Ingredients:
- 2 oz winter bamboo shoots, dried
- 1 tbsp olive oil
- 2-3 slices Ginger fresh
- 2 green onions rinsed and cut into 2-inch length
- 5-6 cloves garlic
- 1 star anise
- 1 tbsp cooking wine
- 2 tbsp premium dark soy sauce
- 1 ½ tbsp light soy sauce
- ½ tsp salt
- 1½ tsp sugar
- 3 tbsp water
- 1 tsp sesame oil

Directions:
1. Soak dried bamboo shoots in cold water for 8 hours. Rinse under water and drain well.
2. Remove membrane from the back of the ribs. Wash and cut between bones into small pieces, rinse and drain.
3. Heat 1 tablespoon of olive oil in the Instant Pot on the SAUTE function and adjust to High heat.
4. Sauté ginger, green onion, garlic and star anise for about 1 minute. Toss in pork ribs, and cook for 3-4 minutes until the ribs start to turn brown
5. Add bamboo shoots and sauté for another 1-2 minutes. Add in 1 tablespoon cooking wine, 2 tablespoons premium dark soy sauce, 1½ tablespoons light soy sauce, 1/2 teaspoon salt, 1½ teaspoons sugar, and 3 tablespoons water. Bring to a boil.
6. Cover the lid and place the pressure valve to SEAL position. Select MANUAL and cook at HIGH pressure for 36 minutes. When the program is done, wait another 5 minutes. Slowly release the pressure then open the lid.
7. Select SAUTÉ and set temperature to More. Stir occasionally until the sauce is reduced to 1/4 of its original volume. Transfer to a serving bowl, and serve over rice.

Pork Ribs BBQ

(Prep + Cook Time: 45 minutes | Servings: 2-4)

Ingredients:

- 1 pork spare rib (about 6 pounds)
- ½ cup Knob Creek Bourbon (optional)
- ½ cup water
- Barbecue sauce
- Onion powder
- Garlic powder Chipotle

Directions:

1. Set a steamer rack in the Instant Pot and pour in the water and bourbon.
2. Sprinkle the pork ribs with the onion powder, garlic, and chipotle.
3. Coil into a circle and vertically place on the steamer rack. Cover and lock the lid.
4. Press the MANUAL key, set the pressure to HIGH, and set the timer for 25 minutes.
5. When the Instant Pot timer beeps, release the pressure naturally for 15 minutes.
6. Turn the steam valve to release remaining pressure. Unlock and carefully open the lid.
7. Transfer the pork ribs on a baking sheet lined with foil and coat with barbecue sauce.
8. Broil for a couple minutes to caramelize the sauce. Cut the ribs in-between the bones. Serve with additional sauce.

Back Baby Ribs

(Prep + Cook Time: 60 minutes | Servings: 2-3)

Ingredients:

- 1 rack baby back ribs
- 2 carrots roughly chopped
- 2-3 drops liquid smoke
- 3 tbsp brown sugar
- 2 tsp chili powder
- 2 tsp black pepper
- 1 tsp onion powder
- 1 tsp garlic powder
- 1 tsp cinnamon powder
- 1 tsp kosher salt
- ½ tsp cumin seed ground
- ½ tsp fennel seed ground
- ¼ tsp cayenne pepper
- 1 medium onion minced
- 3 garlic cloves minced
- 1 cup ketchup
- ½ cup water
- 1/8 cup maple syrup
- 1/8 cup honey
- 2 tbsp apple cider vinegar
- 2 tbsp Dijon mustard

Directions:

1. Remove the membrane from the back of the ribs with a butter knife and a paper towel.
2. Mix all the dry rub ingredients and rub it all over the baby back ribs. Then, set aside while you prepare other ingredients.
3. Pour the homemade BBQ sauce into the pressure cooker. Add 2 – 3 drops of liquid smoke into the BBQ sauce. Place the baby back ribs into the BBQ sauce.
4. Close and lock the lid. Select MANUAL and cook at HIGH pressure for 16 – 25 minutes. Adjust your cooking time according to your preference: 16 minutes (tender with a bit of chew) to 25 minutes (fall off the bone). Turn off the heat and full natural release. Open the lid carefully.
5. While the baby back ribs is cooking in the pressure cooker, preheat the oven to 450F.
6. Carefully place the cooked baby back ribs on a chopping board with kitchen tongs. Cover it with aluminum foil and set aside.
7. Filter the Fat (Optional Step): Filter the BBQ sauce with a strainer and remove the fat with an oil separator.
8. Place roughly chopped carrots into the BBQ sauce and bring your BBQ sauce to a simmer by clicking SAUTÉ button once and click on adjust button twice to get to the Sauté Less

Function. Continue to reduce and thicken the BBQ sauce by simmering until desired thickness (roughly 6 - 8 minutes). Occasionally, stir with a wooden spoon. Taste the seasoning of the BBQ sauce. Stir in more brown sugar and additional 1 – 2 drops of liquid smoke if necessary.

9. Brush the homemade BBQ sauce all over the baby back ribs on all sides including the bones with a silicone basting brush. Place the baby back ribs in the oven on the top rack for 10 – 15 minutes.
10. Serve the baby back ribs immediately with more homemade BBQ sauce along with the carrots. Enjoy!

Fall Off the Bone Ribs in 30 Minutes
(Prep + Cook Time: 45 minutes | Servings: 4)

Ingredients:
- 1 slab baby back ribs
- 2 tsp salt
- 2 tsp pepper
- 1 cup apple juice
- 1 cup BBQ sauce divided, ¼ and ¾ cup

Directions:
1. Liberally salt and pepper both sides of slab of ribs. Cut slab in half if it's too big for your Instant Pot.
2. Pour apple juice into Instant Pot. Place ribs into pot, drizzle with 1/4 cup of BBQ sauce and secure lid. Make sure it's set to Sealing.
3. Select MANUAL and cook at HIGH pressure for 25 minutes. It will take a few minutes to heat up and seal the vent. Once timer counts down, let sit another 5 minutes then use a quick release. Turn on oven to broil (or heat your grill) while you're waiting for the 5 minute resting time.
4. Remove ribs from Instant Pot and place on a baking sheet. Slather on both sides with remaining sauce.
5. Place under broiler (or on grill) for 5-10 minutes, watching carefully so it doesn't burn. Remove and brush with a bit more sauce. Pull apart and dig in!

Maple Spice Rubbed Ribs

(Prep + Cook Time: 55 minutes | Servings: 4)

Ingredients:
- 3 tsp chili powder divided
- 1 ¼ tsp ground coriander
- 1 ¼ tsp garlic powder divided
- ¾ tsp salt
- ½ tsp black pepper
- 3-3 ½ pounds pork baby back ribs trimmed and cut into 4-rib pieces
- 4 tbsp maple syrup divided
- 1 can tomato sauce 8 ounces
- ¼ tsp ground cinnamon
- ¼ tsp ground ginger

Directions:
1. Combine 1½ teaspoons chili powder, coriander, 3⁄4 teaspoon garlic powder, salt and pepper in small bowl; mix well.
2. Brush ribs with 2 tablespoons maple syrup; rub with spice mixture. Place ribs in Instant Pot.
3. Combine tomato sauce, remaining 2 tablespoons maple syrup, 1½ teaspoons chili powder, ½ teaspoon garlic powder, cinnamon and ginger in medium bowl; mix well. Pour over ribs in pot; stir to coat ribs with sauce.
4. Secure lid and move pressure release valve to Sealing position. Press MANUAL and cook at HIGH pressure for 25 minutes.
5. When cooking is complete, use natural release for 10 minutes, then release remaining pressure. Remove ribs to plate; cover loosely to keep warm.
6. Press SAUTÉ; cook sauce about 10 minutes or until thickened.
7. Brush ribs with sauce; serve remaining sauce on the side.

Pork Chops with Mushroom Gravy

(Prep + Cook Time: 35 minutes | Servings: 4)

Ingredients:

- 4 pork chops, bone-in thick
- 2 tbsp vegetable oil
- 1 can condensed cream of mushroom soup
- 1½ cups water
- Lemon pepper

Directions:

1. Pat the pork chops dry and then liberally season with lemon pepper or your preferred seasoning. Put the oil in the pot and press the SAUTE key.
2. When the oil starts to sizzle, brown both sides of the pork chops in the pot. When browned, transfer into a platter.
3. When all the pork chops are browned, pour the water in the pot to deglaze the pot.
4. Stir and scrape any browned bits off from the bottom of the pot.
5. Stir in the mushroom soup and then return the browned pork chops into the pot, along with any meat juices that accumulated on the platter.
6. Press the CANCEL key to stop the SAUTÉ function. Cover and lock the lid.
7. Press the MANUAL key, set the pressure to HIGH, and set the timer for 18 minutes.
8. When the Instant Pot timer beeps, release the pressure naturally for 10-15 minutes or until the valve drops.
9. Turn the steam valve to release remaining pressure. Unlock and carefully open the lid.
10. Transfer the pork chops into a large-sized serving bowl. If needed, thicken the gravy in the pot with slurry of flour and water.
11. Pour the thick gravy over the chops. Serve.

Honey Pork Chops

(Prep + Cook Time: 25 minutes | Servings: 4)

Ingredients:

- 2 pounds pork chops, boneless
- 2 tbsp Dijon mustard
- ¼ tsp cloves, ground
- ¼ tsp black pepper
- ¼ cups honey
- ½ tsp sea salt
- ½ tsp fresh ginger, peeled and minced
- ½ tsp cinnamon
- ½ tbsp maple syrup

Directions:

1. Sprinkle the pork chops with pepper and salt.
2. Put the seasoned pork in the pot.
3. Press the SAUTE key and brown both sides of the pork chops in the pot.
4. In a bowl, combine the honey with the maple syrup, Dijon mustard, cloves, and cinnamon.
5. Pour the mix over the pork chops.
6. Press the CANCEL key to stop the SAUTÉ function. Cover and lock the lid. Press the MANUAL key, set the pressure to HIGH, and set the timer for 15 minutes.
7. When the Instant Pot timer beeps, release the pressure naturally or quickly. Unlock and carefully open the lid. Serve.

Pork Carnitas

(Prep + Cook Time: 2 hours 15 minutes | Servings: 6)

Ingredients:

- 3-4 pounds pork shoulder bone-in
- 2 tbsp cumin
- 2 tbsp oregano
- ½ tsp chipotle powder
- 1 tbsp kosher salt
- ½ tbsp black pepper
- 1 tbsp soy sauce
- 1 yellow onion diced
- 10 garlic cloves minced
- 1 cup vegetable stock
- 2 bay leaves
- Corn tortillas for serving
- Radishes sliced, for serving
- Pico de Gallo for serving
- Cilantro chopped, for serving
- Lime wedges for serving

Directions:
1. Combine spices to make a dry rub, and pat over the pork shoulder.
2. Set Instant Pot to SAUTE, and sear all sides of the shoulder until browned.
3. Add soy sauce, onion, garlic, bay leaves, and vegetable stock, and close the lid. Cook on MANUAL at HIGH Pressure for 90 minutes.
4. Release steam, and remove lid. Lift pork shoulder onto a plate, remove the bone, and shred meat with two forks.
5. Serve hot with your favorite fixing like radishes, cilantro, pico de gallo, and freshly squeezed lime juice. Enjoy!

Teriyaki Pork Tenderloin (E&S)
(Prep + Cook Time: 30 minutes | Servings: 4)

Ingredients:
- 2 pork tenderloins, cut into half
- 2 cups teriyaki sauce (if using a thick kind, thin it out some water so prevent it from burning on the bottom of the pot)
- 2 green onions, chopped
- 2 tbsp canola oil OR a similar oil
- Generous amounts salt and pepper
- Sesame seeds, toasted

Directions:
1. Press the SAUTE button of your Instant Pot and put the oil in the pot.
2. When the pot is hot, put about 1-2 tenderloins in the pot and lightly brown a few sides of the tenderloins.
3. When the meat is browned, lay the roast down and pour the sauce over the top of the tenderloins. Cover and lock the lid.
4. Press the MANUAL key, set the pressure to HIGH, and set the timer for 20 minutes.
5. When the Instant Pot timer beeps, release the pressure naturally for 10 minutes. Turn the steam valve to release remaining pressure.
6. Unlock and carefully open the lid. Slice the meat into pieces.
7. Serve with steamed broccoli and jasmine rice.
8. Garnish with chopped green onions and toasted sesame seeds.

Pork Fried Rice

(Prep + Cook Time: 40 minutes | Servings: 4)

Ingredients:

- 3 cups + 2 tbsp water
- 2 cups white rice
- 8-ounces thin pork loin, cut into ½-inch slices
- 1 beaten egg
- ½ cup frozen peas
- 1 chopped onion
- 1 peeled and chopped carrot
- 3 tbsp olive oil
- 3 tbsp soy sauce
- Salt and pepper to taste

Directions:

1. Turn your Instant Pot to SAUTE.
2. Pour in 1 tablespoon of oil and cook the carrot and onion for 2 minutes.
3. Season the pork. Cook in the pot for 5 minutes.
4. Press CANCEL and take out the onion, carrot, and pork.
5. Deglaze with the water. Add rice and a bit of salt. Lock the lid.
6. Select RICE and cook for the default time.
7. When time is up, press CANCEL and wait 10 minutes. Release any leftover steam.
8. Stir the rice, making a hollow in the middle so you can see the bottom of the pot.
9. Press SAUTE and add 2 tablespoons of oil.
10. Add the egg in the hollow and whisk it around to scramble it while it cooks. When cooked, pour in peas, onion, carrot, and pork.
11. Stir until everything has warmed together.
12. Stir in soy sauce, press CANCEL, and serve.

Pork Ragu

(Prep + Cook Time: 50 minutes | Servings: 8)

Ingredients:

- 2 racks (2 1/4-2 1/2-pound each) baby back ribs, trimmed and cut into fourths
- 2 carrots, large-sized, peeled and chopped fine
- ¼ cup fresh sage, minced
- 1 pound pappardelle OR tagliatelle
- 1 onion, large-sized, chopped fine
- 1 garlic head, outer papery skins removed and top fourth of head cut off and discarded
- 1 fennel bulb, large-sized, stalks discarded, and bulb halved, cored, and chopped fine
- 1 cup dry red wine PLUS 2 tbsp dry red wine
- 1 can (28-ounce) whole peeled tomatoes, drained and then crushed coarse
- 1 ½ tsp fresh rosemary, minced
- 2 tsp ground fennel
- 3 cups chicken broth
- 3 tbsp olive oil
- Grated Parmesan cheese
- Kosher salt and pepper

Directions:

1. Using a good boning knife, remove the pork meat from the bones and cut into 1-inch pieces. Season with salt and pepper. In batches, cook the pork pieces in the Instant Pot with olive oil until browned using the SAUTÉ mode.
2. Transfer the browned meat on a plate and set aside. If needed, add a bit more oil into the Instant Pot.
3. Add the onion, carrots, fennel, rosemary, 2 tablespoons of sage, and 1/2 teaspoon salt.
4. Cook for about 12-15 minutes, occasionally stirring, until the vegetables start to brown, scraping up any browned bits starting to stick on the bottom of the pot.
5. Add 1 cup of the wine; cook for about 5 minutes or until evaporated. Stir in the broth and the tomatoes.
6. Add the garlic and return the pork meat into the pot. Press the CANCEL key to stop the SAUTÉ function.

7. Cover and lock the lid. Press the MANUAL key, set the pressure to HIGH, and set the timer for 20 minutes. When the Instant Pot timer beeps, press the CANCEL key.
8. Let the pressure release naturally for 10-15 minutes or until the valve drops. Using an oven mitt or a long handled spoon, turn the steam valve to Venting to release remaining pressure. Unlock and carefully open the lid.
9. With a large-sized spoon, skim any excess fat off from the surface of the sauce. Using a fork, break the meat into bite-sized pieces. If you want to thicken the sauce, press the SAUTÉ key and cook for about 5 minutes or until thickened.
10. Add the parsley, taste, and season to taste with salt and pepper. Serve over tubular pasta with Parmesan to pass.

Notes: Freeze leftovers and spoon over polenta or pasta.

Pork Satay
(Prep + Cook Time: 35 minutes | Servings: 6)

Ingredients:
- 12 oz pork loin
- 3 tbsp apple cider vinegar
- 1 tbsp olive oil
- 1 tbsp sesame oil
- 1 tsp turmeric
- ½ tsp cayenne pepper
- 1 tsp cilantro
- 1 tsp basil
- 1 tsp brown sugar
- 1 tsp soy sauce
- 11 tbsp fish sauce

Directions:
1. Chop the pork loin into the medium pieces.
2. Place the chopped pork lion in the mixing bowl. Sprinkle the meat with the apple cider vinegar, olive oil, sesame oil, turmeric, cayenne pepper, cilantro, basil, brown sugar, soy sauce, and fish sauce. Mix up the mixture.
3. Then screw the meat into the skewers.
4. Place the skewers in the Instant Pot.
5. Cook the pork satay for 25 minutes at the MEAT mode.
6. When the dish is cooked – remove the pork satay from the Instant Pot.
7. Chill the dish little.
8. Serve the pork satay immediately. Enjoy!

Pork Chops and Applesauce

(Prep + Cook Time: 40 minutes | Servings: 4)

Ingredients:

- 1½ pounds boneless pork chops
- 6 cups apples, sliced
- ½ cup brown sugar
- 2 tbsp flour
- 1 tsp cinnamon
- ½ cup water
- Drizzle olive oil
- Salt and black pepper to taste

Directions:

1. In the inner pot of the pressure cooker, press the SAUTE button and add the oil.
2. Season the pork chops with salt and pepper, then place in the pot. Brown on both sides, then remove from the pot. Press the CANCEL button.
3. In a separate bowl, toss together the apples, flour, brown sugar and cinnamon. Add the water to the inner pot and scrape at any browned bits left from the pork.
4. Pour the apples into the pot and place the pork on top.
5. Close the lid completely and position the steam release handle to sealing position.
6. Select MANUAL and cook at HIGH pressure for 10 minutes, after that use a natural release for 5-10 minutes.
7. Then slide the steam release handle to venting position to fully release the pressure. Open the lid when the float valve has dropped down.
8. Transfer the pork chops to a plate and serve covered in the apple mixture.

Pork Cutlets with the Plum Sauce

(Prep + Cook Time: 40 minutes | Servings: 6)

Ingredients:

- 12 oz ground pork
- 1/3 cup lemon juice
- 6 oz plums, pitted
- 1 tbsp sugar
- 1 tsp cilantro
- ½ tsp thyme
- 1 egg
- 1 tbsp cornstarch
- 1 tbsp ground ginger
- 1 tbsp olive oil
- 1 tbsp flour
- 1 tsp paprika

Directions:
1. Combine the ground pork with the cilantro, thyme, cornstarch, paprika, and egg.
2. Mix up the mixture carefully till you get homogenous mass.
3. Then make the medium cutlets from the ground meat mixture.
4. Pour the olive oil in the Instant Pot and add the pork cutlets. Cook the cutlets at the SAUTE mode for 10 minutes.
5. Stir the cutlets till all the sides are golden brown.
6. Meanwhile, put the plums in the blender and blend them until smooth. Then add sugar, ground ginger, flour, sugar, and lemon juice. Blend the mixture for 1 minute more.
7. When the cutlets are cooked – pour the plum sauce in the Instant Pot. Close the lid and cook the dish at the STEW mode for 10 minutes.
8. Then remove the pork cutlets from the Instant Pot, sprinkle them with the plum sauce. Serve the dish hot!

Pulled Pork
(Prep + Cook Time: 40 minutes | Servings: 8)

Ingredients:
- 2-pound pork shoulder
- ½ cup tomato paste
- ½ cup cream
- ¼ cup chicken stock
- 1 tbsp salt
- 1 tsp ground black pepper
- 1 tsp cayenne pepper
- 3 tbsp olive oil
- 1 tbsp lemon juice
- 1 tsp garlic powder
- 1 onion, peeled

Directions:
1. Transfer the onion to the blender, blend till it is smooth.
2. Pour the olive oil in the Instant Pot and add pork shoulder and roast the meat at the SAUTÉ mode for 10 minutes.
3. Then add tomato paste, cream, chicken stock, ground black pepper, cayenne pepper, lemon juice, and garlic powder.
4. Mix up the mixture and close the Instant Pot lid. Cook the dish at the HIGH pressure mode for 15 minutes.
5. When the time is over – remove the pork shoulder from the Instant Pot and shred it with the help of the folk.
6. After this, return the shredded pork back in the Instant Pot and mix up the mixture carefully.
7. Cook the dish at the manual mode for 2 minutes more.
8. Then transfer the cooked dish in the serving plate.
9. Serve the dish immediately.

Pulled BBQ Pork
(Prep + Cook Time: 1 hour 45 minutes | Servings: 4)

Ingredients:
- 2.6 pounds pork roast
- 2 cups chicken stock OR water
- ¼ cup vegetable oil
- Any of your preferred spices (Worcestershire sauce, pepper, salt)
- BBQ sauce, optional

Directions:
1. Slice the roast into halves to make it easier to handle and fit in the pot.
2. Season and spice the roast with your choice of spices or seasoning or marinade; let sit for about 20 minutes, if desired.
3. Press the SAUTE key. Put the vegetable oil in the pot and heat. When the oil is hot, add the pork and sear each side for 3 minutes.
4. Add 2 cups of liquid – stock or water – into the pot. Press the CANCEL key to stop the SAUTÉ function. Cover and lock the lid.
5. Press the MEAT/STEW key and set the timer for 90 minutes
6. When the Instant Pot timer beeps, release the pressure naturally for 10 minutes.
7. Turn the steam valve to release remaining pressure. Unlock and carefully open the lid. Transfer the pork into a plate and shred.
8. At this point, you can eat this dish as is or continue to the BBQ option. Make sure that there is 1/2 cup water in the pot.
9. Add your preferred BBQ sauce into the pot. Return the shredded pork into the pot. Stir to mix. Cover and lock the lid.
10. Press the MANUAL key, set the pressure to HIGH, and set the timer for 5 minutes.
11. When the Instant Pot timer beeps, turn the steam valve to Venting to quick release the pressure. Unlock and carefully open the lid.
12. Serve with your favorite bread.

Cranberry BBQ Pulled Pork

(Prep + Cook Time: 55 minutes | Servings: 10)

Ingredients:

- 3-4 pounds pork shoulder or roast, boneless, fat trimmed off
- For the sauce:
- 3 tbsp liquid smoke
- 2 tbsp tomato paste
- 2 cups fresh cranberries
- ¼ cup buffalo hot sauce
- 1/3 cup blackstrap molasses
- ½ cup water
- ½ cup apple cider vinegar
- 1 tsp salt, or more to taste
- 1 tbsp adobo sauce
- 1 cup tomato puree
- 1 chipotle pepper in adobo sauce, diced

Directions:

1. Cut the pork against the grain in halves or thirds and set aside.
2. Press the SAUTE key of the Instant Pot.
3. When the pot is hot, add the cranberries and the water.
4. Let simmer for about 4 to 5 minutes or until the cranberries start to pop. Add the remaining sauce ingredients in the pot and continue simmering for 5 minutes more.
5. Add the pork in the pot. Press the CANCEL key to stop the sauté function. Cover and lock the lid.
6. Select MANUAL and cook at HIGH pressure for 40 minutes.
7. When the Instant Pot timer beeps, turn the steam valve to Venting to quick release the pressure. Unlock and carefully open the lid.
8. With a fork, pull the pork apart into shreds.
9. Serve the pork with plenty of sauce on rolls or bread or over your favorite greens.

Mexican Pulled-Pork Lettuce Wraps

(Prep + Cook Time: 1 hour 40 minutes | Servings: 6)

Ingredients:

- 4 pounds pork roast
- 1 head washed and dried butter lettuce
- 2 grated carrots
- 2 tbsp oil
- 2 lime wedges
- 1 chopped onion
- 1 tbsp salt
- 2-3 cups water

Spice Mix:

- 1 tbsp unsweetened cocoa powder
- 2 tsp oregano
- 1 tsp red pepper flakes
- 1 tsp garlic powder
- 1 tsp white pepper
- 1 tsp cumin
- ⅛ tsp cayenne
- ⅛ tsp coriander

Directions:

1. Marinate the pork the night before by mixing all the ingredients in the second list and rubbing into the pork. Store in the fridge.
2. The next day, turn your Instant Pot to SAUTE. When warm, brown roast all over.
3. Pour in 2-3 cups water, so the roast is almost totally submerged. Close and seal the lid.
4. Select MANUAL and cook at HIGH pressure for 55 minutes.
5. When time is up, press CANCEL and let the pressure release naturally.
6. When ready, take out the meat and pull with two forks.
7. Turn the cooker back to SAUTE and reduce the liquid by half.
8. Strain and skim off any excess fat. If you want crispy pork, fry in a pan with some oil until it becomes light brown.
9. Mix pork with the cooking liquid before serving in the lettuce with grated carrots, a squirt of lime, and any other toppings.

Pulled Pork Tacos

(Prep + Cook Time: 70 minutes | Servings: 8)

Ingredients:

For the pork:
- 1 ½ tsp sea salt
- 1 cup chicken broth, OR beef broth
- 1 piece (4 pounds) pork shoulder (a.k.a pork butt, bone out or in)
- 1 tsp freshly ground pepper
- 1 yellow onion, large-sized, peeled and thinly sliced
- ½ tsp chipotle chili powder
- ½ tsp cumin
- ½ tsp garlic powder
- Your favorite or preferred tortillas

Garnish:
- Purple cabbage, sliced
- Cilantro, chopped
- Lime

Directions:

1. In a bowl, combine all of the spices until well mixed.
2. Put the onion in the Instant Pot and pour in the broth.
3. Rub all the sides of the pork with the spice mixture and then put the spice-rubbed pork into the pot. Cover and lock the lid.
4. Press the MEAT key and set the timer for 60 minutes.
5. When the Instant Pot timer beeps, press the CANCEL key and unplug the Instant Pot. Turn the steam valve to quick release the pressure. Unlock and carefully open the lid.
6. Transfer the meat into a cutting board, discard the onion and the cooking liquid.
7. With 2 forks, shred the meat, discarding the fat in the process.
8. If you want crispy, browned edges, you can sear the shredded meat in a hot pan or broil in the oven for a couple of minutes.
9. Use the shredded meat to make tacos, garnishing with sliced purple cabbage and chopped cilantro.
10. Top with your favorite guacamole and salsa.

Cilantro Pork Tacos (E&S)

(Prep + Cook Time: 45 minutes | Servings: 6)

Ingredients:

- 1 tbsp cilantro
- 10 oz ground pork
- 1 tbsp tomato paste
- 1 red onion
- 1 tsp salt
- 1 tsp basil
- 1 tbsp butter
- 1 cup lettuce
- 7 oz corn tortilla
- 1 tsp paprika

Directions:

1. Combine the ground pork, salt, cilantro, paprika, and basil together in the mixing bowl.
2. Add butter and tomato paste. Stir the mixture well.
3. After this, place the ground pork mixture in the Instant Pot and close the lid.
4. Cook the dish at the MEAT mode for 27 minutes.
5. Meanwhile, chop the lettuce and slice the onion.
6. When the meat is cooked – remove it from the Instant Pot and transfer in the corn tortillas.
7. Then add chopped lettuce and sliced onion. Wrap the tacos.
8. Serve the dish immediately.

First Timer's Pork Belly

(Prep + Cook Time: 1 hour 10 minutes | Servings: 4)

Ingredients:

- 1 pound pork belly
- ½ - 1 cup white wine
- 1 garlic clove
- 1 tbsp olive oil
- Rosemary sprig
- Salt to taste
- Black pepper to taste

Directions:

1. Put oil in your Instant Pot and turn to the SAUTE setting.
2. When hot, add pork and sear 2-3 minutes on each side until golden and crispy. Pour in wine, about a quarter inch. Season pork with salt, pepper, and garlic.
3. Add garlic clove. Turn on the cooker to SAUTE to boil the liquid.
4. When boiling, lock the lid. Select MANUAL and cook at HIGH pressure for 40 minutes.
5. If you want the pork to be more like steak, cook for 30 minutes.
6. When time is up, hit CANCEL and wait for the pressure to go down on its own.
7. When the pork is room-temperature, slice and season to taste with more salt.

Red Cooked Pork

(Prep + Cook Time: 50 minutes | Servings: 4)

Ingredients:

- 2 pounds fatty pork belly, cut into 1 ½-inch cubes
- 1/3 cup water OR bone broth
- 1 tsp sea salt
- 1 tbsp blackstrap molasses
- 1 piece (1-inch) ginger, peeled and then smashed
- 2 tbsp coconut aminos (or soy sauce)
- 2 tbsp maple syrup
- 3 tbsp sherry
- A couple sprigs coriander OR cilantro leaves, to garnish

Directions:

1. Put the pork cubes in the pot and pour in enough water to cover the pork cubes.
2. Select SAUTE mode and press the More option.
3. Bring to a boil and boil the pork cubes for 3 minutes.
4. When boiled, press the CANCEL setting. Drain the pork cubes and rinse off any impurities of scum off the meat.
5. Put the pork cubes in a colander and set aside in the sink to drain.
6. Clean and dry the inner pot of the Instant Pot.
7. Pour the maple syrup in the pot and press the SAUTE key and heat.
8. Add the pork cubes and brown the meat for about 10 minutes. Add the rest of the ingredients in the pot.
9. Bring to a boil and then press the CANCEL key to stop the SAUTÉ function. Cover and lock the lid.
10. Select MANUAL and cook at HIGH pressure for 25 minutes.
11. When the Instant Pot timer beeps, release the pressure naturally for 10-15 minutes or until the valve drops. Turn the steam valve to Venting to release remaining pressure. Unlock and carefully open the lid.
12. Press the SAUTE key and bring the contents to a simmer.
13. Cook until the sauce is reduced and thick to your liking.
14. Serve with cilantro or coriander leaves to garnish.
15. Serve the pork cubes with Boston lettuce leaves to wrap them with.

Spare Ribs and Black Bean Sauce
(Prep + Cook Time: 5 minutes | Servings: 4)

Ingredients:
- 1 pound pork spareribs, cut into pieces
- 1 tbsp corn starch
- 1 tbsp oil
- 1 tsp fish sauce, optional
- 1 cup water plus 1-2 tsp water
- Green onions as garnish

For the black bean marinade:
- 1 tbsp black bean sauce
- 1 tbsp ginger, grated
- 1 tbsp light soy sauce
- 1 tbsp Shaoxing wine
- 1 tsp sesame oil
- 1 tsp sugar
- 3 cloves garlic, minced
- A pinch white pepper

Directions:
1. In an oven-safe bowl, combine all the marinade ingredients. Add the pork and marinate for 25 minutes in the refrigerator.
2. When marinated, mix 1 tablespoon oil into the pork and then add the corn starch. Mix well. Add 1 to 2 teaspoon of water and mix well.
3. Pour 1 cup of water into the Instant Pot.
4. Put a steamer rack in the pot and put the bow with the marinated spare ribs on the rack.
5. Press the CANCEL key to stop the SAUTÉ function. Cover and lock the lid. Turn the steam valve to Sealing. Press the MANUAL key, set the pressure to HIGH, and set the timer for 15 minutes.
6. When the Instant Pot timer beeps, release the pressure naturally for 10-15 minutes or until the valve drops.
7. Turn the steam valve to release remaining pressure. Unlock and carefully open the lid.
8. Taste and, if desired, add 1 teaspoon fish sauce and garnish with green onions.

Pork-and-Egg Fried Rice

(Prep + Cook Time: 40 minutes | Servings: 4)

Ingredients:
- 3 cups + 2 tbsp water
- 2 cups long-grain white rice
- 1 beaten egg
- 1 finely-chopped onion
- 1 peeled and finely-chopped carrot
- ½ cup frozen peas
- 8-ounces sliced pork loin chop (½-inch pieces)
- 3 tbsp soy sauce
- 3 tbsp veggie oil
- Salt and pepper to taste

Directions:
1. Preheat the cooker to SAUTE function and add 1 tablespoon of oil. Stir the onion and carrot for about 2 minutes.
2. Add pork after seasoning with salt and pepper. Cook for 5 minutes or until the meat is cooked all the way through.
3. Press CANCEL and take out the onion, carrot, and pork. Pour in water and deglaze, scraping up any bits.
4. Pour in rice, salt, and seal the lid. Select RICE and cook for default time.
5. When time is up, press CANCEL and wait 10 minutes for a natural release. Then quick-release any leftover steam.
6. Create a hole in the rice, and pour in the rest of the olive oil before hitting SAUTE. Add egg and scramble.
7. When the egg is just about ready, add the peas, onion, carrot, and pork.
8. Keep stirring for a few minutes until everything is mixed in well.
9. Serve with soy sauce!

Southern Pork-Sausage Gravy

(Prep + Cook Time: 35 minutes | Servings: 8)

Ingredients:
- 1 pound pork sausage
- 2 cups whole milk
- 4 minced garlic cloves
- ¼ cup flour
- Water as needed

Directions:
1. Turn your Instant Pot to SAUTE and add garlic. If they start to stick, pour in a little water.
2. When fragrant and golden, add the meat. Cook until brown, breaking up with a spatula.
3. Add 1½ cups milk and seal the lid.
4. Select MANUAL and cook at HIGH pressure for 5 minutes.
5. When time is up, turn off the cooker and carefully quick-release the pressure. Wait for 5 minutes. Mix flour and remaining milk in a bowl until smooth.
6. Select SAUTE mode and cook, slowly stirring the gravy.
7. When it starts to bubble and thicken, it's ready to serve!

Seasoned Pork Chops with Cherry-Jam Sauce
(Prep + Cook Time: 40 minutes | Servings: 4)

Ingredients:
- Two 1¼ - 2 inch thick pork loin chops (bone-in and trimmed)
- 1 cup pearl onions
- ½ cup sour cherry jam
- ¼ cup medium-dry red wine
- 2 tbsp olive oil
- 1 tbsp butter
- ½ tsp ground cinnamon
- ¼ tsp ground coriander
- ¼ tsp ground ginger
- ¼ tsp ground cardamom
- ¼ tsp salt

Directions:
1. Mix dry spices in a bowl and coat both sides of the pork chops.
2. Select SAUTE and melt butter.
3. When melted, add one chop at a time and brown lightly on both sides. You want a nice golden color, not too dark, because you don't want the spice rub to burn.
4. When both chops are browned and plated, add onions to the pressure cooker.
5. Stir and cook for about 4 minutes, or until they are browned. Add jam and wine, and deglaze.
6. When the jam has dissolved, add both chops and turn to coat in the sauce. Close and seal the lid.
7. Select MANUAL and cook for 24 minutes at HIGH pressure.
8. When the timer beeps, quick-release the pressure after pressing CANCEL.
9. Cut the chops into strips to serve, with sauce on top.

Milk-Braised Pork

(Prep + Cook Time: 55 minutes | Servings: 4)

Ingredients:

- 2 pounds of pork loin roast, tied together with kitchen string
- 2 ½ cups milk
- 2 tbsp olive oil
- 2 tbsp butter
- 1 bay leaf
- 2 tsp salt
- 2 tsp ground pepper

Directions:

1. Melt the butter in your Instant Pot on SAUTE. Add oil. Put in the meat, fatty-side down, and brown all over.
2. Sprinkle with salt, pepper, bay leaf, and pour in milk. The roast should be half-covered. Close and seal the lid.
3. Select MANUAL and cook at HIGH pressure for 30 minutes.
4. When time is up, press CANCEL and let the pressure release naturally. After 10 minutes, quick-release leftover pressure.
5. Transfer roast to a dish and tent with foil.
6. Wait for the sauce to cool in the pot, and then skim off the fat. Pick out the bay leaf.
7. Turn the pot to SAUTÉ and reduce if you want it to be thicker.
8. Serve roast slices with sauce poured on top.

Pork Roast with Cranberries, Honey, and Herbs

(Prep + Cook Time: 1 hour 25 minutes | Servings: 4)

Ingredients:

- 2 pounds boneless pork roast
- 12-ounces frozen cranberries
- 10-ounces bone broth
- 2 tbsp apple cider vinegar
- 2 tbsp chopped herbs
- 1 tbsp honey
- 1 tbsp grass-fed butter
- ¼ tsp cinnamon
- ¼ tsp ground garlic
- ⅛ tsp cinnamon
- Salt to taste

Directions:

1. Turn your Instant Pot on to the SAUTE setting and add butter.
2. When the butter is melted and coats the bottom, salt the pork and add to the pot. Sear for 2 minutes on each side.
3. Pour in broth and cranberries.
4. Add in vinegar, honey, and herbs. Close and seal the lid.
5. Select MANUAL and cook for 70 minutes on HIGH pressure.
6. When time is up, press CANCEL and carefully quick-release. Take out the pork and shred. Return to the pot and add more salt.
7. Seal the lid again and press MANUAL and cook at HIGH for 10 more minutes.
8. Serve pork with cooked cranberries, cloves, garlic, and cinnamon.

Holiday Brussels Sprouts
(Prep + Cook Time: 35 minutes | Servings: 6)

Ingredients:

- 6 cups Brussels sprouts, chopped
- 5 slices bacon, chopped
- 2 tbsp water
- 2 tbsp balsamic reduction
- ¼ tsp salt
- ¼ cup soft goat cheese, optional
- Pepper to taste

Directions:

1. Press the SAUTE key of the Instant Pot. Add the bacon and sauté until desired crispiness is achieved.
2. Add the Brussels sprouts and stir to coat with the scrumptious bacon fat.
3. Add the water and sprinkle with pepper and salt. Cook for about 4 to 6 minutes, stirring occasionally, and continue sautéing until the Brussels sprouts are crisp. Transfer into a serving dish.
4. Drizzle with balsamic reduction and, if desired, sprinkle with crumbled goat cheese.

Notes: If a bit of bacon stuck in the inner pot, put 1 cup of soapy water in the pot and press SAUTÉ. The browned bits will come right off. Easy to clean up afterwards.

Meat Lover's Crustless Quiche

(Prep + Cook Time: 50 minutes | Servings: 4)

Ingredients:
- 6 large eggs, well beaten
- ½ cup milk
- ¼ tsp salt
- 1/8 tsp ground black pepper
- 4 slices bacon, cooked and then crumbled
- 1 cup ground sausage, cooked
- ½ cup ham, diced
- 2 large green onions, chopped
- 1 cup cheese, shredded
- 1½ cups water

Directions:
1. Pour the water into the Instant Pot and put a stainless steel rack with handle into the bottom of the pot. In a large-sized bowl, whisk the eggs with the milk, salt, and pepper.
2. Add the sausage, bacon, ham, cheese, and green onions into a 1-quart soufflé dish; mix well.
3. Pour the egg mix over the meat; stir well to combine.
4. With an aluminum foil, loosely cover the dish. Put onto the rack. Lock the pot lid. Set the pressure to HIGH and the timer to 30 minutes.
5. When the timer beeps, let the pressure release naturally for 10 minutes, and then turn the valve to Venting to release remaining pressure.
6. Carefully open the lid. Lift out the rack with the dish.
7. Remove the foil covering and, if desired, sprinkle the top of the quiche with additional cheese and broil until melted and slightly browned. Serve immediately.

Glazed Honey Ham

(Prep + Cook Time: 35 minutes | Servings: 8)

Ingredients:
- 6-7 pound ham, boneless
- ½ cup honey
- 1 cup brown sugar
- 1 tsp ground cloves
- 4 tbsp crushed pineapple, juice included
- 1 cup water

Directions:
1. Prepare the ham by slicing it as you would for serving. This will help distribute the glaze.
2. In the Instant Pot add 1 cup of water and the steam rack.
3. Create a sling using tin foil to help remove the ham when it is done cooking.
4. Place the sliced ham in a tinfoil packet. Sprinkle with brown sugar and drizzle with the honey.
5. Distribute the cloves evenly and top with the pineapple and juice. Close the packet and place on the steam rack.
6. Close the lid, select MANUAL and cook at HIGH pressure for 10 minutes.
7. When the pressure cooking cycle is completed use a quick release the pressure. Open the lid when the float valve has dropped down.
8. Transfer the ham to a serving platter and serve immediately with the sauce in a separate serving sauce bowl.

Turnip Greens with Bacon (E&S)
(Prep + Cook Time: 50 minutes | Servings: 4)

Ingredients:
- 1 bag (1-pound) turnip greens
- ½ - 1 cup smoked ham hocks or necks
- 3-4 slices bacon, cut into small pieces
- 2 cups chicken broth
- ½ cup onion, diced (I use frozen)
- Splash extra-virgin olive oil
- Salt and pepper, to taste

Directions:
1. Set the Instant Pot to SAUTE. Pour a splash of olive oil. Add the bacon, the smoked ham, and onion.
2. Season with salt and pepper and sauté until the fat is rendered and the meat is cooked.
3. Add the broth and turnip greens. Close and lock the lid. Turn the steam release valve to Sealing. Cook at HIGH pressure for 30 minutes.
4. When the timer beeps, quick release the pressure and serve warm.

Collard Greens with Bacon

(Prep + Cook Time: 40 minutes | Servings: 6)

Ingredients:

- ¼ pound bacon, cut into 1-inch pieces
- 1 pound collard greens, cleaned and then stems trimmed
- ½ tsp kosher salt
- ½ cup water
- Fresh ground black pepper

Directions:

1. Spread the bacon in the bottom of the Instant Pot.
2. Select SAUTÉ and cook for about 5 minutes, occasionally stirring until the bacon is crispy and browned.
3. Stir in a big handful of collard greens to coat with bacon grease until they wilt slightly. Then start stirring and packing in the rest of the collards.
4. The pot will be filled – just pack them enough to close the lid since they will quickly wilt.
5. Sprinkle the collards with salt and pour water over everything. Close and lock the lid. Turn the steam release valve to Sealing, set the pressure to HIGH, and the timer to 18 minutes.
6. When the timer beeps, turn the steam valve to Venting and quick release the pressure. Carefully open and remove the lid.
7. Pour the collard into a serving dish.
8. Sprinkle with freshly ground black pepper and then serve.

Lamb and Avocado Salad

(Prep + Cook Time: 45 minutes | Servings: 10)

Ingredients:

- 1 avocado, pitted
- 1 cucumber
- 8 oz lamb fillet
- 3 cups water
- 1 tsp salt
- 1 tsp chili pepper
- 3 tbsp olive oil
- 1 garlic clove
- 1 tsp basil
- 1 tbsp sesame oil
- 1 cup lettuce

Directions:

1. Place the lamb fillet in the Instant Pot and add water.
2. Sprinkle the mixture with the salt.
3. Peel the garlic clove and add it to the lamb mixture. Close the lid and cook the dish at the MEAT mode for 35 minutes.
4. Meanwhile, slice the cucumbers and chop the avocado. Combine the ingredients together in the mixing bowl.
5. Chop the lettuce roughly and add it to the mixing bowl.
6. After this, sprinkle the mixture with the chili pepper, olive oil, basil, and sesame oil.
7. When the meat is cooked – remove it from the Instant Pot and chill it well.
8. Chop the meat roughly and add it to the mixing bowl.
9. Mix up the salad carefully and transfer it to the serving bowl.
10. Serve the dish warm. Enjoy!

Lamb Shanks

(Prep + Cook Time: 1 hour 10 minutes | Servings: 4)

Ingredients:

- 3 pounds lamb shanks
- 3 carrots, peeled and chopped
- 1 can (14 ounces) fire-roasted tomatoes
- ¼ tsp pepper
- ½ tsp salt
- ½ tsp crushed red pepper flakes
- 1 yellow onion, diced
- 1 tbsp tomato paste
- 1 tbsp coconut oil
- 1 tbsp balsamic vinegar
- 1 cup beef stock
- 3 stalks celery, diced
- 4 cloves garlic, minced Italian parsley, chopped, for garnish

Directions:

1. Sprinkle the lamb shanks with pepper and salt.
2. Press the SAUTE key of the Instant Pot and wait until hot.
3. Add the coconut oil and heat.
4. When the oil hot, cook the lamb shanks for about 8 to 10 minutes or until all sides are browned. Transfer into a platter.
5. Add the garlic, onion, celery, and carrots in the pot.
6. Season with pepper and salt. Cook, frequently stirring, until the onion is translucent – be careful not to burn the garlic.
7. Add the fire-roasted tomatoes and the tomato paste. Stir to mix. Return the lamb shanks in the pot. Add the beef stock and balsamic vinegar.
8. Press the CANCEL key to stop the SAUTÉ function. Cover and lock the lid.
9. Press the MANUAL key, set the pressure to HIGH, and set the timer for 45 minutes.
10. When the Instant Pot timer beeps, release the pressure naturally for 10-15 minutes or until the valve drops.
11. Turn the steam valve to release remaining pressure. Unlock and carefully open the lid.
12. Transfer the lamb shanks in a serving plate. Ladle the sauce over the shanks.
13. Garnish with chopped fresh parsley.

Ground Lamb Curry

(Prep + Cook Time: 55 minutes | Servings: 4)

Ingredients:
- 1 pound ground lamb
- 3 carrots, chopped
- 1 can (13.5 ounce) tomato sauce
- 2 potatoes, chopped
- 1 cup frozen peas, rinsed
- 1 onion, diced
- 1 tbsp coriander powder
- 1 tsp meat masala, homemade
- 1 tsp paprika
- 1 tsp salt
- ½ tsp cumin powder
- ½ tsp Kashmiri chili powder (or 1/4 tsp cayenne)
- ½ tsp black pepper
- ¼ tsp turmeric powder
- 1-2 Serrano peppers, minced, or more to taste
- 1-inch fresh ginger, minced
- 2 tbsp ghee OR grass-fed butter
- 4 garlic cloves, minced
- 4 tomatoes, chopped
- Cilantro, garnish

Directions:
1. Prepare the Instant Pot by select SAUTE mode. Add the ghee and the onions. Cook until the onion starts to brown.
2. Add the garlic, ginger, and Serrano pepper. Stir-fry for 1 minute.
3. Add the tomatoes. Cook for 5 minutes or until the tomatoes begin to break down.
4. Add the spice and stir-fry for 1 minute.
5. Add the ground lamb and cook until the meat is browned.
6. Add the potatoes, carrots, peas, and tomato sauce. Mix well until combined. Press the CANCEL button to stop the SAUTÉ function. Cover and lock the lid.
7. Press the CHILI button and cook on preset time (30 minutes).
8. When the Instant Pot timer beeps, release the pressure naturally for 10-15 minutes or until the valve drops.
9. Turn the steam valve to Venting to release remaining pressure.
10. Unlock and carefully open the lid. Serve.

Half-Hour Rosemary Lamb
(Prep + Cook Time: 35 minutes | Servings: 6)

Ingredients:
- 4 pounds cubed, boneless lamb
- 1 ½ cups veggie stock
- 1 cup sliced carrots
- 4 minced garlic cloves
- 4-6 rosemary sprigs
- 3 tbsp flour
- 2 tbsp olive oil
- Salt and pepper to taste

Directions:
1. Preheat your cooker with oil, using the SAUTE setting.
2. Season the lamb with salt and pepper. Put in the cooker along with minced garlic.
3. Cook until the lamb has browned all over.
4. Add the flour and stir. Slowly pour in the stock.
5. Add rosemary and carrots. Seal the lid.
6. Select MANUAL and adjust time to 20 minutes on HIGH pressure.
7. When the timer beeps, select CANCEL and quick release the pressure. Open up the lid and pick out the rosemary stems.
8. Serve lamb with plenty of sauce.

Thyme Lamb (E&S)
(Prep + Cook Time: 55 minutes | Servings: 8)

Ingredients:
1 cup fresh thyme
1 tbsp olive oil
2-pound lamb
1 tsp oregano
1 tbsp ground black pepper
1 tsp paprika
¼ cup rice wine
1 tsp sugar
4 tbsp butter
¼ cup chicken stock
1 tbsp turmeric

Directions:
1. Chop the fresh thyme and combine it with the oregano, ground black pepper, paprika, rice wine, sugar, chicken stock, and turmeric. Mix up the mixture.
2. Sprinkle the lamb with the spice mixture and stir it carefully.
3. After this, transfer the lamb mixture in the Instant Pot and add olive oil.
4. Close the Instant Pot lid and cook the dish at the MEAT mode for 45 minutes.
5. When the meat is cooked – remove it from the Instant Pot.
6. Chill the lamb little and slice it. Enjoy!

Garlic Lamb Shanks with Port

(Prep + Cook Time: 1 hour 7 minutes | Servings: 4)

Ingredients:

- 4 pounds lamb shanks
- 1 cup chicken broth
- 1 cup port wine
- 20 peeled, whole garlic cloves
- 2 tbsp tomato paste
- 2 tbsp butter
- 2 tsp balsamic vinegar
- 1 tsp dried rosemary
- Salt and pepper to taste

Directions:

1. Trim any fat you don't want from the lamb and season generously with salt and pepper.
2. Heat oil in your Instant Pot on the SAUTE setting, and when hot, add the lamb. Brown all over.
3. When the lamb is golden, add garlic and stir until they've browned.
4. Pour in port and stock, and stir in tomato paste and rosemary.
5. When the tomato paste has dissolved, close and seal the lid.
6. Select MANUAL and cook on HIGH pressure for 32 minutes.
7. When time is up, press CANCEL and wait 20 minutes for a natural pressure release. Carefully remove lamb.
8. Turn the pot back to SAUTE to boil the cooking liquid. Boil for 5 minutes to reduce it down and thicken.
9. Mix in butter, and then vinegar.
10. Serve with sauce poured over the lamb.

Lamb and Feta Meatballs

(Prep + Cook Time: 15 minutes | Servings: 6)

Ingredients:

- 1 ½ pounds ground lamb
- 4 minced garlic cloves
- One, 28-ounce can of crushed tomatoes
- 6-ounce can of tomato sauce
- 1 beaten egg
- 1 chopped green bell pepper
- 1 chopped onion
- ½ cup crumbled feta cheese
- ½ cup breadcrumbs
- 2 tbsp chopped parsley
- 2 tbsp olive oil
- 1 tbsp chopped mint
- 1 tbsp water
- 1 tsp dried oregano
- ½ tsp salt
- ¼ tsp black pepper

Directions:

1. In a bowl, mix lamb, egg, breadcrumbs, mint, parsley, feta, water, half of the minced garlic, pepper, and salt.
2. With your hands, mold into 1-inch meatballs.
3. Turn your Instant Pot to SAUTE and add oil.
4. When hot, add the bell pepper and onion. Cook for 2 minutes before adding the rest of the garlic.
5. After another minute, add crushed tomatoes with their liquid, the tomato sauce, and oregano. Sprinkle with salt and pepper.
6. Put the meatballs in the pot and seal the lid.
7. Select MANUAL and cook at HIGH pressure for 8 minutes.
8. When time is up, select CANCEL and use a quick release.
9. Serve meatballs with parsley and more cheese!

Braised Lamb Shanks with Carrots and Tomatoes

(Prep + Cook Time: 50 minutes | Servings: 4)

Ingredients:

- 2 pounds lamb shanks
- 2 carrots, peeled and sliced
- 2 cups whole canned tomatoes, sliced
- 1 white onion, large
- 3 sprigs fresh oregano, chopped
- 3 sprigs fresh rosemary, chopped
- 3 sprigs fresh thyme, chopped
- 6 cloves garlic, sliced
- 6 tbsp oil
- 1½ cups veal stock or beef stock
- Flour, for dredging
- Salt and pepper to taste

Directions:

1. Press SAUTE and preheat the Instant Pot.
2. Dredge the lamb shanks with flour and cook in the pot until all the sides are browned.
3. When the lamb shanks are browned, add all the ingredients in the pot, except for the canned tomatoes. Press the CANCEL key to stop the SAUTÉ function. Cover and lock the lid.
4. Press the MANUAL key, set the pressure to HIGH, and set the timer for 25 minutes.
5. When the Instant Pot timer beeps, turn the steam valve to Venting to quick release the pressure. Unlock and carefully open the lid. Add the canned tomatoes. Cover and lock the lid again.
6. Press the MANUAL key, set the pressure to HIGH, and set the timer for 5 minutes.
7. When the Instant Pot timer beeps, turn the steam valve to Venting to quick release the pressure. Unlock and carefully open the lid. If desired, thicken the gravy.
8. Pour the gravy over the lamb shanks and other food. Serve.
9. Serve!

Ginger-Spiced Lamb Shanks with Figs

(Prep + Cook Time: 1 hour 45 minutes | Servings: 6)

Ingredients:

- Four, 12-ounce lamb shanks
- 1 ½ cups bone broth
- 10 halved and stemmed dried figs
- 3 minced garlic cloves
- 1 sliced onion
- 2 tbsp coconut oil
- 2 tbsp coconut aminos (or soy sauce)
- 2 tbsp fresh, minced ginger
- 2 tbsp apple cider vinegar
- 2 tsp fish sauce
- Salt and pepper to taste

Directions:

1. Turn your Instant Pot to SAUTE and add 1 tablespoon of oil. When hot, brown the lamb all over. You'll probably have to do two at a time and add more coconut oil.
2. When all the shanks are browned, take out them on a plate.
3. Add onion and ginger to the pot and stir for 3 minutes. Add vinegar, fish sauce, coconut aminos, and minced garlic.
4. Pour the broth and add the figs; deglazing any stuck-on meat or onion.
5. Put the meat back into the pot. Close and seal the lid.
6. Select MANUAL and cook at HIGH pressure for 60 minutes.
7. When time is up, press CANCEL and let the pressure release naturally (30 minutes).
8. Open the lid and move the shanks to clean plates.
9. With a tablespoon, skim off any excess fat from the sauce. Season with salt and pepper as needed.
10. Pour sauce over the lamb and serve!

Seafood Cranberries Plov (E&S)

(Prep + Cook Time: 40 minutes | Servings: 4)

Ingredients:

- 1 package (16 ounces) frozen seafood blend, (I used Trader Joe's)
- 1 lemon, sliced
- 1 onion, large-sized, chopped
- 1½ cups basmati rice, organic
- 1 pepper, red or yellow, sliced
- ½ cup dried cranberries
- 2-3 tbsp butter
- 3 cups water
- 3-4 big shredded carrots
- Salt and pepper to taste

Directions:

1. Press the SAUTE key of the Instant Pot and wait until the word 'Hot' appears on the display.
2. Put the butter in the pot. Add the onion, carrots, pepper, and cook stirring for about 5-7 minutes.
3. Add the rice, seafood blend, and cranberries, stir.
4. Season generously and add 3 cups water.
5. Press RICE and lock the lid.
6. Just before servings, squeeze fresh lemon juice over the dish.

Quick Seafood Paella

(Prep + Cook Time: 55 minutes | Servings: 4)

Ingredients:

- 1 ¾ cups seafood stock or vegetable stock
- 1 cup seafood mix (meaty white fish, squid, scallops)
- 2 cups mixed shellfish (clams, shrimp, and mussels)
- 2 cups rice, short-grain
- 1 green bell pepper, diced
- 1 red bell pepper, diced
- 1 yellow onion, medium-sized, diced
- 1/8 tsp ground turmeric
- 2 tsp sea salt
- 4 tbsp extra-virgin olive oil
- Large pinch saffron threads

Directions:

1. Press SAUTE, add the olive oil and heat. When the oil is hot, add the onions and peppers, and sauté for about 4 minutes or until the onions are soft.
2. Add the rice, saffron, seafood, and sauté for 2 minutes.
3. Add stock, salt, and turmeric, and stir to mix.
4. Arrange the shellfish on top – do not mix. Lock the lid and close the steam valve. Cook on HIGH pressure for 6 minutes.
5. When the timer is up, let the pressure release naturally for 15 minutes.
6. Open the steam valve to release any remaining pressure. Carefully open the lid.
7. Mix the paella, close the lid, and let stand for 1 minute. Serve!

Notes: If you don't want to make your own fish stock, you can use vegetable stock instead. You can use avocado oil instead of olive oil to sauté the aromatic.

Fast Salmon with Broccoli (E&S)

(Prep + Cook Time: 10 minutes | Servings: 1)

Ingredients:
- 2.5 oz broccoli
- 2.5 oz salmon fillet
- 1 cup water
- Salt and pepper to taste

Directions:
1. Pour the water in the Instant Pot and set a steamer rack in the pot.
2. Chop the broccoli into florets. Season both the salmon and the broccoli with pepper and salt.
3. Put broccoli and salmon on the steamer rack in the pot. Cover and lock the lid.
4. Press the STEAM key and set the timer for 2 minutes.
5. When the Instant Pot timer beeps, let the pressure release naturally for 10-15 minutes or until the valve drops. Turn the steam valve to release remaining pressure.
6. Unlock and carefully open the lid. Serve.

Notes: This dish is good for a small lunch. If you are doubling this recipe, then add an additional 1 minute to the cooking time.

Spicy Lemony Salmon

(Prep + Cook Time: 10 minutes | Servings: 4)

Ingredients:

- 3-4 pieces (1-inch thick) salmon fillets, wild sockeye
- 1-2 tbsp assorted chili pepper (I used Nanami Togarashi)
- 1 lemon, sliced
- 1 lemon, juiced
- 1 cup water
- Salt and pepper to taste

Directions:

1. Season the salmon fillets with the lemon juice, salt, pepper, and Nanami Togarashi.
2. Pour 1 cup water in the Instant Pot and set the steam rack in the pot.

3. Place the salmon fillets on the rack, arranging them in a single layer, if possible, without overlapping.
4. Pour any leftover lemon juice and seasoning over the fillets. Lock the lid and close the steam valve.
5. Select MANUAL and cook at HIGH pressure for 5 minutes.
6. When the timer beeps, release the pressure quickly. Carefully open the lid and transfer the fillets into a serving plate. Enjoy!

Notes: You can find Nanami Togarashi in the Asian section of the grocery store. If you want a spicier dish, sprinkle a bit of red pepper flakes over the fillets before cooking.

Dijon Salmon (E&S)
(Prep + Cook Time: 10 minutes | Servings: 2)

Ingredients:

- 2 pieces firm fish fillets or steaks, such as salmon, scrod, cod, or halibut (1-inch thick)
- 1 cup water
- 1 tsp Dijon mustard per fish fillet
- Steamer basket or trivet

Directions:

1. On the fleshy portion of the fish fillets, spread 1 teaspoon of Dijon mustard over.
2. Pour 1 cup of water into the Instant Pot.
3. Set the steamer basket or trivet in the pot.
4. With the skin side faced down, put the fish fillets in the steamer basket/ trivet. Cover and lock the lid.
5. Select MANUAL and cook at HIGH pressure for 5 minutes.
6. When the timer beeps, turn the steam valve to quick release the pressure. Serve.

Teriyaki Salmon (E&S)

(Prep + Cook Time: 20 minutes | Servings: 4)

Ingredients:

- 1 ½ cups boiling water
- 5 salmon fillets
- 2-ounces dried mushrooms
- 4 washed and halved bok choy
- 3 sliced spring onions
- ¼ cup soy sauce
- 2 tbsp sweet rice wine
- 1 tbsp sesame oil
- 1 tbsp sugar

Directions:

1. Pour the boiling water over the mushrooms to rehydrate them.
2. Put the bok choy in your Instant Pot.
3. Add all the ingredients (except the salmon). Add mushrooms with water. Put the salmon on top. Close and seal the lid.
4. Select MANUAL and cook for 4 minutes at HIGH pressure.
5. When time is up, press CANCEL and let the pressure release naturally for 10 minutes, then quick release the remaining pressure. Serve!

Spicy Sockeye Salmon

(Prep + Cook Time: 10 minutes | Servings: 4)

Ingredients:

- 4 wild sockeye salmon fillets
- 1 cup water
- ¼ cup lemon juice
- 1 sliced lemon
- 2 tbsp assorted chili pepper seasoning
- Salt and pepper to taste

Directions:

1. Prep your salmon by seasoning with chili pepper, salt, pepper, and lemon juice.
2. Put the steamer basket in your cooker with 1 cup of water.
3. Put the fish in the basket, trying not to overlap too much. Close and seal the lid.
4. Select MANUAL and cook at HIGH pressure for 5 minutes.
5. If the fillets are smaller, cut 1 minute off the time for every ¼-inch smaller than 1-inch, or add 1 minute for fillets ¼-inch bigger than 1-inch.
6. When time is up, press CANCEL and quick release the pressure.
7. Serve with fresh greens, rice pilaf, or another favorite side.

Crispy Skin Salmon Fillet

(Prep + Cook Time: 20 minutes | Servings: 2)

Ingredients:

- 2 salmon fillets, frozen (1-inch thickness)
- 1 cup tap water, running cold
- 2 tbsp olive oil
- Salt and pepper to taste

Directions:

1. Pour 1 cup of water in the Instant Pot.
2. Set the steamer rack and put the salmon fillets in the rack. Lock the lid and close the steamer valve.
3. Press MANUAL, set the pressure on LOW, and set the timer for 1 minute.
4. When the timer beeps, turn off the pot and quick release the pressure.
5. Carefully open the lid. Remove the salmon fillets and pat them dry using paper towels.
6. Over medium-high heat, preheat a skillet.
7. Grease the salmon fillet skins with 1 tablespoon olive oil and generously season with black pepper and salt.
8. When the skillet is very hot, with the skin side down, put the salmon fillet in the skillet.
9. Cook for 1-2 minutes until the skins are crispy.
10. Transfer the salmon fillets into serving plates and serve with your favorite side dishes.
11. This dish is great with rice and salad.

Notes: You can use a nonstick skillet to make sure the skin does not stick to the skillet. If you do not like the skin on your salmon, you can remove it after pressure cooking. Increase the cooking time to 2 minutes.

Herbed Garlic Salmon Fillet

(Prep + Cook Time: 30 minutes | Servings: 2)

Ingredients:
- 2 fresh salmon fillets
- ½ cup garlic and herb butter or homemade compound butter with garlic and herbs
- Salt and pepper to taste
- 2 tbsp white wine
- ¼ cup cream
- 1 tsp lemon zest
- 2 cups water

Directions:
1. Add 2 cups of water in the Instant Pot and the trivet. Place the fish, skin side down on the trivet and season, to taste.
2. Close the lid. Press the MANUAL button and cook at HIGH pressure for 5 minutes.
3. When the pressure cooking cycle is completed, quick release the pressure.
4. Open the lid when the float valve has dropped down.
5. Remove the fish and cover to keep warm. Remove the trivet and drain the water.
6. Select SAUTE and melt the garlic butter. Add the wine and stir, cook until bubbling. Add the cream and stir. Top with the lemon zest. Mix well and cook until warm.
7. Transfer salmon to serving plates. Top with the creamy sauce and serve.

Shrimp Creole

(Prep + Cook Time: 20 minutes | Servings: 4)

Ingredients:
- 1 can (28 ounces) crushed tomatoes
- 1 pound jumbo shrimp, frozen, peeled and deveined
- 1 onion, medium-sized, chopped
- 1 tsp thyme
- ¼ tsp cayenne pepper, or to taste
- 2 cloves garlic, minced
- 2 stalks celery, diced
- 1 bay leaf
- 1 bell pepper, diced
- 1 tbsp tomato paste
- 1 tsp salt
- ½ tsp pepper
- 2 tsp olive oil

Directions:
1. Press the SAUTE key of the Instant Pot. Add the oil and heat.
2. When the oil is hot, add the vegetables and sauté for 3 minutes or until the veggies starts to soften.
3. Add the tomato paste. Stir and cook for 1 minute.
4. Add the crushed tomatoes, shrimp, seasoning, and stir to combine.
5. Press MANUAL, set the pressure to HIGH, and set the timer to 1 minute.
6. When the timer beeps, quick release the pressure.
7. Carefully open the lid. If the shrimp is not fully cooked, press the SAUTE key and cook the shrimp for 1 minute, constantly stirring.
8. Serve over rice.

Steamed Asparagus and Shrimp
(Prep + Cook Time: 25 minutes | Servings: 4)

Ingredients:
- 1 pound shrimp, frozen or fresh, peeled and deveined
- 1 bunch asparagus (about 6 ounces)
- 1 tsp olive oil
- ½ tbsp Cajun seasoning (or your choice of seasoning.
- Lemon juice with salt and pepper would be delicious too)

Directions:
1. Pour 1 cup of water in the Instant Pot.
2. Set the steam rack in the pot. In a single layer, put the asparagus on the rack.
3. Put the shrimp on top of the asparagus.
4. Drizzle the shrimp with olive oil and season with Cajun seasoning or your choice of seasoning. Lock the lid and close the steam valve.
5. Press STEAM, set the pressure to Low, and set the timer for 2 minutes if using frozen shrimp or set to 1 minute if using fresh shrimp.
6. When the timer beeps, quickly release the pressure.
7. Carefully open the lid and enjoy!

10 Minute Scampi Shrimp Paella

(Prep + Cook Time: 10 minutes | Servings: 4)

Ingredients:

- 1½ cups water or chicken broth
- 1 cup jasmine rice
- 1 lemon, medium-sized, juiced
- 1 pinch crushed red pepper, or to taste
- 1 pinch saffron
- 1 pound frozen shrimp, wild caught, shell and tail on
- 1 tsp sea salt (real salt)
- ¼ cup butter
- ¼ cup fresh Parsley, chopped
- ¼ tsp black pepper
- 4 cloves garlic, pressed or minced

Optional garnishes:

- Butter
- Hard parmesan cheese, asiago, or romano, grated
- Fresh Parsley, chopped
- Fresh squeezed lemon juice

Directions:

1. Except for the shrimp, combine the rest of the ingredients in the Instant Pot.
2. Layer the frozen shrimp on top of the rice. Lock the lid and close the steam valve.
3. Cook at HIGH pressure for 5 minutes.
4. When the timer beeps, quickly release the pressure. Garnish each serving with grate cheese, butter, and fresh parsley.

Notes: If you don't like shells on your shrimp, carefully remove the cooked shrimp from the top of the rice mix and peel the shells off. Return the peeled shrimp on the rice. Serve. Discard the shells.

Shrimp Risotto

(Prep + Cook Time: 20 minutes | Servings: 4)

Ingredients:

- 4 ½ cups chicken broth
- 1 pound peeled and cleaned shrimp
- 1½ cups Arborio rice
- ¾ cup parmesan cheese
- ¼ cup fresh herbs
- 4 tbsp butter
- 1 chopped yellow onion
- 2 minced garlic cloves
- 2 tbsp dry white wine

Directions:

1. Press SAUTE and melt the butter in your Instant Pot. Add garlic and onion and cook for 4 minutes.
2. Add the rice and stir to toast for 1 minute. Pour the wine and cook until it evaporates.
3. Pour 3 cups of broth and sprinkle with salt and pepper. Close and seal the lid.
4. Select MANUAL and cook at HIGH pressure for 9 minutes.
5. When time is up, press CANCEL and quick release the pressure. Open the lid and add shrimp with the rest of the broth.
6. Turn the pot to SAUTE and cook for 3-5 minutes, or until the shrimp has become bright pink and solid.
7. Add cheese and the rest of the butter. Sprinkle with herbs and serve!

Creamy Shrimp Pasta

(Prep + Cook Time: 15 minutes | Servings: 4)

Ingredients:

- 2½ cups chicken broth
- 8-ounces bowtie pasta
- 12-ounces cleaned frozen shrimp
- 1 cup Parmesan cheese
- ½ cup heavy cream
- 1 chopped yellow onion
- 1 tbsp olive oil
- 1 tbsp minced garlic
- 1 tsp all-purpose flour
- Salt and pepper to taste
- Handful of chopped parsley

Directions:

1. Heat the oil in your Instant Pot on the SAUTE setting. Cook onion until it becomes clear.
2. Add pasta, broth, garlic, salt, pepper, and shrimp. Close and seal the lid.
3. Select MANUAL and cook for 7 minutes at HIGH pressure.
4. When time is up, press CANCEL and quick-release the pressure.
5. Open the lid and press SAUTE. Add cream, Parmesan, and flour.
6. Simmer until the sauce has thickened a little, which should take about 2 minutes.
7. Serve with chopped parsley on top!

Shrimp and Tomatillo Casserole
(Prep + Cook Time: 20 minutes | Servings: 4)

Ingredients:

- 1 ½ pounds peeled and cleaned shrimp
- 1 ½ pounds peeled and chopped tomatillos
- 1 stemmed, seeded, and minced jalapeno
- 1 cup shredded cheddar cheese
- 1 chopped yellow onion
- ½ cup clam juice
- ¼ cup chopped cilantro
- 2 tbsp lime juice
- 2 tbsp olive oil
- 2 tsp minced garlic

Directions:

1. Heat the oil in your Instant Pot on the SAUTE setting.
2. When shiny and hot, add the onion and stir until it becomes clear.
3. Add the garlic and jalapeno. Stir until aromatic; this should only take a minute or so.
4. Add tomatillos, lime juice, and clam juice.
5. Close and seal the lid. Select MANUAL and cook at HIGH pressure for 9 minutes.
6. When the timer beeps, press CANCEL and quick-release. Open the lid and press SAUTE again.
7. Add cilantro and shrimp, and stir for 2 minutes. Add cheese, stir and cover the lid, but don't bring to pressure.
8. Wait 2 minutes for the cheese to melt. Open the lid and stir before serving.

Tuna and Capers Tomato Pasts

(Prep + Cook Time: 20 minutes | Servings: 2)

Ingredients:

- 1 can (15 ounces) fire-roasted diced tomatoes
- 1 can (3.5 ounces) solid tuna packed in vegetable oil
- 2 cups pasta, your choice (I used Orecchiette)
- 2 garlic cloves, sliced
- 2 tbsp olive oil
- 2 tbsp capers
- Grated parmesan
- Red wine (just enough to fill 1/2 of the tomato can)
- Salt and pepper to taste
- Seasonings (I use oregano and dried chilies)

Directions:

1. Set the Instant Pot to SAUTE and wait until hot. Add the garlic and sauté until fragrant.
2. Add the pasta, seasonings, and tomatoes. Fill the empty can of tomatoes with red wine until 1/2 full and then pour enough water into the can until full.
3. Pour the wine mix in the Instant Pot. Lock the lid and turn the steam valve to Sealing.
4. Select MANUAL and cook at HIGH pressure for 6 minutes. When the timer beeps, turn the steam valve to quick release the pressure.
5. Carefully open the capers and tuna. Gently add into the pot and stir.
6. Divide the pasta into serving bowls.

Cheesy Tuna Helper

(Prep + Cook Time: 15 minutes | Servings: 6)

Ingredients:

- 1 can (5 ounces) tuna, drained
- 1 cup frozen peas
- ¼ cup bread crumbs (optional)
- 16 ounces egg noodles
- 28 ounces canned cream mushroom soup
- 3 cups water
- 4 ounces cheddar cheese

Directions:

1. Put the noodles in the Instant Pot. Pour the water to cover the noodles.
2. Add the frozen peas, tuna, and the soup on top of the pasta layer. Cover and lock the lid.
3. Select MANUAL and cook at HIGH pressure for 4 minutes. When the Instant Pot timer beeps, press the CANCEL key and unplug the Instant Pot. Turn the steam valve to quick release the pressure.
4. Unlock and carefully open the lid. Add the cheese and stir.
5. If desired, you can pour the pasta mixture in a baking dish, sprinkle the top with bread crumbs, and broil for about 2 to 3 minutes. Serve.

Tuna and Buttery Crackers Casserole

(Prep + Cook Time: 25 minutes | Servings: 8)

Ingredients:

- 8 ounces fresh tuna
- 3 tbsp butter
- 3 tbsp all-purpose flour
- 3 ½ cups chicken stock
- 2 tsp salt
- 2 cups pasta (I used elbow mac)
- ¼ cup heavy cream
- 1 cup onion
- 1 cup frozen peas
- 1 cup cheddar, shredded
- 1 cup celery
- 1 cup buttery crackers, crushed
- Fresh ground black pepper

Directions:

1. Press SAUTE to preheat the Instant Pot. When hot, put the celery and onion.
2. Sauté until the onion is translucent. Pour the chicken stock and pasta, and season with salt and pepper.
3. Stir to combine for a bit. Put the fresh tuna on top of the pasta mix. Press CANCEL to stop the SAUTÉ function. Close and lock the lid.
4. Select MANUAL and cook at HIGH pressure for 5 minutes. Meanwhile, heat the sauté pan over medium-high.
5. Put the butter in the pan and melt. Add the flour and stir, cook for 2 minutes. Remove the pan from the heat and set aside.
6. When the timer beeps, turn the steam valve to Venting to quick release the pressure. Transfer the tuna onto a plate and set aside.
7. Pour the butter mix into the Instant Pot. Press the SAUTÉ key. Stir until the mixture is thick. Turn off the Instant Pot. Add the heavy cream, peas, tuna and stir.
8. Cover the mix with the crackers and then with the grated cheese.
9. Cover and let stand for 5 minutes. Serve.

Cod Fillets with Almonds and Peas

(Prep + Cook Time: 10 minutes | Servings: 4)

Ingredients:

- 1 pound frozen cod fish fillet
- 2 halved garlic cloves
- 10-ounces frozen peas
- 1 cup chicken broth
- ½ cup packed parsley
- 2 tbsp fresh oregano
- 2 tbsp sliced almonds
- ½ tsp paprika

Directions:

1. Take the fish out of the freezer.
2. In a food processor stir together garlic, oregano, parsley, paprika, and 1 tablespoon almonds.
3. Turn your Instant Pot to SAUTE and heat a bit of olive oil.
4. When hot, toast the rest of the almonds until they are fragrant.
5. Take out the almonds and put on a paper towel.
6. Pour the broth in the cooker and add your herb mixture.
7. Cut the fish into 4 pieces and put in the steamer basket.
8. Lower into the cooker and close the lid.
9. Select MANUAL and cook at HIGH pressure for 3 minutes.
10. Press CANCEL and quick release the pressure.
11. The fish is done when it is solid, not translucent.
12. Add the frozen peas and close the lid again.
13. Cook at HIGH pressure for 1 minute. Use a quick release.
14. Serve with the toasted almonds on top.

Notes: If you want a thicker sauce, remove the fish before mixing 1 tablespoon of cornstarch with 1 tablespoon of cold water, and pouring into the cooker. Turn the cooker to SAUTÉ and bring to a simmer until thickened.

Lemon-Dill Cod with Broccoli (E&S)
(Prep + Cook Time: 5 minutes | Servings: 4)

Ingredients:
- 1 pound, 1-inch thick frozen cod fillet
- 2 cups of broccoli
- 1 cup water
- Dill weed
- Lemon pepper
- Dash of salt

Directions:
1. Cut the fish into four pieces.
2. Season with lemon pepper, salt, and dill weed.
3. Pour 1 cup of water into the Instant Pot and lower in the steamer basket.
4. Put the fish and broccoli florets in the basket. Close the cooker.
5. Select MANUAL and cook for 2 minutes at LOW pressure.
6. Quick-release the pressure after time is up, and turn off the cooker. Serve right away.

Wild Alaskan Cod In The Pot
(Prep + Cook Time: 15 minutes | Servings: 2)

Ingredients:
- 1 large filet wild Alaskan cod (the big fillets can feed easily 2-3 people)
- 1 cup cherry tomatoes
- Salt and pepper to taste
- Your choice of seasoning
- 2 tbsp butter
- Olive oil

Directions:
1. Choose an ovenproof dish that will fit your Instant Pot.
2. Put the tomatoes in the dish.
3. Cut the large fish fillet into 2-3 serving pieces. Lay them on top of the tomatoes. Season the fish with salt, pepper, and your choice of seasoning.
4. Top each fillet with 1 tablespoon butter and drizzle with a bit of olive oil. Put 1 cup water in the Instant Pot and set a trivet.
5. Place the dish on the trivet. Lock the lid and close the steam valve.
6. Press MANUAL and set the timer for 5 minutes if using thawed fish or for 9 minutes if using frozen fish.
7. When the timer beeps, let the pressure release naturally. Enjoy!

Cod Chowder

(Prep + Cook Time: 40 minutes | Servings: 6)

Ingredients:
- 2 pounds cod
- 4 cups potatoes, peeled and diced
- 4 cups chicken broth, organic
- 2 tbsp butter
- ½ mushrooms, sliced
- ½ cup flour
- 1 tsp old bay seasoning (or more)
- 1 cup onion, chopped
- 1 cup half-and-half OR heavy cream OR 1 can evaporated milk
- 1 cup clam juice
- 4-6 bacon slices, optional
- Salt and pepper to taste

Directions:
1. Pour 1 cup of water into the Instant Pot and set a trivet. Put the cod on the trivet. Close and lock the lid.
2. Press MANUAL, set the pressure to HIGH, and set the timer for 9 minutes. Once cooking is complete, use a quick release.
3. Transfer the cod onto a large-sized plate. With a fork or a knife, cut the fish into large chunks. Set aside.
4. Remove the trivet and pour the liquid out from the inner pot.
5. Press the SAUTE key. Add the butter, onion, and mushrooms; sauté for 2 minutes or until soft.
6. Add the chicken broth and the potatoes.
7. Press the CANCEL key to stop the SAUTÉ function. Close and lock the lid.
8. Select MANUAL and cook at HIGH pressure for 8 minutes.
9. When the timer beeps, turn the steam valve to quick release the pressure.
10. Add and stir the seasoning, pepper, salt, and fish.
11. In a bowl, mix the clam juice with the flour until well blended.
12. Pour the mix into the pot. Turn off the Instant Pot.
13. Add the half-and-half and stir well until blended. Serve with fresh baked buttered rolls.

Notes: If you are using bacon, cook the bacon until crisp and then transfer into a paper towel lined plate. Add the onions and the mushrooms, cooking them in the bacon fat before adding the broth and potatoes.

Coconut Fish Curry

(Prep + Cook Time: 45 minutes | Servings: 4)

Ingredients:
- 1½ pounds white fish fillet rinsed and cut into bite sized pieces
- 1 heaping cup cherry tomatoes
- 2 green chilies sliced into stripes
- 2 medium onions sliced into strips
- 2 cloves garlic finely chopped
- 1 tbsp Ginger freshly grated
- 6 curry leaves, bay leaves, basil or kaffir leaves work too
- 1 tbsp ground coriander
- 1 tbsp ground cumin
- ½ tsp ground turmeric
- 1 tsp chili powder
- ½ tsp ground fenugreek
- 2 cups coconut milk unsweetened, about one small can
- 1 tsp olive oil
- Salt to taste
- Lemon juice to taste

Directions:
1. Press SAUTE to pre-heat the Instant Pot. When "Hot" appears on the display, add the oil and the curry leaves.
2. Lightly fry the leaves until golden around the edges (about 1 minute).
3. Add in the onion, garlic, and ginger. Sauté until the onion is soft
4. Add all of the ground spices: coriander, turmeric, chili powder and fenugreek. Sauté them together with the onions until they have released their aroma (about 1 minute).
5. Deglaze the pot with the coconut milk, scraping everything from the bottom of the pot to incorporate it into the sauce.
6. Add the green chilies, tomatoes and fish. Stir to coat.
7. Close and lock the lid. Select MANUAL and cook at HIGH pressure for 3 minutes. When time is up, use a quick release. Open the lid.
8. Add salt and lemon juice to taste before serving. Enjoy!

Fish in Orange Ginger Sauce
(Prep + Cook Time: 20 minutes | Servings: 4)

Ingredients:
- 4 pieces white fish fillets
- 3-4 spring onions
- 1 piece (thumb-sized) ginger, chopped
- 1 orange for juice and zest
- 1 tsp orange zest
- 1 cup white wine or fish stock
- Olive oil
- Salt and pepper to taste

Directions:
1. Using a paper towel, pat the fish fillets dry. Rub the fillets with the olive oil and then season them lightly.
2. Add the white wine/ fish stock, orange zest, orange juice, ginger, and spring onion into the Instant Pot.
3. Set a steamer basket in the pot and then put the fish in the steamer basket. Close and lock the lid.
4. Press MANUAL and cook at HIGH pressure for 7 minutes.
5. Once cooking is complete, use a quick release. Open the lid.
6. Serve. The sauce will serve as the dressing.

Caramelized Haddock
(Prep + Cook Time: 55 minutes | Servings: 4)

Ingredients:
- 1 pound of haddock
- 3 garlic cloves, chopped
- 1 cup of coconut water
- 1 minced red chili
- 1 minced spring onion
- ⅓ cup water
- ¼ cup white sugar
- 3 tbsp fish sauce
- 2 tsp black pepper

Directions:
1. Marinate the fish in garlic, fish sauce, and pepper for at least 30 minutes.
2. Put the sugar and water in the Instant Pot and heat on SAUTE mode until the sugar has browned into a caramel.
3. Add fish and coconut water to the cooker. Close and seal lid.
4. Select MANUAL and cook at HIGH pressure for 10 minutes.
5. When time is up, press CANCEL and let the pressure release naturally. Serve with chili and onion.

Mackerel Salad

(Prep + Cook Time: 25 minutes | Servings: 6)

Ingredients:

- 1 cup lettuce
- 8 oz mackerel
- 1 tsp salt
- 1 tsp paprika
- 1 tbsp olive oil
- ½ tsp rosemary
- 1 garlic clove
- ½ cup fish stock
- 1 tsp oregano
- 7 oz tomatoes
- 1 big cucumbers
- 1 red onion

Directions:

1. Wash the lettuce and chop it. Rub the mackerel with the salt, paprika, and rosemary.
2. Place the spiced mackerel in the Instant Pot.
3. Add the fish stock and close the lid. Select MANUAL and cook at HIGH pressure for 10 minutes.
4. Peel the garlic clove and slice it. Peel the red onion and slice it.
5. Combine the sliced red onion with the chopped lettuce. Slice the cucumber and chop tomatoes.
6. Add the vegetables to the lettuce mixture.
7. Once cooking is complete, use a quick release. The mackerel is cooked – remove it from the Instant Pot and chill it little. Chop the fish roughly.
8. Add the chopped fish in the lettuce mixture.
9. Sprinkle the salad with the olive oil and stir it carefully with the help of the fork, do not damage the fish.
10. Serve the cooked salad immediately. Enjoy!

Green Chili Mahi-Mahi Fillets

(Prep + Cook Time: 10 minutes | Servings: 2)

Ingredients:

- ¼ cup green chili enchilada sauce, homemade or store-brought
- 2 Mahi-Mahi fillets, thawed
- 2 tbsp butter
- Salt and pepper to taste
- 1 cup water

Directions:
1. Pour 1 cup of water into the Instant Pot and set a steamer rack.
2. Grease the bottom of each mahi-mahi fillet with 1 tablespoon of butter, spreading the butter from end to end – this will prevent the fish from sticking to the rack.
3. Put the fillets on the rack. Spread 1/4 cup of enchilada sauce between each fillet using a pastry brush – cover them well.
4. Top with more enchilada sauce, if desired. Season fillets with salt and pepper. Lock the lid and close the steam valve. Press MANUAL, set the pressure to HIGH, and set the timer for 5 minutes.
5. When the timer beeps, quickly release the pressure and transfer the fillets into serving plates. Serve.

Notes: The cooking time is sufficient to cook the fillets if they are thawed. Test the fish before taking out. If they are not done, close the lid and let cook with the residual heat of the pot for 1 minute.

Trout-Farro Salad
(Prep + Cook Time: 55 minutes | Servings: 4)

Ingredients:
- 12-ounces skinned and chopped cooked trout
- 1 cup semi-pearled Farro
- 1 large, shaved fennel bulb
- ½ cup low-fat mayonnaise
- ¼ cup low-fat sour cream
- 3 tbsp lemon juice
- 2 tbsp Dijon mustard
- 1 tsp white sugar
- 1 tsp ground black pepper
- Water as needed

Directions:
1. Put the farro in your Instant Pot and pour in just enough water so the grain is covered by two inches. Close and seal the lid.
2. Select MANUAL and cook at HIGH pressure for 17 minutes.
3. When time is up, press CANCEL and use a quick-release.
4. Shave your fennel and put in a colander. Pour farro right on top of it, draining.
5. Toss fennel and farro together, and set aside for about 30 minutes.
6. When you're just about ready to serve, mix the mayo, sour cream, lemon juice, Dijon, white sugar, and pepper together.
7. Add the farro, fish and fennel. Serve right away.

Tasty Cuttlefish

(Prep + Cook Time: 40 minutes | Servings: 6)

Ingredients:

- 1 pound squid
- 1 tbsp minced garlic
- 1 tsp onion powder
- 1 tbsp lemon juice
- 2 tbsp starch
- 1 tbsp chives
- 1 tsp salt
- 1 tsp white pepper
- 3 tbsp fish sauce
- 2 tbsp butter
- ¼ chili pepper

Directions:

1. Slice the squid.
2. Combine the minced garlic, onion powder, starch, chives, salt, and white pepper together. Stir the mixture.
3. Then chop the chili and add it to the spice mixture.
4. Then combine the sliced squid and spice mixture together. Stir it carefully.
5. After this, sprinkle the seafood mixture with the lemon juice and fish sauce. Stir it. Leave the mixture for 10 minutes.
6. Toss the butter in the Instant Pot and melt it.
7. Then place the sliced squid mixture in the Instant Pot and close the lid. Cook the dish for 13 minutes at the STEW mode.
8. When the dish is cooked – remove it from the Instant Pot.
9. Sprinkle the dish with the liquid from the cooked squid. Serve.

Tilapia Bites

(Prep + Cook Time: 20 minutes | Servings: 8)

Ingredients:

- 3 eggs
- ½ cup half and half
- 1 tsp salt
- 1-pound tilapia fillets
- 1 tsp red pepper
- 1 tbsp lemon juice
- 3 tbsp olive oil
- 1 tsp coriander
- 1 tsp cinnamon
- ½ lemon

Directions:

1. Beat the eggs in the bowl and whisk them with the help of the hand whisker.
2. After this, add salt, red pepper, and half and half in the whisked eggs mixture. Stir it.
3. Grate 1 teaspoon of lemon zest and squeeze the juice from lemon in the bowl.

4. Chop the tilapia fillets into the big cubes.
5. Sprinkle the fish with the coriander and cinnamon. Stir the mixture. Spray the Instant Pot with the olive oil inside.
6. Dip the tilapia cubes in the egg mixture. Then transfer the fish in the Instant Pot.
7. Select SAUTE and cook the fish for 4 minutes on the each side or till you get golden brown color.
8. Then transfer the cooked tilapia bites in the paper towel and chill the dish. Serve.

Fish Pho

(Prep + Cook Time: 40 minutes | Servings: 6)

Ingredients:

- 4 oz salmon
- 7 oz squid
- 5 cups water
- 1 garlic clove
- ½ cup fresh dill
- 1 tbsp salt
- ¼ cup soy sauce
- 1 tsp ground black pepper
- ½ tbsp coriander
- ¼ tsp thyme
- 1 jalapeno pepper
- 8 oz rice noodles
- 5 oz bok choy
- 1 tsp chili flakes

Directions:

1. Select SAUTE and preheat the Instant Pot.
2. Add the water, salt, fresh dill, soy sauce, ground black pepper, coriander, thyme, and chili flakes.
3. Stir the mixture and SAUTE it for 15 minutes.
4. Meanwhile, chop the salmon and squid. Peel the garlic clove and slice it.
5. When the time is over – open the lid and remove all the ingredients from the Instant Pot except the liquid.
6. Put the chopped salmon and squid. Add sliced garlic clove. Stir the mixture gently and add more salt if desired.
7. Then close the Instant Pot and cook the dish at HIGH pressure for 10 minutes.
8. Then open the lid and ladle the seafood Pho in the serving bowls.
9. Serve the dish immediately. Enjoy!

Catfish with Herbs

(Prep + Cook Time: 20 minutes | Servings: 6)

Ingredients:

- 1 tsp fresh parsley
- 1 tsp dill
- 1 tbsp olive oil
- 14 oz catfish
- ¼ cup fresh thyme
- 3 garlic cloves
- ¼ cup water
- 2 tbsp soy sauce
- 1 tbsp salt

Directions:

1. Wash the fresh parsley and fresh thyme. Chop the greens.
2. Combine the chopped greens with the dill and salt. Stir the mixture.
3. Peel the garlic cloves and slice them.
4. Select SAUTE and preheat the Instant Pot. Pour the olive oil in the pot.
5. Add the sliced garlic and sauté for 1 minute.
6. Then combine the catfish with the green mixture. Add soy sauce and water.
7. Stir the mixture and transfer it to the Instant Pot.
8. Sauté the fish for 4 minutes on the each side.
9. When is cooked – you will get the light golden brown color of the fish. Serve the dish hot! Enjoy!

Oysters-in-the-Shell (E&S)

(Prep + Cook Time: 15 minutes | Servings: 6)

Ingredients:

- 36 in-shell oysters
- 6 tbsp melted butter
- Salt and pepper to taste
- 1 cup water

Directions:

1. Clean the oysters.
2. Toss in the Instant Pot with 1 cup of water.
3. Select MANUAL and cook on HIGH pressure for 3 minutes.
4. When time is up, press CANCEL and quick release the pressure.
5. Serve right away with melted butter.

Lobster Tails
(Prep + Cook Time: 25 minutes | Servings: 4)

Ingredients:
- 4 lobster tails (1-pound each)
- 1 cup water
- ½ cup white wine
- ¼ cup melted butter

Directions:
1. Defrost your lobster tails in a bowl of cold water.
2. Cut the tails in half tip-to tip, so the meat is exposed.
3. Pour the wine and water in your Instant Pot.
4. Lower the steamer basket into the pressure cooker.
5. Put the lobster tails shell-side down in the steamer basket.
6. Select MANUAL and cook at LOW pressure for 4 minutes.
7. When time is up, quick release the pressure after turning off the cooker.
8. You know the meat is done when it is firm and white, not translucent. Serve with melted butter.

Crab Legs with Garlic-Butter Sauce
(Prep + Cook Time: 10 minutes | Servings: 2)

Ingredients:
- 1 cup water
- 2 pounds frozen or fresh crab legs
- 1 minced garlic clove
- 4 tbsp salted butter
- 1 halved lemon
- 1 tsp olive oil

Directions:
1. Pour water in your Instant Pot and lower in the steamer basket. Add the crab legs.
2. Choose the STEAM option adjust time to 3 minutes for fresh, and 4 for frozen. In the meantime, heat the oil in a skillet.
3. Cook garlic for just 1 minute, stirring so it doesn't burn.
4. Add the butter and stir to melt. Squeeze the halved lemon in the butter.
5. By now, the crab will be done, so select CANCEL and quick release the pressure.
6. Serve crabs with the garlic butter on the side.

Tender Octopus
(Prep + Cook Time: 20 minutes | Servings: 6)

Ingredients:
- 1 tsp salt
- 10 oz octopus
- 1 tsp cilantro
- 2 tbsp olive oil
- 1 tsp garlic powder
- 1 tsp lime juice
- 1 cup water

Directions:
1. Place the octopus in the Instant Pot. Sprinkle it with the cilantro, garlic powder, and salt. Stir it.
2. After this, pour the water in the Instant Pot and close the lid. Cook the dish at the HIGH pressure for 8 minutes and quick release the pressure
3. Then remove the dish from the Instant Pot and put in the tray. Sprinkle the seafood with the olive oil.
4. Preheat the oven to 360F and transfer the tray to the oven. Cook the dish for 7 minutes more.
5. When the octopus is cooked – remove it from the oven and sprinkle with the lemon juice. A little chill and serve it. Enjoy!

Red chili anchovy
(Prep + Cook Time: 25 minutes | Servings: 2)

Ingredients:
- 1 red chili pepper
- 10 oz anchovy
- 4 tbsp butter
- 1 tsp sea salt
- ½ tsp paprika
- 1 tsp chili flakes
- 1 tbsp basil
- 1 tsp dry dill
- 1 tsp rosemary
- 1/3 cup bread crumbs

Directions:
1. Remove the seeds from the chili pepper and slice it.
2. Combine the chili flakes, paprika, sea salt, basil, dry dill, and rosemary together in the shallow bowl. Stir the mixture.
3. Then stir the anchovy with the spice mixture. Mix up it carefully with the help of the hands. Add sliced chili pepper and leave the mixture for 10 minutes. *Meanwhile*, toss the butter in the Instant Pot and melt it at the SAUTÉ mode.
4. Then dip the spiced anchovy in the bread crumbs and put the dipped fish in the melted butter.
5. Cook the anchovy for 4 minutes from the each side.
6. When the fish is cooked – remove it from the Instant Pot and put in the paper towel to avoid the excess oil.
7. Serve the anchovy immediately. Enjoy!

Mussels with Red Pepper Garlic Sauce

(Prep + Cook Time: 20 minutes | Servings: 4)

Ingredients:

- 3 pounds mussels
- 1 tbsp extra-virgin olive oil
- 4 cloves garlic minced
- 1 large red bell pepper roasted, minced or puréed
- ¾ cup Fish Stock clam juice, or water
- ½ cup dry white wine
- 1/8 tsp red pepper flakes
- 2 tbsp heavy cream whipping
- 3 tbsp parsely fresh, chopped

Directions:

1. Clean the mussels. Scrub the mussels and de-beard if necessary.
2. Make the steaming liquid. Preheat the Instant Pot by selecting SAUTÉ and adjust to Normal for medium heat. Heat the olive oil until it shimmers.
3. Add the garlic and cook, stirring frequently, until it is fragrant, about 1 minute. Add the roasted red pepper, fish stock, wine, and red pepper flakes. Stir to combine.
4. Add the mussels to the pot. Lock the lid into place. Select MANUAL; adjust the pressure to HIGH and the time to 1 minute. After cooking, quick release the pressure.
5. Unlock and remove the lid. Check the mussels; if they are not opened, replace the lid but don't lock it into place. Let the mussels steam for another 1 minute, until they've opened. (Discard any that do not open.)
6. Finish the dish. Add the cream, parsley and stir. Serve with the cooking liquid. Enjoy!
7. You might also like

Lentil, Potato and Carrot Soup (V)

(Prep + Cook Time: 25 minutes | Servings: 6)

Ingredients:

For the sauté:

- 1 clove garlic, minced
- 1 onion, small-sized, minced
- 1 tbsp olive oil (or dry sauté with no added oil)

For the soup:

- 1 cup lentil blend (pachraya massoor, autumn blend, or mix of red lentils, yellow split peas, brown lentil and Beluga lentils)
- 2 carrots, medium-sized, cubed
- 1 potato, medium-sized, peeled and cubed
- 1 sweet potato, small-sized, peeled and cubed
- 1 tsp marjoram
- 1 tsp thyme
- ½ tsp smoked paprika
- ¼ tsp rosemary powder (OR 1 teaspoon dried whole rosemary)
- 5 cups water
- 1 bay leaf

After cooking:

- ¼ cup nutritional yeast
- Salt and pepper to taste

Directions:

1. Select SAUTE; add the olive oil and heat. Add the onion and sauté until translucent.
2. Add the garlic and sauté for 1-2 minutes. Press the CANCEL key to turn off the SAUTÉ function.
3. Add all the soup ingredients in the pot.
4. Lock the lid and close the steam valve. Select MANUAL and cook at HIGH pressure for 10 minutes.
5. When the timer beeps, let the pressure release naturally. Open the steam valve to release any remaining pressure.
6. Carefully open the lid, stir to mix, and ladle into bowls.
7. Serve with crusty bread.

Spiced-Carrot Chilled Soup (V)

(Prep + Cook Time: 1 hour 40 minutes | Servings: 4)

Ingredients:

- 2 pounds trimmed, peeled, and chopped carrots
- 3 tbsp olive oil
- Salt to taste
- Dukkah to taste
- Water as needed

Directions:

1. Put carrots in your Instant Pot with ½ cup of water.
2. Seal the lid. Select MANUAL and cook at HIGH pressure for 30 minutes.
3. When time is up, press CANCEL and quick release the pressure.
4. Remove carrots and blend with olive oil until smooth.
5. Pour soup through a sieve to get a really smooth texture.
6. Add water if necessary to get the right consistency.
7. Add salt to taste before storing in the fridge until chill.
8. Before serving, whisk and sprinkle on dukkah.

Notes: Dukkah is a spice blend made from sesame seeds, cumin, salt, pepper, coriander, and hazelnuts. You can find it online, or at Trader Joe's and Whole Foods.

Instant Pot Vegetable Soup (V)

(Prep + Cook Time: 30 minutes | Servings: 6)

Ingredients:

- 1 can (14 oz) petite diced tomatoes
- 1 yellow onion, chopped
- ½ tsp ground pepper
- ½ tsp salt
- ¼ cup flat-leaf parsley, chopped
- 12 oz Green Beans (Simple Truth Frozen Organic)
- 12 oz Mixed Vegetables (Simple Truth Frozen Organic)
- 2 ¾ cups vegetable broth
- 2 tsp olive oil
- ¾ tsp dried oregano
- ¾ tsp dried thyme
- 4 garlic cloves, minced
- Salt and pepper to taste

Directions:

1. Press the SAUTE key of the Instant Pot. Put the olive oil in the pot and let heat for 1 minute.
2. Add the onion, cook, occasionally stirring for about 5 minutes until softened.
3. Add the garlic, thyme and oregano, stir and cook for 1 minute.
4. Add the mixed frozen veggies, green beans, tomatoes, salt and pepper to taste, and pour the broth. Stir until combined.
5. Press the CANCEL key to stop the SAUTÉ function. Cover and lock the lid. Press the MANUAL key, set the pressure to HIGH, and set the timer for 4 minutes.
6. When the Instant Pot timer beeps, press the CANCEL key. Let the pressure release naturally for 5 minutes.
7. Using an oven mitt or a long handled spoon, turn the steam valve to release remaining pressure. Unlock and carefully open the lid.
8. Add the parsley, season to taste and stir. Serve.

Fresh Garden Soup (V, E&S)

(Prep + Cook Time: 20 minutes | Servings: 4)

Ingredients:

- 4 cups vegetable broth
- 4 cups baby spinach
- Two, 15-ounce cans white beans, drained
- Two, 15-ounce cans of red beans, drained
- One, 14-ounce can of diced tomatoes
- 3 cups water
- 1 cup chopped onion
- ½ stalk celery, chopped
- ½ cup chopped zucchini
- ½ cup green beans
- ½ cup shredded carrots
- 4 minced garlic cloves
- 3 tbsp olive oil
- 2 tbsp minced parsley
- 1 ½ tsp salt
- 1 ½ tsp dried oregano
- ½ tsp dried basil
- ½ tsp black pepper
- ¼ tsp dried thyme

Directions:

1. Turn your cooker to the SAUTE setting and heat oil.
2. When hot, cook celery, garlic, green beans, and onions until the onion begins to turn clear.
3. Pour the broth, (drained) tomatoes, red beans, water, carrots, and spices. Stir before sealing the lid.
4. Press SOUP and adjust time to 3 minutes.
5. When time is up, press CANCEL and quick release the pressure. Add white beans and spinach. Put the lid back on, but do not bring to pressure.
6. Let the soup sit for 10 minutes. Taste and season as needed before serving.

Sweet Potato Soup (V)

(Prep + Cook Time: 35 minutes | Servings: 4)

Ingredients:

- 6 carrots, peeled and diced
- 3-4 large red sweet potatoes, peeled and diced
- 1 whole onion, chopped
- 3-4 cloves garlic, chopped
- 2 tbsp butter
- ½ tsp thyme
- ½ tsp ground sage
- 1 quart vegetarian broth
- Salt and pepper to taste

Directions:

1. Set the Instant Pot to SAUTE. Put the butter and then add the garlic, onion, and carrots. Sauté until the onions are translucent.
2. Add the sweet potatoes, broth, and seasonings.
3. Press CANCEL. Close and lock the lid. Press MANUAL. Set the pressure to HIGH and set the timer for 20 minutes.
4. When the timer beeps, quick release the pressure. Carefully open the lid and stir the soup to blend.
5. With an immersion blender, blend until soft and serve.

Turmeric Sweet Potato Soup (V)

(Prep + Cook Time: 45 minutes | Servings: 8)

Ingredients:

- 6 carrots, peeled and sliced
- 4 cups vegetable broth
- 4 cloves garlic, coarsely chopped
- 3-4 sweet potatoes, large-sized, peeled and diced
- 2 tsp ground turmeric
- 2 tbsp coconut, OR vegetable oil
- 1 tsp paprika
- 1 onion, large-sized, chopped
- Salt and pepper to taste

Directions:

1. Select SAUTE mode. Put the oil in the Instant Pot. Add the garlic, onion, and carrots and sauté until the onion is transparent.
2. Add the sweet potatoes, paprika, turmeric, pepper, salt, and pour the broth.

3. Press the CANCEL key to stop the SAUTÉ function. Cover and lock the lid. Press the MANUAL key, set the pressure to HIGH, and set the timer for 20 minutes.
4. When the Instant Pot timer beeps, press the CANCEL key and unplug the Instant Pot.
5. Quick release the pressure. Unlock and carefully open the lid.
6. When the ingredients are cooked, puree right in the pot using an immersion blender.
7. Alternatively, you can puree in batches in a blender on HIGH speed.
8. Serve garnished with spiced pumpkin seeds or crispy fried shallots.

Lentil Soup (V)
(Prep + Cook Time: 20 minutes | Servings: 6)

Ingredients:
- 1 pound waxy potatoes, such as Red Bliss or Yukon Gold (I used a blend that included purple potatoes)
- 1 bunch Rainbow Chard OR similar greens, such as spinach, chopped
- 1 cup green or brown lentils, sorted and rinsed
- 1 cup red lentils, sorted and rinsed
- 1 ½ tsp smoked paprika
- 1 medium onion, chopped
- 1 tsp salt
- 2 carrots, sliced into ¼ inch pieces
- 2 celery stalks, diced (optional)
- 2 tsp cumin
- 3 cloves garlic, minced
- 8 cups water
- Salt and pepper to taste

Directions:
1. Set the Instant Pot to SAUTE. Add the garlic, onions, celery, carrots, potatoes, and spices. Sauté for 3-5 minutes until the onions are soft.
2. Add the lentils and water, stir. Press CANCEL. Close and lock the lid. Set the pressure to HIGH and set the timer to 3 minutes.
3. When the timer beeps, quick release the pressure. Carefully open the lid.
4. Add the chard and season with salt and pepper to taste, stir. Serve.

Lentil Soup with Sweet Potato (V)

(Prep + Cook Time: 20 minutes | Servings: 6)

Ingredients:

- 2 tsp olive oil
- ½ yellow onion, chopped
- 1 large celery stalk, diced
- 4 garlic cloves, minced
- 1 tsp ground cumin
- 1 tsp paprika
- ½ tsp salt
- ½ tsp red pepper flakes
- 1 cup green lentils
- ¾ lb. sweet potato, peeled & cut into ½-inch dice
- 3½ cups low sodium vegetable broth
- 1 cup water
- 1 (14 oz) can petite diced tomatoes
- 4 oz spinach leaves (about 4 cups packed)
- Salt and pepper to taste

Directions:

1. Set Instant Pot to SAUTE setting. Add the olive oil and allow to heat for 30 seconds. Add the onion and celery, and cook, stirring, until softened about 4 minutes. Add the garlic, cumin, paprika, salt and red pepper flakes, and stir.
2. Add the lentil, sweet potato, vegetable broth, water and diced tomatoes, and stir to combine.
3. Close and lock the lid, select MANUAL and cook at HIGH pressure for 12 minutes. It will take about 15 minutes for the Instant Pot to reach pressure.
4. Once the time is expired, wait for 10 minutes, then carefully use the quick release valve (it may sputter a bit) to release the steam.
5. Add the spinach and stir until wilted. Season to taste. Serve.

Dried Beans Vegetarian Soup (V)
(Prep + Cook Time: 45 minutes | Servings: 6)

Ingredients:
- 1 bag (20 oz) 15 bean soup blend of Hurst Beans (save a seasoning packet for another use)
- 1 can (14.5 oz) Red Gold petite diced tomatoes, undrained
- 1 dried bay leaf
- 1 lemon, fresh squeezed juice
- 1 red bell pepper, seeded and chopped
- 1 sweet onion, small-sized, chopped
- 1 tbsp olive oil
- ½ tsp ground red pepper
- 2 carrots, peeled and chopped
- 2 stalks celery, chopped with tops
- 2-3 sprigs fresh thyme
- 3 cloves garlic, chopped
- 8 cups vegetable stock, OR 4 cups water plus 4 cups stock
- Kosher salt and fresh black pepper to taste

Directions:
1. Sort the beans, rinse, and drain.
2. Except for the lemon juice and tomatoes, put all of the ingredients into a 6-quart Instant Pot, ending with the olive oil.
3. Cover and lock the lid. Press the MANUAL key, set the pressure to HIGH, and set the timer for 45 minutes.
4. When the Instant Pot timer beeps, press the CANCEL key. Let the pressure release naturally for 10-15 minutes or until the valve drops.
5. Using an oven mitt or a long handled spoon, turn the steam valve to release remaining pressure.
6. Unlock and carefully open the lid. Taste, and if needed, adjust seasoning. Stir in the lemon juice and tomatoes. If desired, slightly mash a couple of beans. Serve.

Notes: If desired, you can cook the dish a bit longer on SAUTE mode after adding the lemon, tomato, and seasoning to meld the new added ingredients.

Split Pea Soup (V, E&S)

(Prep + Cook Time: 55 minutes | Servings: 6)

Ingredients:
- 1 bay leaf
- 1 pound split peas
- 1 yellow onion, diced
- ½ tbsp smoked paprika
- ¼ tsp thyme
- 2 cloves garlic, minced
- 2 tbsp coconut oil (butter or your choice of oil)
- 3 carrots, sliced
- 3 stalks celery, sliced
- 6 cups vegetable broth
- Fresh ground pepper

Directions:
1. Put the onion, celery, carrots, and garlic in the pot. Add the rest of the ingredients.
2. Lock the lid and close the steam valve. Select MANUAL and cook at HIGH pressure for 15 minutes.
3. When the timer beeps, let the pressure release naturally. Open the steam valve to release any remaining pressure in the pot and carefully open the lid.
4. Stir the soup, taste, and adjust seasoning as needed.
5. Serve hot with crusty bread.

Quinoa Soup (V, E&S)

(Prep + Cook Time: 40 minutes | Servings: 6)

Ingredients:
- 3 cups boiling water
- 2 bags of frozen mixed veggies (12 oz)
- 1 15 oz can of white beans
- 1 15 oz can of fire-roasted diced tomatoes
- 1 15 oz can of pinto beans
- ¼ cup rinsed quinoa
- 1 tbsp dried basil
- 1 tbsp minced garlic
- 1 tbsp hot sauce
- ½ tbsp dried oregano
- Dash of salt
- Dash of black pepper

Directions:

1. Put everything in the Instant Pot and stir. Close and seal the lid.
2. Select MANUAL and set time to 2 minutes on HIGH pressure.
3. When time is up, press CANCEL and quick release the pressure.
4. When all the pressure is gone, open the cooker and season to taste. Serve.

Notes: The reason the time range is so wide is because it can take between 15-20 minutes for the Instant Pot to reach pressure if you're using frozen veggies. Using boiling water helps with that, and if you use fresh veggies, it takes very little time to get to pressure)

Turkish Soup (V, E&S)

(Prep + Cook Time: 15 minutes | Servings: 2)

Ingredients:

- 2 ½ cups water
- 1 cup red lentils
- 1 chopped carrot
- 1 chopped potato
- 1 chopped onion
- ½ cup celery
- 3 minced garlic cloves
- ½ tbsp rice
- 3 tsp olive oil
- ½ tsp paprika
- ½ tsp coriander
- Salt to taste

Directions:

1. Turn your Instant Pot to SAUTE and add oil.
2. While that heats up, prep your veggies.
3. When oil is hot, cook the garlic for a few minutes until fragrant. Rinse off the rice and lentils, and put them in the Instant Pot.
4. Add 2 ½ cups of water, paprika, salt, and veggies. Close and seal the lid.
5. Select MANUAL and cook at HIGH pressure for 10 minutes.
6. When time is up, press CANCEL and quick release the pressure.
7. Let the mixture cool for a little while before pureeing in a blender. Serve.

Rainbow Soup (V)

(Prep + Cook Time: 25 minutes | Servings: 8)

Ingredients:

- 5 cups veggie broth
- 3 minced garlic cloves
- 3 cups cooked black beans
- 2 diced carrots
- 15-ounce can diced tomatoes
- 1 chopped small red cabbage
- 1 chopped onion
- 1 diced jalapeno chili
- 1 chopped yellow bell pepper
- 6-ounces quartered mushrooms
- 2 tbsp tomato paste
- 1 tbsp oregano
- 1 tbsp chili powder
- 1 tsp cumin
- Salt to taste

Directions:

1. Mix everything in your pressure cooker, except the salt.
2. Close the lid, select MANUAL and cook at HIGH pressure for 6 minutes.
3. When time is up, turn off the cooker and wait 15 minutes.
4. Release any remaining pressure.
5. Add salt to taste and serve!

Wintery Stew (V)

(Prep + Cook Time: 25 minutes | Servings: 4)

Ingredients:

- 2 tbsp olive oil
- 3 cloves garlic, crushed and minced
- 1 cup yellow onion, diced
- 1 cup green bell pepper, chopped
- 2 cups carrots, chopped
- 2 cups parsnips, chopped
- 2 cups red potatoes, cubed
- 1 cup beets, cubed
- 2 cups tomatoes, chopped
- 1 tbsp fresh tarragon, chopped
- 1 tbsp fresh dill, chopped
- 1 tsp salt

- 1 tsp black pepper
- 1 tbsp molasses
- 4 cups vegetable stock

Directions:
1. Place the olive oil in the Instant Pot and turn on the SAUTE setting.
2. Add the garlic and onion, stir. Sauté for 2 minutes.
3. Add the green bell pepper, carrots, parsnips, red potatoes, beets and tomatoes, stir well.
4. Season with tarragon, dill, salt, black pepper and molasses. Mix well. Add the vegetable stock.
5. Cover and seal the pressure cooker. Set the pressure to HIGH and cook for 7 minutes.
6. Use the natural release method to release the steam before serving.

Tomato-Coconut Soup (V, E&S)

(Prep + Cook Time: 20 minutes | Servings: 4)

Ingredients:
- 1 can coconut milk
- 1 tsp Ginger minced
- 1 red onion diced
- 1 tsp salt
- 6 large tomatoes cut into quarters
- ½ tsp ground cayenne pepper
- ¼ cup cilantro freshly chopped
- 1 tsp ground turmeric
- 1 tbsp agave nectar or honey
- 1 tsp garlic minced

Directions:
1. Combine all of the ingredients in the Instant Pot.
2. Lock the lid. Select MANUAL and cook at HIGH pressure for 5 minutes.
3. When the cooking is complete, let the pressure release naturally. Unlock the lid.
4. Using an immersion blender, mix the soup until smooth, and serve.

Sweet Peanut Stew (V)

(Prep + Cook Time: 35 minutes | Servings: 4)

Ingredients:

- 1 cup brown rice
- 2 tbsp olive oil
- 2 tbsp shallots, diced
- 2 cloves garlic, crushed and minced
- 1 tsp salt
- 1 tsp black pepper
- 2 tsp crushed red pepper flakes
- 4 cups vegetable stock
- ½ cup chunky natural peanut butter
- 2 cups fresh pineapple, chunked
- 3 cups fresh spinach, torn
- ½ cup peanuts, chopped
- ½ cup fresh cilantro, chopped

Directions:

1. Place the olive oil in the Instant Pot and press SAUTE.
2. Add the shallots, garlic, salt, black pepper and crushed red pepper flakes. Sauté for 2 minutes.
3. Add the rice, vegetable stock and peanut butter.
4. Cover and seal the pressure cooker. Cook at HIGH pressure for 15 minutes.
5. Once cooking is complete, use a quick release.
6. Add the pineapple and spinach. Cover and bring the pressure back up to LOW. Continue to cook for 2 minutes.
7. Use the natural release method to release the steam.
8. Serve garnished with chopped peanuts and fresh cilantro.

Cheddar Broccoli and Potato Soup

(Prep + Cook Time: 25 minutes | Servings: 4)

Ingredients:

- 1 broccoli head, medium-sized, broken into large florets
- 1 cup cheddar cheese, shredded
- 1 cup half and half
- 2 cloves garlic, crushed
- 2 pounds Yukon Gold Potatoes, peeled and then cut into small chunks
- 2 tbsp butter
- 4 cups vegetable broth
- Chives or green onion, chopped, for garnish
- Salt and pepper to taste

Directions:

1. Press the SAUTE key. When the pot is hot, add the butter and the garlic, and sauté for 1 minute or until the garlic starts to brown.
2. Add the potatoes, broccoli, broth, and season with a bit of salt and pepper. Lock the lid and close the steam valve. Cook for 5 minutes at HIGH pressure.
3. When the timer beeps, press CANCEL and let the pressure release naturally for 10 minutes. Open the steam valve to release remaining pressure.
4. Add the half-and-half and ½ cup cheddar cheese. Using an immersion blender, blend until smooth.
5. Alternatively, you can blend in batches in a large-sized blender. If you want a thinner soup, just add more broth.
6. Season with salt and pepper to taste.
7. Serve hot with remaining cheddar.

Potato Soup with Leek and Cheddar

(Prep + Cook Time: 25 minutes | Servings: 8)

Ingredients:

- 4 medium gold potatoes, peeled and diced, I used Yukon
- 1½ cups cream or half and half
- 1/3 cup cheddar cheese, grated
- 3 tbsp leeks, cleaned and thinly sliced, white and light green (reserve 2 for serving)
- 1½ tsp dried oregano
- 1 tsp kosher salt
- 2 bay leaves
- 2 tbsp unsalted butter
- ¾ cup white wine
- 4 cloves garlic, crushed
- 4 sprigs fresh thyme
- 5 cups vegetable broth
- Leeks, and cheese, for topping

Directions:

1. Set the Instant Pot to SAUTE.
2. Put the butter in the pot and melt. When melted, add the leek and season with salt and sauté until soft.
3. Add the garlic and sauté for 30 seconds. Press CANCEL. Reserve a few portion of the leek and set aside for serving.
4. Add the thyme, bay leaves, oregano, broth, white wine, and potatoes into the pot. Stir to mix.
5. Close and lock the lid. Set the pressure to HIGH and set the timer to 10 minutes.
6. When the timer beeps, quick release the pressure. Carefully open the pot.
7. Add the cream and with an immersion blender, puree the soup until desired consistency. Press the WARM button and heat the soup through.
8. When the soup is hot, sprinkle with the sautéed leeks, and sprinkle with cheese.

Mushroom Barley Soup (E&S)

(Prep + Cook Time: 35 minutes | Servings: 8)

Ingredients:

- 1 onion, medium-sized, diced
- 1 pound baby Bella mushrooms, sliced
- 1 sage sprig
- 1 tsp salt
- ¼ tsp freshly ground pepper
- ¼ tsp garlic powder
- 2 carrots, diced
- 2 stalks celery, diced
- ¾ cup pearl barley (do not use instant)
- 4 garlic cloves, chopped
- 4 thyme sprigs
- 8 cups beef broth or stock

Directions:

1. Pour all of the ingredients in the Instant Pot and stir to mix. Cover and lock the lid.
2. Press the MANUAL key, set the pressure to HIGH, and set the timer for 20 minutes.
3. When the Instant Pot timer beeps, press the CANCEL key and unplug the Instant Pot. Let the pressure release naturally for 10 minutes. Turn the steam valve to release remaining pressure.
4. Unlock and carefully open the lid. Serve and enjoy!

Butternut Squash Sweet Potato Soup (E&S)
(Prep + Cook Time: 40 minutes | Servings: 4)

Ingredients:

- 3 cups bone broth or vegetable broth or chicken broth
- 2 tbsp coconut oil
- 2 cups sweet potatoes, peeled and cubed
- 2 cups butternut squash, peeled, seeded, and cubed
- 2 cloves garlic, crushed
- ½ tsp turmeric
- ½ tsp ground nutmeg
- 1 tsp walnuts, chopped, for garnish, optional
- 1 tsp or pinch of sea salt
- 1 tsp fresh parsley, for garnish, optional
- 1 tsp dried tarragon
- 1 tsp cinnamon
- 1 onion, small-medium, cubed
- 1 inch ginger, peeled
- 1 ½ tsp curry powder

Directions:

1. Press the SAUTE key of the Instant Pot.
2. When the pot is hot, add the coconut oil, ginger, garlic, onions, and pinch of salt. Sauté until the onion is slightly soft.
3. Add the rest of the ingredients and stir to mix. Lock the lid and close the steam valve. Press MANUAL and cook at HIGH pressure for 10 minutes.
4. When the timer beeps, let the pressure release naturally. Carefully open the lid.
5. With an immersion blender, puree the soup right in the pot.
6. Alternatively, transfer the soup in a blender of a food processor, and puree in batches if needed. Be careful because the soup will be hot.
7. Serve immediately and garnish.

Bean Soup

(Prep + Cook Time: 65 minutes | Servings: 6)

Ingredients:

- 1 cup cannellini beans
- 7 cups water
- 1 cup dill
- 4 tbsp salsa
- 1 jalapeno pepper
- 1/3 cup cream
- 2 tsp salt
- 1 tsp white pepper
- 1 white onions
- 1 sweet red pepper
- 1-pound chicken fillet
- 1 tsp soy sauce

Directions:

1. Place the cannellini beans in the Instant Pot.
2. Chop the chicken fillet and add it in the Instant Pot too.
3. Add water and cook the beans at the PRESSURE mode on HIGH for 35 minutes.
4. Meanwhile, chop the dill and jalapeno peppers. Slice the onions and chop the sweet red peppers.
5. Add the vegetables to bean mixture and close the lid. Press SOUP mode and cook the dish for 15 minutes more.
6. Then sprinkle the soup with the cream, salsa, white pepper, and soy sauce. Stir the soup carefully and cook it for 5 minutes more.
7. Remove the soup from the Instant Pot and let it a little chill.
8. Ladle the soup into the serving bowls. Enjoy!

Simple Chicken Soup (E&S)

(Prep + Cook Time: 50 minutes | Servings: 4)

Ingredients:

- 2 cups water
- 2 cups chicken stock
- 2 frozen, boneless chicken breasts
- 4 medium-sized potatoes
- Three peeled carrots
- ½ big diced onion
- Salt and pepper to taste

Directions:

1. Put everything into the Instant Pot, including salt and pepper.
2. Select MANUAL and cook at HIGH pressure for 35 minutes.
3. When time is up, turn off the cooker and let the pressure release naturally for 15 minutes.
4. Carefully open the cooker, stir, and serve!

Chicken Noodle Soup

(Prep + Cook Time: 30 minutes | Servings: 6)

Ingredients:

- 3 TB butter
- 1 medium onion diced
- 2 large carrots diced
- 3 celery stalks diced
- 5 garlic cloves minced
- 1 tsp dried thyme
- 1 tsp oregano
- 1 tsp dried basil
- 8 cups chicken broth or vegetable broth, Homemade broth is preferable for extra nourishment but use a quality store-bought broth if you need.
- 2 cups cooked chicken leftovers cubed, You can add more if you like your soup meatier, or leave it out if you wish for it to be a vegetable-based soup.
- 8 oz spaghetti noodles break them in half
- 2-3 cups chopped spinach amount depends on your preference.
- Salt and black pepper to taste

Directions:

1. Press the SAUTE button and melt the butter in the Instant Pot. Once melted, add the onion, carrot, celery, and a big pinch of salt to bring out their juices. You can cook the veggies for about 5 minutes until they're soft and sweet.
2. Add the garlic, thyme, oregano, and basil. Cook for 1 minute.
3. Add the broth, chicken, and noodles, and turn off the Instant Pot so the sauté mode turns off.
4. Close the lid and press the SOUP button. Cook for 4 minutes.
5. The Instant Pot will take about 10 minutes to come to pressure, and then it will count down the 4 minutes. When the 4 minutes is done, quick release the pressure. It will take 1-2 minutes to release all of the pressure.
6. Take the lid off, stir in your chopped spinach to wilt, and more salt and pepper (to your taste). The soup is hot enough to wilt the spinach - no need to add more heat!
7. Taste the soup, and add salt as needed. Serve warm.

Chicken Cream Cheese

(Prep + Cook Time: 35 minutes | Servings: 6)

Ingredients:

- 1 can black beans, drained and rinsed (15 ounces)
- 1 can corn, undrained (15.25 ounces)
- 1 can rotel tomato, undrained (10 ounces)
- 1 pound chicken breasts, boneless skinless
- 1 package dry ranch seasoning (1 ounce)
- 2 tsp cumin, or to taste
- 2 tsp chili powder, or to taste
- 8 oz of cream cheese

Directions:

1. Put all the ingredients in the Instant Pot. Lock the lid and close the steam valve.
2. Set the PRESSURE to HIGH and set the timer for 20 minutes.
3. When the timer beeps, let the pressure release for 10-15 minutes.
4. Open the steam valve to release any remaining pressure from the pot. Carefully open the lid.
5. Remove the chicken and shred.
6. Break up the cream cheese and stir into the pot. Cover and let the cheese melt.
7. When the cheese is melted, open the lid and return the shredded meat in the pot. Stir everything to mix.

Notes: Serve with tortilla chips or rice.

Chicken Tortilla Soup

(Prep + Cook Time: 30 minutes | Servings: 4)

Ingredients:

- 2, 6-inch corn tortillas cut into 1-inch squares
- 3-4 cups chicken broth
- 3 chicken breasts
- 1 big, chopped tomato
- 1 chopped onion
- 2 minced garlic cloves
- 15 ounces of black beans
- 1 cup frozen corn
- 2 tbsp chopped cilantro
- 1 bay leaf
- 1 tbsp olive oil
- 2 tsp chili powder
- 1 tsp ground cumin
- ¼ tsp ground cayenne pepper

Directions:

1. Turn on the Instant Pot to SAUTE.
2. Pour in the olive oil and cook the onion while stirring until soft.
3. Add the cilantro, garlic, and tortillas. Stir and wait 1 minute.
4. Add the black beans, corn, tomato, 3 cups of broth, chicken, and spices.
5. Turn off the SAUTE function and close the lid.
6. Switch over to SOUP mode and adjust the time to just 4 minutes.
7. When time is up, quick-release the pressure.
8. Carefully take out the chicken and shred before returning back to the pot. Stir everything well.
9. Serve with cilantro, cheese, lime juice, and any other toppings you enjoy.

Buffalo Chicken Soup (E&S)

(Prep + Cook Time: 20 minutes | Servings: 4)

Ingredients:

- 3 cups chicken bone-broth
- 2 tbsp ghee, OR butter
- 2 cups cheddar cheese, shredded
- 2 chicken breasts, boneless, skinless, frozen or fresh
- ¼ cup diced onion
- 1/3 cup hot sauce
- ½ cup celery, diced
- 1 tbsp ranch dressing mix
- 1 cup heavy cream
- 1 clove garlic, chopped

Directions:

1. Except for the cheddar cheese and heavy cream, put the rest of the ingredients into the Instant Pot. Cover and lock the lid.
2. Press the MANUAL key, set the pressure to HIGH, and set the timer for 10 minutes.
3. When the Instant Pot timer beeps, press the CANCEL key and unplug the Instant Pot. Turn the steam valve to quick release the pressure. Unlock and carefully open the lid.
4. Carefully remove the chicken, shred the meat, and then return the shredded meat into the soup.
5. Add the cheese and cream and stir to combine. Ladle into bowls and serve.

Chicken and White Bean Chili with Tomatoes

(Prep + Cook Time: 35 minutes | Servings: 8)

Ingredients:

- 4 ounces canned mild green chilies, diced,
- 3 cups canned great northern beans, drain and rinse
- 3 ¾ cups chicken, boneless breasts, diced
- 2 cups chicken broth or stock, reduced fat
- 14 ounces canned tomatoes, diced
- ¼ tsp cayenne pepper
- ½ tsp paprika
- ½ tsp garlic powder
- 1 tbsp cumin
- 1 ¼ cups onion, diced

Directions:

1. Combine all of the ingredients in the Instant Pot. Lock the lid and close the steam valve.
2. Press the SOUP key and adjust the time for 10 minutes.
3. When the timer beeps, release the pressure quickly.
4. Serve and enjoy.

Fennel Chicken Soup (E&S)

(Prep + Cook Time: 55 minutes | Servings: 6)

Ingredients:

- 4 green onions, chopped
- 4 cups water
- 3 cloves garlic, peeled and chopped
- 2 cups chicken bone broth
- 1/8 tsp salt
- ½ onion, chopped
- 1 tbsp dried oregano
- 1 pound chicken thighs or/ and breast, boneless, skinless, cut into chunks
- 1 cup spinach or kale, chopped
- 1 bulb fennel, large-sized, chopped
- 1 bay leaf

Directions:

1. Put all of the ingredients into the Instant Pot. Cover and lock the lid.
2. Press the SOUP key and set the timer for 30 minutes.
3. When the Instant Pot timer beeps, press the CANCEL key and unplug the Instant Pot. Let the pressure release naturally for 10 minutes. Turn the steam valve to release remaining pressure.
4. Unlock and carefully open the lid.
5. Divide between serving bowls and serve.

Notes: This soup can be frozen and reheated.

Cheese Tortellini and Chicken Soup

(Prep + Cook Time: 35 minutes | Servings: 6)

Ingredients:

- 2 whole chicken breast, skinless and boneless
- 2 small bags frozen cheese tortellini
- 2 cups baby carrots, chopped
- ½ white onion, chopped
- 1 cup celery, chopped
- 2 cartons (32 ounces each) chicken broth

Your choice of spices for chicken (I used the following):

- 1 tbsp garlic, minced
- 1 tbsp paprika
- 1 tbsp parsley
- 1 tsp pepper
- 1 tsp salt

Directions:

1. Pour 1 cup of the chicken broth in the Instant Pot. Add the chicken breast. Sprinkle the top of the chicken with the spices. Lock the pot and close the steam valve.
2. Press the MANUAL key, set the pressure to HIGH, and set the timer to 15 minutes.
3. Meanwhile, prepare the vegetables.
4. When the timer beeps, open the steam valve to quick release the pressure.
5. Remove the chicken from the pot and shred using two forks. Return the shredded meat into the pot.
6. Add the vegetables and the tortellini.
7. Add one container of the chicken broth and add 1/2 of the other container in the pot.
8. If desired, add more parsley or spices. Lock the lead and close the steam valve. Press MANUAL, set the pressure to HIGH and set the timer for 3 minutes.
9. When the timer beeps, let the pressure release quickly.
10. Ladle into bowls and enjoy!

Enchilada Soup

(Prep + Cook Time: 35 minutes | Servings: 6)

Ingredients:

- 1 ½ pounds chicken thighs, boneless, skinless
- 1 bell pepper, thinly sliced
- 1 can (14.5 ounces) fire-roasted crushed tomatoes
- 1 onion, thinly sliced
- 1 tbsp chili powder
- 1 tbsp cumin
- 1 tsp oregano
- ½ cup water
- ½ tsp ground pepper
- ½ tsp sea salt
- ½ tsp smoked paprika
- 2 cups bone broth
- 3 cloves garlic, minced

For garnish:

- Fresh cilantro
- 1 avocado

Directions:

1. Except for the garnish ingredients, put all of the ingredients in the pot in the following order: chicken, tomatoes, bell pepper, onion, garlic, broth, water, cumin, chili powder, oregano, paprika, sea salt, pepper. Cover and lock the lid.
2. Press the MANUAL key, set the pressure to HIGH, and set the timer for 20minutes.
3. When the Instant Pot timer beeps, press the CANCEL key and unplug the Instant Pot. Turn the steam valve to quick release the pressure.
4. Unlock and carefully open the lid. Using 2 forks, shred the chicken right in the Instant Pot.
5. Ladle into servings bowls and top each serving with fresh cilantro and avocado.

Smoked Turkey Soup

(Prep + Cook Time: 1 hour 20 minutes | Servings: 8)

Ingredients:

- 11-ounces smoked turkey drumstick
- 6 cups water
- 2 cups dried black beans
- 2 bay leaves
- 1 chopped onion
- 1 chopped celery stalk
- 1 chopped carrot
- 3 pressed garlic cloves
- ½ cup chopped parsley
- ½ tbsp olive oil
- 1 ¼ tsp salt
- ¼ tsp black pepper

Directions:

1. Put oil in your Instant Pot and heat. Add carrots, celery, onions, and parsley.
2. Cook and stir for 8-10 minutes, until the veggies have softened. Add garlic and cook for another minute.
3. Pour the water, and add beans, turkey, black pepper, and bay leaves.
4. When boiling, close and seal the lid. Select MANUAL and cook at HIGH pressure for 45 minutes.
5. When the timer beeps, turn off cooker and wait for a natural pressure release.
6. When safe, open the lid and pick out the bay leaves.
7. Take out the turkey and pick off the meat, and plate for now.
8. Blend the soup to your desired texture and add meat. Season to taste.

Turkey Chili

(Prep + Cook Time: 60 minutes | Servings: 4)

Ingredients:
- 1 can (15-ounce) fire-roasted diced tomatoes
- 1 can (15-ounce) kidney beans, including their liquid
- 1 pound ground turkey
- 1 tbsp olive oil
- 1 tsp ground cumin
- 1 yellow onion, medium-sized, diced
- ½ tsp dried oregano leaves
- ¼ cup your favorite hot sauce
- 2 fresh cayenne peppers, chopped (seeds included)
- 2 green bell peppers, seeded and diced
- 4 cloves garlic, chopped
- To serve:
- ¼ cup cilantro, chopped
- 1 cup Monterey Jack cheese, grated

Directions:
1. Set the Instant Pot to SAUTE. Put the oil in the pot. Add the garlic, onion, and peppers.
2. Sauté for about 10 minutes until the onions are soft and start to brown.
3. Add the oregano and cumin; sauté for 2 minutes or until fragrant. Add the turkey.
4. With a spatula or a spoon, break the meat. Sauté for 5 minutes or until cooked through and opaque.
5. Add the beans, tomatoes, and hot sauce. Stir to combine. Close and lock the lid.
6. Press BEAN/CHILI. When the timer beeps, release the pressure naturally or do a quick release. Carefully open the lid. Ladle the chili into bowls.
7. Serve hot. If desired, top with grated cheese and cilantro. Serve with cornbread or rice.

Notes: If you have no fresh cayenne chili peppers, use jalapeno, serrano, or canned chipotle for a smoky heat.

Minestrone Soup

(Prep + Cook Time: 25 minutes | Servings: 4)

Ingredients:

- 2 tbsp lard OR olive oil
- 2 stalks celery, diced
- 1 large onion, diced
- 1 large carrot, diced
- 3 cloves garlic, minced
- 1 tsp dried oregano
- 1 tsp dried basil
- Sea salt and pepper to taste
- 1 can (28 ounces) San Marzano tomatoes, diced in a food processor or a blender
- 1 can (15 ounces) white or cannellini beans, (or about 2 cups freshly cooked and drained)
- 4 cups bone broth or vegetable broth
- 1 bay leaf
- ½ cup fresh spinach OR kale (without the rib) torn into shreds
- 1 cup elbow pasta, gluten-free
- 1/3 cup parmesan cheese, finely grated (omit for vegan option)
- 1-2 tbsp fresh pesto, optional

Directions:

1. Press the SAUTE button of the Instant Pot. Pour the olive oil and add the carrot, garlic, onion, and celery. Sauté until softened.
2. Add the oregano, basil, salt, and pepper. Add the tomatoes, broth, bay leaves, kale, and pasta. Press CANCEL. Close and lock the lid.
3. Press MANUAL, set the pressure to HIGH, and set the timer for 6 minutes.
4. When the timer beeps, let it sit for about 1-2 minutes then do a quick release. Carefully open the lid.
5. Add the white kidney beans. Ladle into bowls.
6. Garnish each serving with parmesan cheese and a dollop of pesto.

Seafood Stew

(Prep + Cook Time: 25 minutes | Servings: 4)

Ingredients:
- 3 tbsp extra-virgin olive oil
- 2 bay leaves
- 2 tsp paprika
- 1 small onion thinly sliced
- 1 small green bell pepper thinly sliced
- 1½ cups tomatoes diced
- 2 cloves garlic smashed
- Sea salt to taste
- Pepper freshly ground, to taste
- 1 cup Fish Stock
- 1½ pounds meaty fish like cod or striped bass, cut into 2-inch chunks
- 1 pound Shrimp cleaned and deveined
- 12 Little Neck Clams
- ¼ cup cilantro for garnish
- 1 tbsp extra-virgin olive oil to add when serving

Directions:
1. Press SAUTE function on the Instant Pot. When display reads "Hot", add olive oil.
2. Add the bay leaves, and paprika and stir for about 30 seconds
3. Add the onion, bell pepper, tomatoes, garlic and 2 tablespoons of the cilantro; season with salt and pepper. Stir for a few minutes.
4. Add fish stock or water.
5. Season the fish with salt and pepper. Nestle the clams and shrimps among the vegetables in the pot. Add the fish pieces on top.
6. Close the lid tightly, and close the vent. Select MANUAL and cook at HIGH pressure for 10 minutes.
7. When the timer goes off, let the pressure naturally release for 10 minutes. Carefully release remaining pressure.
8. Divide the stew among bowls. Drizzle with the remaining 1 tablespoon olive oil and sprinkle with the remaining 2 tablespoons cilantro and serve immediately. Enjoy!

An English Fish Stew

(Prep + Cook Time: 20 minutes | Servings: 6)

Ingredients:

- 2 tbsp of butter
- 1 giant onion peeled up and diced
- 2 celery stalks diced up
- 4 massive carrots and peeled up and dice
- 4 medium sized potatoes peeled and reduced to half
- 1 pound of firm flesh white fish fillets reduce to half size
- 2 cups of fish broth
- 1 cup of chilly water
- 1 piece of bay leaf
- Half a teaspoon of dried thyme
- 1 cup of heavy cream
- 1 cup of fresh thawed frozen corn kernels
- Salt and freshly ground white or black pepper
- Fresh parsley

Directions:

1. Put your Instant Pot to SAUTE mode and toss in the butter and let it melt down.
2. Add the onions and sauté them for three minutes.
3. Stir in the celery, carrot, potatoes and sauté for another minute.
4. Add the fish, bay leaf, thyme, and pour the fish stock Lock up the lid of your cooker and let it cook at HIGH pressure for 4 minutes.
5. Once done, release your pressure quickly and take out the bay leaf.
6. Stir in some cream to make the mix a bit heavy alongside corn.
7. Season with some pepper and salt. Simmer until the corn is fully cooked and the chowder is scorching.
8. Serve by garnishing with parsley.

Egg Roll Soup

(Prep + Cook Time: 50 minutes | Servings: 8)

Ingredients:

- 4 cups chicken broth, OR beef broth
- 2/3 cup coconut aminos (or soy sauce)
- 2 cups carrots, shredded
- ½ head cabbage, chopped
- 1 tsp sea salt
- 1 tsp onion powder
- 1 tsp ground ginger
- 1 tsp garlic powder
- 1 tbsp ghee, OR avocado oil, OR olive oil
- 1 pound ground pork, pastured
- 1 onion, large-sized, diced

Optional:

- 2-3 tbsp tapioca starch

Directions:

1. Press the SAUTE key of the Instant Pot. Put your choice of cooking fat in the pot and add the ground pork and diced onion. Sauté until the meat is no longer pink. Add the rest of the ingredients into the pot.
2. Press CANCEL to stop the SAUTÉ function. Cover and lock the lid.
3. Select MANUAL and cook at HIGH pressure for 25 minutes.
4. When the Instant Pot timer beeps, press CANCEL to stop SAUTE function. Use a quick release.
5. Unlock and carefully open the lid. Ladle the soup into serving bowls and Serve.
6. If you want to thicken the soup, remove 1/4 cup of broth from the pot and stir in 2 to 3 tablespoons tapioca starch to make slurry.
7. Pour the slurry back into the pot and stir well for a couple of minutes or until thick.

Italian Soup

(Prep + Cook Time: 25 minutes | Servings: 6)

Ingredients:

- 3 large potatoes (Russet or red), unpeeled and sliced into ¼-inch thick pieces
- 2 cups fresh kale, chiffonade (sliced into ribbons)
- 1 pound hot Italian sausage, casing removed
- 4 slices bacon, rough chopped
- 1 cup heavy cream OR half & half
- 1 ½ quarts chicken broth or stock
- 1 onion, chopped
- ¼ cup water
- 4 garlic cloves, minced

Directions:

1. Set to SAUTE mode and preheat the Instant Pot. When hot, add the bacon and cook until crisp.
2. Transfer the bacon into a plate with paper towel to drain most of the grease. Put the onions in the pot, sauté for 3 minutes.
3. Add the sausage, sauté for about 5 minutes, breaking them into pieces.
4. Add the garlic and sauté for 1 minute. If needed, turn off the pot and drain excess grease.
5. Add the potatoes, water, and broth. Lock the lid and close the steam valve. Press MANUAL, set the pressure to HIGH, and set the timer to 5 minutes.
6. When the timer beeps, let the pressure release naturally for 10 minutes. Open the steam valve to release any remaining pressure.
7. Add the kale and stir until wilted. Add the cream and stir to combine.
8. Ladle into serving bowls and top each serving with crisp bacon.

Notes: You can substitute hot sausage with mild sausage, then add hot pepper flakes to add heat.

Bacon-y Potato Chowder

(Prep + Cook Time: 15 minutes | Servings: 8)

Ingredients:

- 5 pounds russet potatoes, peeled and cubed
- 1 pound bacon, fried crisp and rough chopped
- 1 cup heavy cream
- ¼ cup butter
- ½ cup whole milk
- 4 cups chicken stock
- 3 stalks celery, sliced thin
- 1 tsp ground black pepper
- 1 tbsp seasoning salt (I used Country Bob's)
- 1 large onion, small diced
- 1 clove garlic, minced
- Shredded cheddar cheese, sour cream, and diced green onion for garnish

Directions:

1. Put the potato chunks in the pot.
2. Add the garlic, onion, celery, seasoning salt, pepper, and butter. Stir to mix.
3. Add the chicken stock and the bacon. Close and lock the lid. Press MANUAL and cook at HIGH pressure for 5 minutes.
4. When the timer beeps, quick release the pressure. Carefully open the lid.
5. With a potato masher, crush the veggies until the mixture is a semi-smooth mash. If you want, you can leave a few big chunks of potato for texture.
6. Add the whole milk and the cream. Stir to mix. Ladle into bowls.
7. Top each serving with sour cream, shredded cheddar cheese, and sliced green onion.

Navy Bean, Spinach, and Bacon Soup

(Prep + Cook Time: 45 minutes | Servings: 6)

Ingredients:

- 4 slices bacon, center cut, chopped
- 4 cups chicken broth, reduced sodium
- 3 cups baby spinach
- 3 cans (15 ounces each) navy beans, rinsed and drained
- 2 tbsp tomato paste
- 2 bay leaves
- 1 sprig fresh rosemary (I used a bouquet garni for tosing)
- 1 onion, medium-sized, chopped
- 1 celery stalk, large-sized, chopped
- 1 carrot, large-sized, chopped

Directions:

1. Put 1 can beans and 1 cup of water in a blender, and blend. Press the SAUTÉ key of the Instant Pot.
2. Put the bacon in the pot and cook until crisp. Remove and transfer into a plate lined with paper towel.
3. Add the onion, celery, and carrots into the pot, and sauté for about 5 minutes or until soft. Stir in the tomato paste.
4. Add the beans, pureed beans, bay leaves, rosemary, and broth. Lock the lid and close the steam valve. Cook for 15 minutes on HIGH pressure.
5. When the timer beeps, release the pressure quickly or naturally. Carefully open the lid.
6. Remove the bay leaves and the rosemary. Pour 2 cups of the soup in a blender and blend. Return into the soup.
7. Add the spinach and stir until wilted.
8. Ladle between 6 bowls ad top each serving with bacon.

Butternut Squash and Apple Soup

(Prep + Cook Time: 25 minutes | Servings: 6)

Ingredients:

- 1 apple, peeled and then cut up
- 1 whole butternut squash, peeled and then cut up into small cubes
- 4 cups chicken broth or vegetable broth
- Ginger powder or pureed ginger (I like the ginger that comes in the tube from the supermarket)
- Olive oil to taste

Directions:

1. Press the SAUTÉ key of the Instant Pot.
2. When the pot is hot, add the oil and some butternut squash cubes.
3. Cook for about 5 minutes or until the squash are slightly brown.
4. Add the rest of the squash cubes and the rest of the ingredients. Lock the lid and close the steam valve.
5. Press MANUAL, set the pressure to HIGH, and set the time to 10 minutes.
6. When the timer beeps, press CANCEL and release the pressure quickly.
7. With an immersion blender, puree the soup in the pot.
8. Alternatively, puree the soup in a high-powered blender.

Easy Weeknight Stew (E&S)

(Prep + Cook Time: 65 minutes | Servings: 4)

Ingredients:
- 1 can (14 ounces) diced fire-roasted tomatoes (you can use regular tomatoes)
- 1 can (14 ounces) full-fat coconut milk
- 1 handful cilantro, fresh chopped, to garnish
- 1 onion, diced
- 1 pound string beans, cut into 1-inch pieces
- 1 tbsp salt
- 1 tbsp cumin
- 1 tsp fresh ginger, minced
- 2 cloves garlic, minced
- 2 cups broth (chicken or you can use pork)
- 3 medium-sized bulbs celeriac, peeled and then chopped (you can use 6 stalks celery, chopped)
- 3 pounds pork shoulder or country style ribs, cut into 1-2 inch squares
- 3 tbsp curry powder
- 6 carrots, peeled and chopped
- Sea salt and pepper to taste

Directions:
1. In a large-sized bowl, combine the cubed meat with the ginger, curry powder, salt, and cumin, and mix well.
2. Except for the cilantro, pepper, and salt, put all the ingredients into the Instant Pot. Lock the lid and close the steam valve.
3. Turn on the pot and press the STEW key.
4. When the timer beeps, turn off the pot, and let the pressure release quickly or naturally.
5. Carefully open the lid, if needed, season with salt and pepper, and then garnish with cilantro.
6. If you want a thicker stew, stir in some arrowroot starch.

Notes: Beef and lamb would also work great for this stew. Choose cuts with more connective tissue and not lean steaks. You can use butternut squash instead of the carrots and you can add freshly chopped spinach once the stew has cooled so the leaves are still bright green with a crunch.

Speedy Chili Texas Trail

(Prep + Cook Time: 20 minutes | Servings: 8)

Ingredients:

- 2 tbsp canola oil
- 1 large onion, peeled, chopped
- 1½ pounds ground beef, turkey or chicken
- 2 cups of your favorite Bloody Mary (spicy preferred)
- 2 cans (14 ounces each) diced tomatoes with green chilies (or 28-ounce can diced tomatoes with juice)
- 2 cans (14 ounces each) kidney beans, drained and rinsed well
- 4 tbsp of your favorite chili powder, divided, or more if desired
- 1½ cups water

For serving, optional:

- Corn chips Cheese,
- Shredded Green onions,
- Sliced Sour cream

Directions:

1. Press the SAUTE key of the Instant Pot. Add the oil and heat.
2. Add the onion and sauté until golden brown, about 8 minutes.
3. Add the meat and cook until browned, breaking them while cooking.
4. Stir in the Bloody Mary mix and press the More SAUTÉ mode to increase heat. Stir and scrape any browned bits from the pot.
5. Add the beans, tomatoes, 2 tablespoons chili powder, and stir well.
6. Bring to just boiling, then add the water. Lock the lid and close the steam valve. Cook for 5 minutes at HIGH pressure.
7. When the timer beeps, quick release the pressure. Carefully open the lid. Just before serving, stir in chili pepper to desired spiciness.
8. Let stand for 5 minutes and ladle into bowls.
9. Garnish each serving as desired. Serve!

Bone Broth

(Prep + Cook Time: 1 hour 40 minutes | Servings: 8)

Ingredients:

- 1 tsp unrefined sea salt
- 1-2 tbsp apple cider vinegar
- 2-3 pounds bones (2-3 pounds lamb, beef, pork, or non-oily fish, or 1 carcass of whole chicken)
- Assorted veggies (1/2 onion, a couple carrots, a couple stalks celery, and fresh herbs, if you have them on hand)
- Filtered water

Directions:

1. Put the bones in the Instant Pot. Top with the veggies. Add the salt and apple cider vinegar.
2. Pour in enough water to fill the pot 2/3 full.
3. If you have enough time, let the pot sit for 30 minutes to allow the vinegar to start pulling the minerals out of the bones.
4. Cover and lock the lid. Press the SOUP key, set the pressure to LOW, and set the timer for 120 minutes.
5. When the Instant Pot timer beeps, press the CANCEL key and unplug the Instant Pot. Let the pressure release naturally for 10-15 minutes or until the valve drops.
6. Unlock and carefully open the lid. Strain the broth.
7. Discard the veggies and bones. Pour the broth into jars. Store in the refrigerator or freeze.

Notes: If you are using pork, lamb, or beef bones, roast them in a preheated 350F oven for 30 minutes. This step is optional, but it does wonders to the flavors of the broth.

Beef Bone Broth

(Prep + Cook Time: 90 minutes | Servings: 8)

Ingredients:
- 5 ounces carrots
- 4-5 sprigs thyme
- 4 cloves garlic
- 3 pounds beef bones (oxtail or neck bones preferred)
- 3 bay leaves
- 1 onion, roughly chopped
- Half head celery, chopped
- Filtered water
- Pepper to taste
- Salt to taste

Directions:
1. Cut the celery and onion. Add into the Instant Pot.
2. Add the rest of the ingredients into the pot.
3. Fill the pot with water up to the line before the max line of the Instant Pot.
4. Cover and lock the lid. Turn the steam valve to Sealing. Press the MANUAL key, set the pressure to HIGH, and set the timer for 90 minutes.
5. When the Instant Pot timer beeps, press the CANCEL key and unplug the Instant Pot. Turn the steam valve to quick release the pressure. Unlock and carefully open the lid.
6. Strain the broth and store in freezer.

Chicken Stock

(Prep + Cook Time: 120 minutes | Liters: 4)

Ingredients:
- 1 chicken carcass
- 1 onion, cut into quarters
- 10-15 whole pieces peppercorns
- 2 bay leaves
- 2 tbsp apple cider vinegar
- Veggie scraps, optional
- Water Equipment: 4-5 mason jars

Directions:
1. Put the chicken carcass in the Instant Pot. If desired, feel free to add the skin.
2. Add the vegetable scraps, onion, apple cider vinegar, peppercorns, and bay leaves.
3. Fill the pot with water to 1/2-inch below the max line. Cover and lock the lid. Press the SOUP key and set the timer for 120 minutes.

4. When the Instant Pot timer beeps, press the CANCEL key and unplug the Instant Pot. Let the pressure release naturally for 10-15 minutes or until the valve drops – do not turn the steam valve for at least 30 minutes. Turn the steam to release remaining pressure.
5. Unlock and carefully open the lid. Strain out everything else from the stock and discard.
6. Pour the stock into the mason jar – do not overfill. If you are planning to freeze your stock, use 5 mason jars.
7. Let the stock cool and then store in the fridge or freeze within 3 days.

Notes: Let the jars cool completely before putting them in the fridge or freezing them. If not freezing, be sure to use in 3 days. If not using within 3 days, then freeze.

Fish Stock
(Prep + Cook Time: 65 minutes | Quarts: 3)

Ingredients:
2 salmon heads, large-sized, cut into quarters
2 lemongrass stalks, roughly chopped
1 cup carrots, roughly chopped
1 cup celery, roughly chopped
2 cloves garlic
Filtered water
Handful fresh thyme, including stems
Oil, for frying the fish heads

Directions:
1. Wash the fish heads with cold water – make sure there is no blood – and then pat them dry.
2. Put the oil in a pan and lightly sear the fish heads – this will minimize the fish meat from falling apart.
3. Slice the vegetables and put them in the Instant Pot.
4. Add the fish and thyme. Pour water in the pot until the level reaches 3 quarts or just cover the fish. Cover and lock the lid.
5. Press the SOUP key, set the pressure to HIGH, and set the timer for 45 minutes.
6. When the Instant Pot timer beeps, press the CANCEL key and unplug the Instant Pot. Let the pressure release naturally for 10-15 minutes or until the valve drops. Unlock and carefully open the lid.
7. Strain the fish and vegetable and store the stock.

Vegetable Stock (V)

(Prep + Cook Time: 30 minutes | Cups: 8)

Ingredients:

- 2 green onions, sliced
- 2 tsp minced garlic
- 4 medium-sized carrots, peeled and chopped
- 4 celery stalks, chopped
- 6 parsley sprigs
- 4 thyme sprigs
- 8 cups water
- 2 bay leaves
- 8 black peppercorns
- 1½ tsp salt

Directions:

1. Prepare vegetables. In a 6-quarts Instant Pot, pour the water and add all the ingredients except salt.
2. Plug in and switch on the Instant Pot, and secure pot with lid.
3. Select SOUP option, and adjust cooking time to 30 minutes and let cook.
4. When the timer beeps, switch off the Instant Pot and let pressure release naturally for 10 minutes and then do quick pressure release.
5. Then uncover the pot and pass the mixture through a strainer placed over a large bowl to collect stock and vegetables on the strainer.
6. Stir salt into the stock and let cool completely before storing or use it later for cooking.

Vegan Alfredo Sauce (V)

(Prep + Cook Time: 20 minutes | Servings: 4)

Ingredients:

- 12-ounces cauliflower florets
- ½ cup water
- Almond milk if needed
- Garlic salt to taste
- Black pepper to taste

Directions:

1. Pour water into your Instant Pot. Put cauliflower florets into your steamer basket and lower into cooker. Seal the lid.
2. Select MANUAL and cook at HIGH pressure for 3 minutes.
3. When the timer beeps, press CANCEL and wait for a natural pressure release.
4. Remove steamer basket and cool cauliflower for a few minutes.
5. Pulse cauliflower with pot liquid in a blender until very smooth. If it isn't quite creamy enough, add a splash of almond milk.
6. Season with garlic salt and black pepper.

Mixed-Veggie Sauce (V)

(Prep + Cook Time: 30 minutes | Cups: 2)

Ingredients:

- 4 chopped tomatoes
- 4-5 cubes of pumpkin
- 4 minced garlic cloves
- 2 chopped green chilies
- 2 chopped celery stalks
- 1 sliced leek
- 1 chopped onion
- 1 chopped red bell pepper
- 1 chopped carrot
- 1 tbsp sugar
- 2 tsp olive oil
- 1 tsp red chili flakes
- Splash of vinegar
- Salt to taste

Directions:

1. Prep your veggies.
2. Heat your oil in the Instant Pot.
3. Add onion and garlic, and cook until the onion is clear.
4. Add pumpkin, carrots, green chilies, and bell pepper. Stir before adding the leek, celery, and tomatoes.
5. After a minute or so, toss in salt and red chili flakes.
6. Close and seal the pressure cooker. Select MANUAL and cook at HIGH pressure for 6 minutes.
7. When time is up, press CANCEL and let the pressure come down on its own.
8. The veggies should be very soft. Let the mixture cool a little before moving to a blender.
9. Puree until smooth. Pour back into the pot and add vinegar and sugar.
10. Simmer on the lowest SAUTE setting for a few minutes before serving.

Tomato Sauce (V)

(Prep + Cook Time: 50 minutes | Cups: 8)

Ingredients:

- 4,2 pounds tomatoes, cut into halves or quarters, less or more to fill the Instant Pot to the max level
- 1 onion, minced
- 1 tbsp oregano
- 1 tbsp salt
- 1 tbsp sugar
- 2 bay leaves
- 2 tbsp basil, chopped
- 2-3 tbsp parsley, chopped
- Lemon juice (1 tbsp per jar)

Directions:

1. Put all of the ingredients in the Instant Pot. Cover and lock the lid. Press the MANUAL key, set the pressure to HIGH, and set the timer for 30-40 minutes.
2. While the sauce is cooking, sterilize the mason jars and new lids in a pot of boiling water for 15 minutes.
3. Drain the sterilized jars and lids on a paper towel.
4. When the Instant Pot timer beeps, press the CANCEL key and unplug the Instant Pot. Let the pressure release naturally for 10-15 minutes or until the valve drops.
5. Unlock and carefully open the lid. Set a food mill over another pot.
6. Scoop out the tomatoes into the food mill. The tomatoes will mush up quickly and go through the pot, leaving the seeds and the skins behind.
7. Put 1 tablespoon lemon juice or 1/4 teaspoon citric acid on each mason jar and immediately fill the mason jars with the hot sauce.
8. Wipe the rims to ensure that the lids will seal. Put the lids on and screw them down.
9. Put the jars in the boiling water where you sterilized the jars and rims. Sterilize for 30 minutes.
10. Remove the jars and let them cool – make sure that each lid pops and is concave.

Basil Fresh Tomato Sauce (V)

(Prep + Cook Time: 40 minutes | Cups: 8)

Ingredients:

- 4 ½ -5 pounds Roma tomatoes, diced
- ½ cup fresh basil, chopped
- 2 tbsp olive oil
- ¼ tsp crushed peppers
- ½ tbsp pepper
- ½ tbsp garlic powder
- 1 tbsp salt
- 1 onion, diced
- 1 bay leaf
- 1 ½ tbsp Italian seasoning
- 6 cloves garlic, minced

Directions:

1. Press the SAUTE key of the Instant Pot and select the More option. Put the olive in the pot.
2. Add the onions and garlic. Sauté for about 5 minutes or until the onions are soft.
3. Add the tomatoes, crushed pepper, Italian seasoning, garlic powder, pepper, salt, and bay leaf in the pot. Stir to combine.
4. Cover and lock the lid. Press the MANUAL key, set the pressure to HIGH, and set the timer for 10 minutes.
5. When the Instant Pot timer beeps, press the CANCEL key and unplug the Instant Pot. Use a quick release.
6. Unlock and carefully open the lid. Add the basil in the pot and stir.
7. Press the SAUTE key and select the More option. Simmer for 5 minutes.
8. Remove the bay leaf and serve or use in a different recipe.
9. This sauce can be kept for up to 5 days in the fridge or you can freezer for a much later use.

Pasta and Spaghetti Sauce

(Prep + Cook Time: 25 minutes | Servings: 6)

Ingredients:

- 2 pounds Italian sausage, casings removed (hot or mild), optional
- 1 can (28 ounces) diced tomatoes
- 1 onion, small-sized, chopped, optional
- 1 tbsp olive oil
- ½ cup red wine (use a cabernet)
- ½ cup water
- ¼ tsp coarse black pepper, fresh ground
- ¼ - ½ tsp crushed red pepper flakes
- 2 cans (15 ounces) tomato sauce
- 2 tsp brown sugar
- 2 tsp dried parsley flakes
- 2 tsp fennel seed, crushed
- 2 tsp salt
- 3 tsp basil
- 3-4 cloves garlic, minced
- 6 ounces tomato paste
- Parmesan cheese OR a piece of rind, optional

Directions:

1. Press the SAUTE key of the Instant Pot and wait until hot. Put 1 tablespoon olive oil in the pot and add the sausage.
2. Cook until browned, breaking the sausages in the process as you stir.
3. Add the rest of the ingredients in the pot. If you are not using any meat, then start at this step.
4. Press the CANCEL key to stop the sauté function. Cover and lock the lid.
5. Press the MANUAL key, set the pressure to HIGH, and set the timer for 10 minutes.
6. When the Instant Pot timer beeps, press the CANCEL key and unplug the Instant Pot. Let the pressure release naturally for 10-15 minutes or until the valve drops. Using an oven mitt or a long handled spoon, turn the steam valve to Venting to release remaining pressure. Unlock and carefully open the lid.
7. Serve with your spaghetti or your favorite pasta.

Meat Sauce

(Prep + Cook Time: 15 minutes | Servings: 4)

Ingredients:
- 1 can Hunts traditional pasta sauce
- 1 pound extra-lean ground beef
- ¼ cup fresh parsley, chopped
- 3-4 cloves garlic, minced
- 3-4 fresh basil leaves, chopped

Directions:
1. Put all of the ingredients into the Instant Pot. With a spatula, break the meat up and mix to combine.
2. Cover and lock the lid. Press the MANUAL key, set the pressure to HIGH, and set the timer for 8 minutes.
3. When the Instant Pot timer beeps, press the CANCEL key and unplug the Instant Pot. Turn the steam valve to quick release the pressure.
4. Unlock and carefully open the lid. Serve.

Cheesy Sauce

(Prep + Cook Time: 25 minutes | Servings: 8)

Ingredients:
- 1 cup carrot, chopped
- 1 tbsp turmeric, chopped OR 1 tsp turmeric powder
- 1 tsp salt
- ½ cup nutritional yeast
- ½ cup onion, chopped
- ½ cup raw cashews
- 2 cups potato, peeled and then chopped
- 2 cups water
- 3 cloves garlic, peeled and left whole

Directions:
1. Put all of the ingredients in the Instant Pot. Cover and lock the lid.
2. Press the MANUAL key, set the pressure to HIGH, and set the timer for 5 minutes.
3. When the Instant Pot timer beeps, press the CANCEL key and unplug the Instant Pot. Turn the steam valve to quick release the pressure. Unlock and carefully open the lid. Let cool for about 10-15 minutes.
4. Transfer into a blender and blend for about 2 minutes or until super smooth and creamy.

Mushroom Sauce (V)
(Prep + Cook Time: 15 minutes | Cups: 2)

Ingredients:
- 10 mushrooms, chopped
- 1 yellow onion, chopped
- 2 garlic cloves, minced
- 1 tsp thyme, dried
- 2 cups veggie stock
- ½ tsp rosemary, dried
- ½ tsp sage
- 1 tsp sherry
- 1 tbsp water
- 1 tbsp nutritional yeast
- 1 tbsp coconut aminos (or soy sauce)
- Salt and black pepper to the taste
- ¼ cup almond milk
- 2 tbsp rice flour

Directions:
1. Set your Instant Pot on SAUTE mode, add onion and brown for 5 minutes.
2. Add mushrooms and the water, stir and cook for 3 minutes.
3. Add garlic, stir again and cook for 1 minute.
4. Add stock, yeast, sherry, soy sauce, salt, pepper, sage, thyme and rosemary, coconut aminos, stir, cover and cook on HIGH pressure for 4 minutes.
5. Meanwhile, in a bowl, mix milk with rice flour and stir well.
6. Quick release the pressure from the pot, open the lid.
7. Add milk mix, stir well, cover and cook at HIGH pressure for 6 more minutes. Quick release the pressure and serve sauce.

Plant Based Smokey Gouda Sauce (V, E&S)
(Prep + Cook Time: 25 minutes | Cups: 4)

Ingredients:
- 1 zucchini, chopped, about 1½ cups
- ½ cup Daikon, chopped
- 1 small head cauliflower cut into chunks, about 4 cups
- 2 cloves garlic peeled and left whole
- 1½ cups water divided
- ½ cup raw cashews soaked in water for at least 10 minutes
- ¼ cup nutritional yeast
- ¾ tsp salt
- 1 tbsp smoked paprika
- 2 tbsp ume plum vinegar
- 1 tsp brown rice vinegar

Directions:
1. Place all of the ingredients into your IP and lock the lid.
2. Select MANUAL and cook at HIGH pressure for 3 minutes. Use the natural release method when the timer is up.
3. When all of the pressure is out of the pot, open the lid and allow to cool for about 10 – 15 minutes, and then transfer the mixture to your blender and blend until super creamy and smooth, about 2 full minutes. You may have to blend this in batches.
4. Enjoy on veggies, nachos, pastas, or as a dip!

Apple Sauce (V)
(Prep + Cook Time: 30 minutes | Cups: 3)

Ingredients:
- 12 apples, organic, peeled if preferred and then quartered
- ¼ tsp sea salt
- ½ lemon, organic, fresh juiced
- 1 tbsp raw honey, light colored
- 1 tbsp ground cinnamon
- 1 cup water, filtered
- 2 tbsp ghee (optional)

Directions:
1. Wash and prepare all the apples. If you don't like apple skin, you can peel them off. If you don't mind the skin, you can leave them on. Cut apples into quarters and put them in the IP.
2. Add ghee, honey, cinnamon, water, and sea salt in the pot.
3. Cover and lock the lid. Press the MANUAL key, set the pressure to HIGH, and set the timer for 3 minutes.
4. When the Instant Pot timer beeps, press the CANCEL key and unplug the Instant Pot. Let the pressure release naturally for 10-15 minutes or until the valve drops. Turn the steam valve to release remaining pressure. Unlock and carefully open the lid.
5. Ladle the apple mix in a high-powered blender or a food processor.
6. If there is a lot of excess liquid left in the Instant Pot, use only about 1/2 of the cooking liquid.
7. Pulse until the apples and cooking liquid are completely combines and the mixture is smooth.
8. If needed, add remaining liquid in the blender/ food processor to achieve desired consistency.
9. Alternatively, you can use a hand-held immersion blender to puree the sauce.

BBQ Sauce

(Prep + Cook Time: 25 minutes |Cups: 2)

Ingredients:

- ¾ cup seedless dried plums (or prunes), tightly packed into the measuring cup
- 1/8 tsp ground clove powder
- 1/8 tsp cumin powder
- ½ tsp granulated garlic
- ½ cup water
- ½ cup tomato puree OR passata
- 1 tsp sea salt
- 1 tsp liquid smoke
- 1 tsp hot sauce, OR home-made Tabasco
- 1 tbsp sesame seed oil OR avocado, peanut, or grape seed oil or any high smoke-pint oil
- 1 onion, medium-sized, roughly chopped
- 4 tbsp honey
- 4 tbsp white vinegar OR apple cider vinegar

Directions:

1. Press the SAUTE key of the Instant Pot and wait until hot.
2. Add the sesame oil and the onion; sauté, stirring occasionally, until the edges of the onion start to brown.
3. In a 2-cup measuring cup or a small-sized mixing bowl, add the tomato puree, honey, water, and vinegar.
4. Add the salt, hot sauce, garlic, cumin powder, liquid smoke, and clove.
5. Mix well until the contents are combined and the honey is evenly dissolved in the liquid.
6. Pour the mixture into the Instant Pot, scraping the bottom of the pot using a spatula to remove any browned bits.
7. Add the plums. Press the CANCEL key to stop the SAUTÉ function. Cover and lock the lid.
8. Press the MANUAL key, set the pressure to HIGH, and set the timer for 10 minutes.
9. When the Instant Pot timer beeps, press the CANCEL key and unplug the Instant Pot. Let the pressure release naturally. Unlock and carefully open the lid.
10. With an immersion blender, puree the contents in the Instant Pot. You may need to tilt the pot to immerse the blender in the liquid. Serve.

Chipotle Honey BBQ Sauce

(Prep + Cook Time: 25 minutes | Cups: 2)

Ingredients:
- 1 tsp olive oil
- 1 onion, medium-sized, chopped
- ½ tsp cumin
- ¼ cup honey
- 2 chipotles in adobo sauce
- 1 tbsp adobo sauce
- 2 tsp apple cider vinegar
- 1 cup ketchup
- 1 tsp chili powder
- 1 tsp paprika
- 1 tsp salt
- ½ tsp pepper
- ¼ cup orange juice
- 2 cloves garlic, chopped

Directions:
1. Press the SAUTE key of the Instant Pot. Put the olive oil in the pot and heat until shimmering.
2. Add the garlic and onion; sauté for about 3 minutes or until soft. While the veggies are sautéing, whisk the ketchup with the orange juice, honey, and apple cider vinegar.
3. Pour the ketchup mix over the veggies.
4. Add the adobo sauce, chipotles, seasoning, and spices. Press the CANCEL key to stop the SAUTÉ function. Cover and lock the lid.
5. Turn the steam valve to Sealing. Press the MANUAL key, set the pressure to HIGH, and set the timer for 8 minutes.
6. When the Instant Pot timer beeps, press the CANCEL key and unplug the Instant Pot.
7. Using an oven mitt or a long handled spoon, turn the steam valve to Venting to quick release the pressure. Unlock and carefully open the lid.
8. Pour the sauce carefully into a blender and puree.
9. Pour the sauce in a glass jar and store in the refrigerator for up to 1 week.

Chili Dog Sauce

(Prep + Cook Time: 35 minutes | Cups: 3)

Ingredients:

- 8 ounces ground beef
- 2 tsp chili powder
- 2 tsp prepared yellow mustard
- 2 cups pinto beans, cooked
- ¼ cup tomato paste
- ½ cup onion, minced
- 1 tsp white vinegar
- 1 tsp garlic powder
- 1 tsp cumin powder
- 1 tbsp Worcestershire sauce
- 1 cup beef stock
- Kosher salt, to taste
- 2 tsp hot sauce, optional

Directions:

1. Put the ground beef, beans, and beef stock into the Instant Pot. Stir to combine.
2. With a potato masher, mash the ground beef and the beans until very fine.
3. Add the Worcestershire sauce, vinegar, garlic, cumin, chili powder, onion, mustard, and tomato paste into the pot. Cover and lock the lid.
4. Press the MANUAL key, set the pressure to HIGH, and set the timer for 5 minutes.
5. When the Instant Pot timer beeps, press the CANCEL key and unplug the Instant Pot. Use a quick release. Unlock and carefully open the lid. Stir and taste the sauce.
6. Adjust seasoning as needed.

Notes: You can use canned beans for this recipe. If using dry beans, pressure cook 2 cups of pinto beans with 6 cups water for 40 minutes at HIGH pressure. When cooking time is up, release the pressure naturally. Rinse and strain the beans, whether pressure-cooked or canned, before using in this recipe.

Sneaky Marinara Sauce (V)

(Prep + Cook Time: 25 minutes | Cups: 8)

Ingredients:

- 2 cans (28 oz) crushed tomatoes
- 1 sweet potato, large-sized, diced (about 2 cups)
- ½ cup red lentils
- 1 tsp salt
- 1½ cups water
- 2-3 cloves garlic, minced

Directions:

1. Pick over the lentils. Remove any shriveled lentils or any stones. Put in a fine mesh sieve and rinse to clean.
2. Press the SAUTE key of the Instant Pot. Add the sweet potatoes, lentils, and garlic. Sprinkle with the salt and sauté for about 1-2 minutes to bring the garlic flavor out and warm the pot.
3. Add the crushed tomatoes and pour in the water. Stir very well to combine, making sure that the lentils are not stuck on the bottom of the pot.
4. Press the CANCEL key to stop the SAUTÉ function. Cover and lock the lid. Press the MANUAL key, set the pressure to HIGH, and set the timer for 13 minutes.
5. When the Instant Pot timer beeps, press the CANCEL key and unplug the Instant Pot. Let the pressure release naturally for 10-15 minutes or until the valve drops.
6. Using an oven mitt or a long handled spoon, turn the steam to release remaining pressure. Unlock and carefully open the lid.
7. Stir the marinara to combine. If desired, puree using an immersion blender.
8. Serve.

Notes: You can double this recipe in the Instant Pot without going over the maximum volume limit. It makes 4 quarts with some leftover.

Cranberry Apple Sauce (V)

(Prep + Cook Time: 20 minutes | Cups: 2)

Ingredients:
- 1-2 apples, medium-sized, peeled, cored, and then cut into chunks
- 10 oz cranberries, frozen or fresh, preferably organic
- ¼ tsp sea salt
- ¼ cup lemon juice
- ½ cup maple syrup OR honey OR omit
- 1 tsp cinnamon

Directions:
1. Put all of the ingredients in the Instant Pot and combine.
2. Cover and lock the lid. Press the MANUAL key, set the pressure to HIGH, and set the timer for 1 minute.
3. When the Instant Pot timer beeps, let the pressure release naturally for 10-15 minutes or until the valve drops. Press the CANCEL key and unplug the Instant Pot.
4. Unlock and carefully open the lid. Using a wooden spoon, mash the fruit a bit.
5. Select the SAUTE key and simmer for 1-2 minutes to allow some of the water to evaporate and the mix to thicken.
6. Press the CANCEL key. If you omitted the maple syrup/ honey and want to sweeten with stevia, then add to taste.
7. Stir to combine. Transfer into a pint jar and refrigerate.

Tabasco Sauce (V)

(Prep + Cook Time: 25 minutes | Cups: 2)

Ingredients:
- 12 oz fresh hot peppers OR any kind, stems removed
- 2 tsp smoked or plain salt
- 1¼ cups apple cider

Directions:
1. Press the SAUTE key of the Instant Pot.

2. Roughly chop the hot peppers and put into the Instant Pot. Pour in just enough apple cider to cover the peppers. Add the salt.
3. Press the CANCEL key to stop the SAUTÉ function. Cover and lock the lid.
4. Press the MANUAL key, set the pressure to HIGH, and set the timer for 1 minute.
5. When the Instant Pot timer beeps, press the CANCEL key and unplug the Instant Pot. Let the pressure release naturally for 10-15 minutes or until the valve drops. Turn the steam valve to release remaining pressure. Unlock and carefully open the lid.
6. Using an immersion blender, puree the contents and strain into a fresh dished-washed or sterilized bottle.
7. Refrigerate for up to 3 months or transfer into a suitable container and freeze for up to 1 year.

Salted Caramel Sauce
(Prep + Cook Time: 20 minutes | Cups: 1)

Ingredients:
- ½ tsp sea salt
- 1/3 cup heavy cream
- 3 tbsp butter, cut into ½-inch pieces
- 1 cup sugar
- ½ tsp vanilla
- 1/3 cup water

Directions:
1. Press the SAUTE key of the Instant Pot.
2. Add the water and the sugar. Stir to combine and let cook for 13 minutes without touching the pot.
3. When 13 minutes are up, immediately whisk the butter in the pot, followed by the cream. Whisk until smooth.
4. Add the vanilla and the salt.
5. Press the CANCEL key and with an oven mitt gloved hand, remove the inner pot from the housing to remove from heat.
6. Pour the salted caramel into a heat-safe glass and let cool. Store in the fridge for up to 5 days.

Breakfast Potato Hash (V, E&S)
(Prep + Cook Time: 20 minutes | Servings: 6)

Ingredients:
- 1 large sweet potato, diced to about 1-inch (about 1 cup)
- 1 large potato, diced to about ½-inch cubes (about 1 cup)
- 1 cup bell pepper, chopped (about 2 peppers)
- 1 clove garlic, minced
- 1 tbsp olive oil
- 1 tsp cumin
- 1 tsp paprika
- ½ tsp black pepper
- ½ tsp kosher salt
- ½ cup water
- Pinch cayenne

Directions:
1. Stir the veggies with the oil and the spices.
2. Add the mix into the Instant Pot and add 1/2 cup of water in the pot.
3. Set the pressure to HIGH and the timer to 0 minutes.
4. When the timer beeps, turn the valve to release pressure naturally.
5. Open the pot and press the SAUTE button. Sauté for about 5 to 6 minutes or until the potato cubes begin to brown. Serve.

Baked Potatoes (V, E&S)
(Prep + Cook Time: 15 minutes | Servings: 8)

Ingredients:
- 5 pounds potatoes, peeled, if desired, chopped into roughly the same size
- 1½ cups water

Directions:
1. Pour the water into the Instant Pot container and then insert a steam rack. Put the potatoes on the rack.
2. Close and lock the lid and make sure that the steam release valve is sealed. Press MANUAL and cook at HIGH pressure for 10 minutes.
3. When the timer beeps, let the pressure release naturally for about 20 minutes.
4. Open the steam valve to release any remaining pressure.
5. Serve and enjoy.

Fingerling Potatoes (E&S)

(Prep + Cook Time: 35 minutes | Servings: 4)

Ingredients:
- 1½ pounds fingerling potatoes, 1-inch thick (or less)
- ½ cup chicken broth
- 2 tbsp butter
- Leaves from 1 rosemary sprig
- Salt and pepper to taste

Directions:
1. Prick the potatoes, so they don't explode in the cooker.
2. Turn the Instant Pot to SAUTE and add butter.
3. When melted, add the potatoes and stir. Cook for the next 10 minutes, stirring once and awhile.
4. When the skins are crispy and the butter smells rich and nutty, pour in the broth. Close and seal the lid.
5. Select MANUAL and cook at HIGH pressure for 7 minutes.
6. When time is up, press CANCEL and wait 10 minutes before quick-releasing.
7. Season well with salt, pepper, and rosemary before serving.

Perfect Mashed Potatoes and Parsnips (E&S)

(Prep + Cook Time: 20 minutes | Servings: 4-6)

Ingredients:
- 3 pounds Yukon gold potatoes peeled and cut into 1½-inch cubes
- 1 pound parsnips cut into 1-inch thick circles
- 1 tsp salt
- 1 tsp pepper
- 4 tbsp butter, room temperature
- 4 tbsp half and half

Directions:
1. Pour 2 cups of water into the Instant Pot. Place steamer basket in the inner pot.
2. Place cut potatoes in the steamer basket. Place cut parsnips on top of potatoes.
3. Close the Instant Pot. Select MANUAL and cook at HIGH pressure for 7 minutes. Use a quick release.
4. Open the Instant Pot and carefully remove the steamer basket from the Instant Pot. Place the vegetables into a large bowl. Sprinkle with salt and pepper.

5. Using a potato masher or fork, mash the potatoes and parsnips. Add in the butter and half and half and mix well.
6. Garnish with fresh herbs (e.g. parsley, chives, rosemary) if desired.

Scalloped Potatoes
(Prep + Cook Time: 15 minutes | Servings: 6)

Ingredients:
- 6 peeled and thinly-sliced potatoes
- 1 cup chicken broth
- ⅓ cup milk
- ⅓ cup sour cream
- 2 tbsp potato starch
- 1 tbsp chopped chives
- 1 tsp salt
- Dash of pepper
- Dash of paprika

Directions:
- Pour the broth into your Instant Pot. Add chives, potatoes, salt, and pepper. Close and seal the lid.
- Select MANUAL and adjust time to 5 minutes on HIGH pressure.
- When time is up, turn off the cooker and use a quick release.
- Move the potatoes to a broiler-safe dish. Pour milk, sour cream, and potato starch into the liquid in your Instant Pot.
- Turn back to SAUTE and whisk for 1 minute.
- Pour everything over the potatoes and mix.
- Add paprika and cook under the broiler for a few minutes, until the top is brown.

Garlicky Mashed Potatoes (V)
(Prep + Cook Time: 20 minutes | Servings: 4)

Ingredients:
- 4 medium russet, yellow finn or yukon gold potatoes
- ¼ cup parsley, chopped
- ½ cup milk, non-dairy
- 1 cup vegetable broth
- 6 cloves garlic, peeled and cut in half
- Salt to taste

Directions:
1. Cut each potato into 8-12 chunks. Put into the Instant Pot.
2. Add the broth and the garlic.
3. Close and lock the lid. Select MANUAL and cook at HIGH pressure for 4 minutes.
4. When the timer beeps, use a quick release.
5. With a hand blender or a masher, mash the potatoes.
6. Depending on the consistency you want, add all the soymilk or just the amount you need.
7. Add salt to taste and then add the parsley, stir to combine. If desired, add pepper. Serve hot.

Coconut Butter Garlic New Potatoes (V, E&S)
(Prep + Cook Time: 10 minutes | Servings: 2)

Ingredients:
- 1.1 lb potatoes
- 3 tbsp coconut butter
- Handful fresh herbs
- Salt and pepper to taste
- 2/3 cup water

Directions:
1. Pour the water in the Instant Pot and set a steamer basket in the pot. Put the new potatoes in the steamer basket.
2. Add the fresh herbs, garlic, coconut butter, and a generous sprinkle of pepper and salt. Cover and lock the lid.
3. Press the MANUAL key, set the pressure to HIGH, and set the timer for 4 minutes. When the Instant Pot timer beeps, keep warm for 5 minutes. Quick release the pressure.
4. When the potatoes are cool enough, transfer into a serving bowl and remove the excess coconut butter mixture.
5. Serve with additional fresh herbs, such as rosemary, parsley, chives, or whatever you have on hand.

Dum Aloo (V)

(Prep + Cook Time: 35 minutes | Servings: 3-4)

Ingredients:

- 10 baby potatoes, peeled (if using large potatoes, then cube them to equal size)
- 2 tbsp ghee
- 1 onion, finely chopped
- 2 tsp ginger, grated
- 2 tsp garlic, grated
- 2 red tomatoes, pureed
- ½ tsp turmeric
- ½ - 1 tbsp kashmiri red chili powder or any other mild red chili powder
- ½ -1 tsp garam masala
- 1 tsp salt
- 8-10 cashews
- ¼ cup milk warm
- 1 tbsp dried fenugreek leaves
- Cilantro leaves chopped for garnish

Directions:

1. Soak cashews in warm milk for 10 minutes and set aside.
2. Set Instant Pot to SAUTE mode. Once the 'Hot' sign displays, add ghee. Add onions and cook for 2 minutes with a glass lid on, stirring few times.
3. Add ginger and garlic paste, cook for 30 seconds.
4. Add tomato paste, turmeric, red chili powder, garam masala and salt. Cook everything on SAUTE mode for 2 minutes, stirring a couple of times.
5. With a small spoon, very carefully fill the potatoes with the cooked masala/gravy and line them all in the Instant Pot insert.
6. Add 1/2 cup of water. Close the Instant Pot, select MANUAL and cook at HIGH pressure for 8 minutes. When time is up, quick release the pressure
7. Blend milk and cashews together to make smooth paste.
8. Stir in dried fenugreek leaves, cashew paste and chopped cilantro.
9. Set Instant Pot to SAUTE mode, mix everything together. Add salt to taste. Bring to gentle boil and then turn Instant Pot off.
10. Serve with hot parathas. Enjoy!

Potato Mini Cakes

(Prep + Cook Time: 30 minutes | Servings: 6)

Ingredients:
- 9 oz mashed potato
- 2 eggs
- 1 tbsp starch
- 1 onion
- 1 tbsp sour cream
- 1 tsp salt
- 4 oz scallions
- 1 tbsp olive oil
- 1/3 cup flour
- 1 tsp onion powder

Directions:
1. Place the mashed potato in the blender and add eggs. Blend the mixture until you get a smooth texture.
2. Transfer the potato mixture to the mixing bowl.
3. Chop the scallions and add in the mixture.
4. Then add flour, onion powder, salt, starch, and sour cream. Peel the onion and grate it.
5. Add the grated onion on the potato mixture.
6. Mix up the mixture and knead the soft non-sticky dough.
7. Make the medium balls from the potato mixture and flatten them well.
8. After this, pour the olive oil in the Instant Pot.
9. Add the potato mini cakes in the Instant Pot and SAUTE them for 3 minutes from the each side.
10. When all the potato mini cakes are cooked – let them a little chill and cut the dish into the strips.
11. Serve the dish immediately. Enjoy!

Instant Potatouille (V, E&F)

(Prep + Cook Time: 15 minutes | Servings: 6-8)

Ingredients:
- ½ cup water
- 8 ounces yellow crookneck squash
- 8 ounces zucchini
- 12 ounces Chinese eggplant or Japanese
- 1 orange bell pepper about 8 ounces
- 2-3 portobello mushrooms about 6 ounces
- ½ red onion chopped, about 6 ounces
- 24 ounces yukon gold potatoes about 1½ pounds
- 2 cans fire roasted tomatoes, 14.5 ounce cans
- ½ cup basil fresh, finely chopped into threads (chiffonade cut)

Directions:
1. Place all the ingredients except for the fresh basil in an 8 quart Instant Pot and cook at HIGH pressure for 10 minutes.
2. Quick release pressure and stir in the basil.
3. Serve with rice if desired. I enjoy adding 2 to 3 cups of cooked rice into the stew prior to serving. Enjoy!

Notes: This recipe was made in an 8 quart Instant Pot. If you don't have the 8 quart, cut the recipe in half.

Tempeh and Potato Coconut Curry
(Prep + Cook Time: 25 minutes | Servings: 4)

Ingredients:
- 1 package tempeh steamed
- ¾ cup yellow curry broth
- 2 cups onion sliced
- ½ tsp Ginger ground
- ¼ tsp turmeric
- 1 tsp cumin
- 3 cups potatoes diced
- 5,4 ounces coconut milk unsweetened
- Salt to taste
- Pepper to taste

Directions:
1. Press SAUTE and preheat the Instant Pot
2. In a covered Instant Pot (with a glass lid), heat about 1/4 cup of the yellow curry broth on medium to high heat.
3. Add onions, ginger, turmeric and cumin and sauté. Add potatoes and sauté a few minutes.
4. Crumble tempeh into tiny pieces (resembling ground meat), mix well, then add coconut milk.
5. Close the Instant Pot and Cook at LOW pressure for 4 minutes by using the MANUAL setting, adjusting pressure to Low, and setting cook time to 4 minutes.
6. When time is up, use a quick release.
7. Remove the lid and, uncovered, simmer until liquid is absorbed. Add salt and pepper (if desired). Enjoy!

Smokey Sweet Potato and Black Bean Chili (V)

(Prep + Cook Time: 25 minutes | Servings: 6)

Ingredients:
- 1 tbsp canola oil
- 2 onions finely diced
- 6 garlic cloves minced
- 2 red bell peppers chopped
- 2 tbsp chili powder
- 2 tsp ground cumin
- 1 tsp dried oregano
- ½ tsp chipotle chili powder or 1 chipotle chili, chopped, seeds removed
- 1½ cups broth or water
- 2 sweet potatoes peeled and cut into 2-inch dice
- 2 cups black beans soaked overnight or quick soaked and drained
- 3 cups tomatoes finely chopped fresh or canned, (1-28 ounce can)
- ¼ cup tomato paste
- ¼ tsp salt
- Cilantro chopped for garnish

Directions:
1. Heat the oil in the Instant Pot on SAUTÉ. Add the onions and cook for 3 minutes.
2. Add the garlic, red peppers and spices and cook another 2 minutes. Turn off SAUTÉ. Add the water and stir to be sure that none of the spices are stuck on the bottom of the pot.
3. Add the sweet potatoes and black beans. Close and lock the lid. Select MANUAL and cook at HIGH pressure for 8 minutes.
4. When 8 minutes is up let the pressure release naturally, this takes about 10 minutes or longer.
5. When the pressure is down, remove the lid.
6. Add the tomatoes and tomato paste and salt. Select SAUTÉ and cook at Low about 5 minutes until the tomatoes have broken down into a sauce.
7. Remove the whole chipotle pepper if you used it. Taste and adjust seasonings.
8. Serve over rice, or other grain, garnished with cilantro. Enjoy!

Potato Stew Mixed With Chard

(Prep + Cook Time: 10 minutes | Servings: 2)

Ingredients:

- 2 tbsp olive oil
- 1 tsp cumin seed
- 1 medium sized diced up onion
- 1 jalapeno pepper
- ½ tsp turmeric
- 1 tbsp peeled minced fresh ginger
- 1 tsp salt
- 2 medium sized sweet potatoes peeled up and cut into ½ a inch cubes
- 1 tsp ground coriander
- ¾ cup water
- 1 bunch Swiss chard
- 1 can unsweetened coconut milk
- ¼ cup finely chopped up fresh cilantro
- Lime wedges for serve

Directions:

1. Put your Instant Pot to SAUTE mode and pour some oil over medium heat.
2. Add the cumin seeds and wait until they are 'dancing' in the oil.
3. After 3 minutes, add the jalapeno, ginger, turmeric, salt, sweet potatoes and cook it for another 3 minutes while stirring it.
4. Add the coriander now and keep stirring it until it has a nice fragrance.
5. Pour in some water and a bit salt followed by the coconut milk, chard.
6. Close up the lid and lock it up. Let it cook for 3 minutes at HIGH pressure keeping the heat at HIGH.
7. Once done, wait for a while and quickly release the pressure.
8. Take the dish out from the pot and serve with some cilantro, decorate it with lime wedges.

Sweet Potato Spinach Curry with Chickpeas

(Prep + Cook Time: 20 minutes | Servings: 2)

Ingredients:

- 1 small can of drained chickpeas
- 1 ½ cups chopped sweet potatoes
- 3 chopped garlic cloves
- 2 cups chopped fresh spinach
- 1½ cups water
- 2 chopped tomatoes
- ½ chopped red onion
- ½-inch thumb of ginger, chopped
- 1 tsp olive oil
- 1 tsp coriander powder
- ½ tsp garam masala
- ¼ tsp cinnamon
- Salt and pepper to taste
- Squeeze of lemon

Directions:

1. Pour oil in your Instant Pot and heat on SAUTE.
2. When the oil is hot, add the ginger, onion, and garlic.
3. When the onions are clear, add the spices and mix. After 30 seconds, add tomatoes and mix to coat everything.
4. Add sweet potatoes, chickpeas, 1½ cups water, and a dash of salt. Close and seal the lid. Select MANUAL and cook at HIGH pressure for 8-10 minutes.
5. When time is up, press CANCEL and do a natural pressure release.
6. Add the fresh spinach and stir so the heat wilts the leaves.
7. Taste and season more if necessary. Serve with a squirt of fresh lemon.

Sweet Potato Chili (V)

(Prep + Cook Time: 35 minutes | Servings: 4)

Ingredients:

- 2 cups veggie broth
- 1 medium-sized peeled and chopped sweet potato
- One 28 oz can of diced tomatoes with liquid
- 1 15 oz can rinsed and drained kidney beans
- 1 15 oz can rinsed and drained black beans
- 4 minced garlic cloves
- 1 chopped green bell pepper
- 1 chopped red bell pepper
- 1 chopped red onion
- 1 tbsp olive oil
- 1 tbsp chili powder
- 2 tsp unsweetened cocoa powder
- 1 tsp ground cumin
- 1 tsp cayenne pepper
- ¼ tsp ground cinnamon
- Sea salt and pepper to taste

Directions:

1. Select SAUTE and preheat the Instant Pot. Add oil.
2. When shiny, add bell peppers, sweet potato, and onion.
3. Cook while stirring until the onions begin to turn clear.
4. Add all the spices and beans, broth, and tomatoes. Stir.
5. Close and seal the lid. Select MANUAL and cook at HIGH pressure for 10 minutes.
6. When time is up, press CANCEL and wait for a natural pressure release.
7. When the pressure is gone, open the cooker. The potatoes should be fork-tender.
8. Taste and season more if necessary before serving.

Sweet Potatoes (V, E&S)

(Prep + Cook Time: 25 minutes | Servings: 6)

Ingredients:
- 6 sweet potatoes, medium-sized (about 4-5 oz each)
- 2 cups water

Directions:
1. Wash the sweet potatoes clean and prick.
2. Pour 2 cups of water into the Instant Pot and put the steamer rack.
3. Layer the sweet potatoes on the rack.
4. Close and lock the lid. Press the MANUAL, set the pressure to HIGH, and the timer to 10 minutes.
5. When the timer beeps, turn the valve to Venting for quick pressure release.
6. Let the sweet potatoes cool and serve or store in an airtight container for up to 5 days.

Notes: If you are using large-sized sweet potatoes, set the timer to 12-15 minutes.

Steamed Broccoli (V)

(Prep + Cook Time: 10 minutes | Servings: 2)

Ingredients:
- 2-3 cups broccoli florets
- ¼ cup water
- A bowl with ice and cold water
- Salt and pepper to taste

Directions:
1. Pour the water into the Instant Pot.
2. Put the steamer basket in the pot. Place the broccoli in the steamer.
3. Press MANUAL, set the pressure to HIGH, and the timer to 0 minutes.
4. Prepare the bowl with iced water.
5. When the timer beeps after the end of the cooking cycle, immediately open the valve to quick pressure release.
6. Remove the steamer basket and then put the broccoli in the ice bath to stop cooking and helps keep the broccoli's bright green color.
7. Serve seasoned with salt and pepper.

Garlicky Broccoli (V)

(Prep + Cook Time: 20 minutes | Servings: 4)

Ingredients:
- 1-2 heads broccoli (about 0.8 pound), cut into 2-4 cups florets
- ½ cup water
- 6 garlic cloves, minced
- 1 tbsp peanut oil
- Fine sea salt, roughly 1/8-1/4 tsp, to taste
- 1 tbsp rice wine, optional
- Bowl with ice and cold water

Directions:
1. Pour 1/2 cup of water into the Instant Pot and put the steamer rack in the pot.
2. Put the broccoli florets on the steamer rack. Close and lock the lid. Set the PRESSURE to LOW and the timer to 0 minutes.
3. When the timer beeps, turn the steamer valve to Venting. Carefully open the lid.
4. Immediately put the broccoli florets in the ice bath or put them under running cold water to stop cooking.
5. Drain and set aside to air dry. Pour out the hot water from the pot and dry.
6. Select SAUTE and preheat the Instant pot. Add 1 tablespoon peanut oil, coating the whole bottom of the pot.
7. Add the minced garlic and sauté for about 25 to 30 seconds; do not let the garlic burn.
8. Add the broccoli florets and, if using, the rice wine; stir for 30 seconds.
9. Season with salt to taste and stir for 30 second more. Serve.

Broccoli Salad

(Prep + Cook Time: 25 minutes | Servings: 6)

Ingredients:
- 1 white onion
- 1-pound broccoli
- ½ cup chicken stock
- 1 tbsp salt
- 1 tsp olive oil
- 1 tsp garlic powder
- 3 tbsp raisins
- 2 tbsp walnuts, crushed
- 1 tsp oregano
- 1 tbsp lemon juice
- Bowl with ice and cold water

Directions:
1. Wash the broccoli carefully and separate it into the small florets.

2. Place the broccoli florets in the Instant Pot and sprinkle them with the salt.
3. Close and lock the lid. Select MANUAL and cook vegetables at HIGH pressure for 10 minutes.
4. Then toss the broccoli into the ice water immediately to save the bright color.
5. Transfer the chilled broccoli in the serving bowl.
6. Peel the onion and slice it. Add the sliced onion in the broccoli.
7. Sprinkle the mixture with the garlic powder, oregano, crushed walnuts, raisins, and lemon juice.
8. Add olive oil and stir the mixture gently to not damage the ingredients of the salad. Serve it!

Tofu, Kale, and Sweet Potato (V)
(Prep + Cook Time: 15 minutes | Servings: 4)

Ingredients:
- 1 peeled and cut sweet potato
- 2 cups sliced kale leaves (stems and ribs removed)
- 8 oz cubed tofu
- 1 chopped onion
- 2 minced garlic cloves
- ¼-½ cup veggie broth
- 1-3 tsp tamari
- 1 tsp ground ginger
- ½ tsp ground cayenne
- 1 tsp olive oil
- Squeeze of lemon juice

Directions:
1. After prepping your ingredients, turn your Instant Pot to SAUTE and add oil.
2. When hot, sauté the tofu for a minute. Mix in the tamari with a few tablespoons of broth. Stir for a minute.
3. Add sweet potatoes, onion, garlic, and the rest of the broth. Select MANUAL and cook at HIGH pressure for 2 minutes.
4. When time is up, press CANCEL and quick-release the pressure.
5. Add the kale, select MANUAL and cook at HIGH pressure for another 1 minute. Use a quick-release.
6. Serve with a splash of fresh lemon.

Coconut Tofu Curry (V, E&S)

(Prep + Cook Time: 35 minutes | Servings: 4)

Ingredients:
- 10 fluid oz coconut milk, full-fat
- 1 tbsp curry powder
- 2 tbsp peanut butter
- 1 tbsp garam masala
- 2 cups cubed green bell pepper
- 2 tsp salt
- 8 oz tomato paste
- 1 cup cubed onion
- 2 tsp mince garlic
- 1 cup diced tofu, firm

Directions:
1. In a food processor or blender place all the ingredients except tofu and pulse until smooth.
2. Place tofu in a 6 quarts Instant Pot and then top with prepared sauce.
3. Close the lid, select MAUAL and cook at HIGH pressure for 4 minutes. Instant Pot will take 10 minutes to build pressure before cooking timer starts.
4. When the timer beeps, switch off the Instant Pot and use a quick pressure release.
5. Uncover pot and stir. Serve immediately.

Vegan Italian Tofu Scramble (V, E&S)

(Prep + Cook Time: 5 minutes | Servings: 4)

Ingredients:
- 1 block of extra firm tofu
- 1 can Italian-style diced tomatoes
- ¼ cup veggie broth
- 2 tbsp jarred banana pepper rings
- 1 tbsp Italian seasoning

Directions:
1. Crumble the tofu in your Instant Pot, and pour over broth, add banana peppers, can of diced tomatoes, and Italian seasoning.
2. Mix well and seal the lid.
3. Select MANUAL and cook at HIGH pressure for 4 minutes.
4. When the timer beeps, press CANCEL and quick release the pressure. Stir and serve!

BBQ Tofu (V)

(Prep + Cook Time: 15 minutes | Servings: 6)

Ingredients:

- Two, 14 oz packages of extra-firm tofu
- One, 12 oz bottle of your favorite BBQ sauce
- 4 peeled and minced garlic cloves
- 1 chopped onion
- 1 cored, seeded, and chopped red bell pepper
- 1 cored, seeded, and chopped green bell pepper
- 1 diced celery stalk
- 2 tbsp olive oil
- Pinch of curry powder

Directions:

1. Turn your Instant Pot on to the SAUTE function and add oil.
2. Add garlic, bell peppers, celery, and onion.
3. Season with curry powder and salt. Cook for just 2 minutes.
4. Add tofu and stir for 5 minutes. Pour in the BBQ sauce.
5. Close and seal the lid. Press MANUAL and adjust time to 2 minutes on HIGH pressure.
6. When time is up, press CANCEL and quick release the pressure. Serve tofu with rice or another side.

Ratatouille (V)

(Prep + Cook Time: 30 minutes | Servings: 8)

Ingredients:

- 4 small zucchini, sliced thin
- 2 small eggplants, peeled and then sliced thin
- 1 can (28 oz) crushed tomatoes
- 1 jar (12 oz) roasted red peppers, drained and sliced
- 1 medium onion, sliced thin
- 1 tbsp olive oil
- 1 tsp salt
- 2 cloves garlic, crushed
- ½ cup water

Directions:

1. With the slicing disk of a food processor, prepare the zucchini, eggplant, and onion.
2. Alternatively, you can slice them thin by hand. Press the SAUTE button of the Instant Pot.
3. Put the olive oil and heat until shimmering.

4. Add the vegetables and sauté for 3 minutes or until they start to soften.
5. Season with the salt and then add the crushed tomatoes and the water; stir to combine.
6. Close and lock the lid. Select MANUAL and cook at HIGH pressure for 4 minutes.
7. When the timer beeps, turn the steam valve to quick release the pressure.
8. Serve immediately. If there are any leftovers, you can store in the refrigerator for up to 5 days.

Maple Mustard Brussels Sprouts

(Prep + Cook Time: 25 minutes | Servings: 8)

Ingredients:
- 16 Brussels sprouts, medium or large-sized (about 1-2 inch diameter), cut into halves or into quarters to make 3 cups total
- 1 ½-2 tbsp Dijon mustard
- 1 tsp olive oil
- ½ cup onion, diced
- ½ cup vegetable stock OR water
- ½-1 tbsp maple syrup
- 2 tsp pure sesame OR sunflower oil, optional
- Salt and freshly ground black pepper

Directions:
1. Set the Instant Pot to SAUTE. Pour the oil in the pot.
2. Add onion and sauté for about 1-2 minutes or until starting to soften.
3. In a glass jar or in a jar, whisk the stock with the mustard. Set aside.
4. Add the Brussels sprouts and then the stock mix in the pot.
5. Stir to coat and then drizzle the maple syrup over the veggies without stirring. Close and lock the lid. Select MANUAL and cook at LOW pressure for 3 minutes.
6. When the timer beeps, turn the steam valve to Venting for quick pressure release. Carefully unlock and open the lid.
7. Transfer the sprouts into a bowl.
8. If desired, season to taste with salt and pepper.

Notes: If you are using small sprouts, do not cut them into halves. The cooking time indicated for this recipe cooks the sprouts al dente. If you want then softer, cook them for 1-2 minutes more.

Brussels Sprouts (V, E&S)

(Prep + Cook Time: 5 minutes | Servings: 4)

Ingredients:

- 1 pound Brussels sprouts
- ¼ cup pine nuts
- Salt and pepper to taste
- Olive oil
- 1 cup water

Directions:

1. Pour the water into the Instant Pot. Set the steamer basket.
2. Put the Brussels sprouts into the steamer basket.
3. Close and lock the lid. Press the MANUAL button. Set the pressure to HIGH and set the time to 3 minutes.
4. When the timer beeps, turn the valve to Venting to quick release the pressure.
5. Transfer the Brussels sprouts into a serving plate, season with olive oil, salt, pepper, and sprinkle with the pine nuts.

Steamed Artichokes (V)

(Prep + Cook Time: 45 minutes | Servings: 4)

Ingredients:

- 2 medium-sized whole artichokes (about 5 ½ oz each)
- 1 lemon wedge
- 1 cup water

Directions:

1. Rinse the artichokes clean and remove any damaged outer leaves.
2. With a sharp knife, trim off the stem and top third of each artichoke carefully. Rub the cut top with a lemon wedge to prevent browning.
3. Pour 1 cup of water into the Instant Pot and set the steamer basket or rack. Pout the artichokes on the steamer/rack.
4. Select MANUAL and cook at HIGH pressure for 20 minutes.
5. When the timer beeps, press CANCEL to turn off the warming function. Let the pressure release naturally for 10 minutes.
6. Open the lid and with tongs, remove the artichokes from the pot.
7. Serve warm with your dipping sauce of choice.

Notes: If cooking larger artichokes, set the timer to 25 minutes and if cooking smaller artichokes, set the timer to 15 minutes.

Breakfast Kale (V)

(Prep + Cook Time: 10 minutes | Servings: 4)

Ingredients:
- 10 oz kale
- 2 tsp vinegar, your favorite flavored

For the faux parmesan cheese:
- 1 cup raw cashews
- ½ cup nutritional yeast
- 1 tbsp salt-free seasoning (I used Benson's)
- ½ cup water

Directions:
1. Fill the Instant Pot container with washed and chopped kale.
2. Pour the water. Close and lock the lid. Select MANUAL and cook at HIGH pressure for 4 minutes.
3. Meanwhile, put all the faux Parmesan ingredients into a food processor. Process until the mixture is powdery. If you prefer it chunkier, process less.
4. When the timer beeps, use a quick release and carefully open the lid. Transfer the kale in a serving plate.
5. Pour about 2 teaspoons of your favorite flavored vinegar.
6. Top with the faux parmesan. Serve over cooked brown rice or with a small potato.

Polenta with Honey and Pine Nuts

(Prep + Cook Time: 25 minutes | Servings: 6)

Ingredients:
- 5 cups water
- 1 cup polenta
- ½ cup heavy cream
- ½ cup honey
- ¼ cup pine nuts
- Salt to taste

Directions:
1. Mix pine nuts and honey with water in your Instant Pot.
2. Turn on the SAUTE function and bring to a boil while stirring.
3. Mix in polenta. Close and seal lid. Select MANUAL and adjust time to 12 minutes.
4. When time is up, press CANCEL and quick release the pressure.
5. Mix in cream and wait 1 minute before serving with a sprinkle of salt.

Polenta with Fresh Herbs (V)

(Prep + Cook Time: 20 minutes | Servings: 6)

Ingredients:

- 4 cups veggie broth
- 1 cup coarse-ground polenta
- ½ cup minced onion
- 1 bay leaf
- 3 tbsp fresh, chopped basil
- 2 tbsp fresh, chopped Italian parsley
- 2 tsp fresh, chopped oregano
- 2 tsp minced garlic
- 1 tsp fresh, chopped rosemary
- 1 tsp salt

Directions:

1. Select SAUTE and preheat your Instant Pot. Dry sauté the onion for about a minute.
2. Add the minced garlic and cook for one more minute.
3. Pour the broth, along with the oregano, rosemary, bay leaf, salt, half the basil, and half the parsley. Stir.
4. Sprinkle the polenta in the pot, but don't stir. Close and seal the lid.
5. Select MANUAL and cook at HIGH pressure for 5 minutes.
6. When the timer beeps, press CANCEL and wait 10 minutes.
7. Pick out the bay leaf. Using a whisk, stir the polenta to smooth it.
8. If it's thin, simmer on the SAUTE setting until it reaches the consistency you like.
9. Season to taste with salt and pepper before serving.

Pumpkin Puree (V, E&S)

(Prep + Cook Time: 30 minutes | Servings: 6)

Ingredients:

- 2 pounds small-sized sugar pumpkin or pie pumpkin, halved and seeds scooped out
- ½ cup water

Directions:

1. Pour the water into the Instant Pot and set the steamer rack.
2. Put the pumpkin halves on the rack. Set the pressure to HIGH and the timer to 13 or 15 minutes.

3. When the timer beeps, turn the valve to quick release the pressure. Let the pumpkin cool.
4. When cool enough, scoop out the flesh into a bowl.
5. Puree using an immersion blender or puree in a blender.

Notes: You can stir pumpkin into your oatmeal, use it to make a dessert, stir some with an applesauce for instant pumpkin applesauce, mix with softened butter with some sugar and spices like cinnamon, nutmeg, or cloves to make a compound butter for biscuits, blend it to make a creamy soup, and much more.

Carrot Puree (V, E&S)
(Prep + Cook Time: 25 minutes | Servings: 4)

Ingredients:

- 1 ½ pounds carrots, peeled and roughly chopped
- 1 tbsp soy butter, softened
- 1 tbsp honey
- ½ tsp salt
- 1 cup water
- Brown Sugar as needed for more sweetness

Directions:

1. Rinse peeled carrots, pat dry and then chop roughly into small pieces. Pour water and then insert a steamer basket in the Instant Pot.
2. Place chopped carrots into the basket and secure pot with lid.
3. Select MANUAL and cook at HIGH pressure for 4 minutes.
4. When the timer beeps, switch off the Instant Pot and do a quick pressure release.
5. Then uncover the pot and transfer carrots to a food processor or blender.
6. Pulse until smooth and transfer puree to a bowl. Stir in honey, salt, and butter.
7. For more sweetness stir in brown sugar to taste and serve immediately.

Maple Glazed Carrots

(Prep + Cook Time: 40 minutes | Servings: 8)

Ingredients:
- 2 pounds carrots, peeled and then diagonally sliced into thick pieces
- ¼ cup raisins
- ½ cup water
- 1 tbsp maple syrup
- 1 tbsp butter
- Pepper to taste

Directions:
1. Wash the carrots. Peel them and then slice into thick diagonal pieces. Put the carrots into the Instant Pot.
2. Add the raisins and the water. Close and lock the lid. Set the PRESSURE to LOW and the timer to 3 or 4 minutes.
3. When the timer beeps, turn the valve to Venting to quick release the pressure.
4. Remove the carrots from the pot and strain. In the still warm Instant Pot bowl, melt the butter and the maple syrup.
5. Add the carrots and gently stir to coat. Sprinkle with pepper and serve.

Carrots with Pancetta, Butter, and Leeks

(Prep + Cook Time: 20 minutes | Servings: 4)

Ingredients:
- 1 pound baby carrots
- 4-ounces diced pancetta
- 1 sliced leek
- 2 cups water
- ¼ cup sweet white wine
- 2 tbsp chopped butter
- Black pepper to taste

Directions:
1. Select SAUTE and cook pancetta until crisp.
2. Add the white and green parts of the leek and wait for 1 minute. Pour the wine and deglaze the pot.
3. Add carrots and a dash of pepper before stirring.
4. Pour pot contents into a 1-quart baking dish. Add the butter.
5. Put a piece of parchment paper on top of the dish followed by foil, which you should seal over the dish.
6. Carefully wipe out the inner pot and add 2 cups of water. Lower in a trivet and then put the dish on top. Seal the lid.
7. Select MANUAL and cook at HIGH pressure for 7 minutes.
8. When time is up, quick-release the pressure.
9. Carefully take out the dish and stir before serving.

Steamed Carrot Flowers (V)

(Prep + Cook Time: 15 minutes | Servings: 4)

Ingredients:
- 1 pound thick carrots, peeled
- 1 cup water

Directions:
1. With a sharp knife, cut 4-5 long groves along the carrot body.
2. Cut the carrots into coins, which now makes them into flowers. Put the carrot flowers in the steaming basket.
3. Pour 1 cup of water into the Instant Pot, then put the steamer basket in the pot.
4. Close and lock the lid. Set the pressure to LOW and the timer to 4 minutes. When the timer beeps, quick release the pressure.
5. Carefully remove the steamer basket from the pot.
6. Transfer the carrot flowers into a serving dish.
7. Serve naked or without seasoning or dressing or at least taste them before drizzling with a bit of olive oil and pinch of salt.

Wrapped Carrot with Bacon

(Prep + Cook Time: 25 minutes | Servings: 8)

Ingredients:
- 1-pound carrot
- 9 oz bacon
- 1 tsp salt
- ½ tsp ground black pepper
- 1 tsp ground white pepper
- 1 tsp paprika
- ¼ cup chicken stock
- 1 tbsp olive oil
- ¼ tsp marjoram

Directions:
1. Wash the carrot carefully and peel it. Sprinkle the carrot with the ground black pepper.
2. Combine the salt, ground white pepper, paprika, and marjoram together. Stir the mixture.
3. Slice the bacon. Then combine the sliced bacon and spice mixture together. Stir it carefully.
4. Then wrap the carrot in the sliced bacon.
5. Pour the olive oil in the Instant Pot and add wrapped carrot. Close the lid and SAUTE the carrot for 10 minutes.
6. Then add the chicken stock, close and lock the lid. Select MANUAL and cook at HIGH pressure for 8 minutes more.
7. When the time is over – quick release the remaining pressure and open the lid. Chill the carrot little. Enjoy!

Zucchini and Mushrooms (V)

(Prep + Cook Time: 20 minutes | Servings: 6)

Ingredients:

- 8-12 oz mushrooms, sliced or separated depending on type of mushroom
- 4 medium zucchini, cut into ½-inch slices (about 8 cups)
- 1 can (15 ounce) crushed or diced tomatoes with juice
- 1 large sprig fresh basil, sliced
- 1 tbsp extra-virgin olive oil
- ½ tsp black pepper, or to taste
- ½ tsp salt, or to taste
- 2 cloves garlic, minced
- 1½ cups onions, diced

Directions:

1. Press the SAUTE button of the Instant Pot. Add the olive oil and heat.
2. Add the garlic, onions, and mushrooms; cook, frequently stirring, until the onions are soft and the mushrooms lose their moisture.
3. Add the basil and sprinkle with the salt and pepper. Sauté for 5 minutes until the mushrooms are soft.
4. Add the zucchini, stir. Add the tomatoes with the juices over the zucchini; do not stir.
5. Close and lock the lid. Press the MANUAL button. Set the pressure to LOW and the timer to 1 minute.
6. When the timer beeps, turn the steam valve to quick release the pressure. Carefully remove the cover.
7. If the zucchini are still a little undercooked, just cover the pot and let rest for 1 minutes to allow the zucchinis to soften.
8. Serve over pasta, rice, baked potatoes, or polenta. If desired, you can stir a can of white beans.

Mushroom Gravy (V)

(Prep + Cook Time: 45 minutes | Servings: 4)

Ingredients:

- 2 tbsp olive oil
- 8 oz sliced white mushrooms
- 4 tbsp all-purpose flour
- 4 tbsp vegan butter
- 2 fluid ounce vegetable broth
- 2 fluid ounce almond milk
- 22 fluid ounce water

Directions:

1. Select SAUTE and preheat the Instant Pot. Add olive oil.
2. Then add mushrooms and cook for 5-7 minutes or until nicely golden brown.
3. Pour in broth and continue cooking until mushrooms turn into dark color.
4. Press CANCEL, then pour the water and stir until just mixed. Close and lock the lid, select MANUAL and cook at HIGH pressure for 5 minutes.
5. Instant Pot will take 10 minutes to build pressure before cooking timer starts.
6. When the timer beeps, switch off the Instant Pot and let pressure release naturally for 10 minutes and then do quick pressure release.
7. Then uncover the pot, drain mushrooms and return to the pot, reserve broth.
8. Place a medium-sized saucepan over medium heat, add butter and let heat until melt completely.
9. Then gradually stir in flour and then slowly whisk in reserved broth until combined.
10. Pour in milk, stir in mushrooms and bring the mixture to simmer, whisk occasionally.
11. Simmer mixture for 8 minutes until gravy reaches desired thickness and then ladle into serving platters. Serve immediately.

Citrus Cauliflower Salad (V)

(Prep + Cook Time: 20 minutes | Servings: 4)

Ingredients:
- Florets from 1 small cauliflower
- Florets from 1 small Romanesco cauliflower
- 1 pound broccoli
- 2 peeled and sliced seedless oranges
- 1 zested and squeezed orange
- 1 sliced hot pepper
- 4 tbsp olive oil
- 1 tbsp capers (not rinsed)
- Salt to taste
- Pepper to taste

Directions:
1. Pour 1 cup of water into your Instant Pot. Add florets into your steamer basket and lower in the cooker.
2. Close and lock the lid. Press STEAM and cook for 6 minutes.
3. While that cooks, make your vinaigrette. Mix the orange juice, zest, hot pepper, capers, olive oil, salt, and pepper. Peel your oranges and slice very thin.
4. When the timer beeps, press CANCEL and quick release the pressure.
5. Mix florets with oranges and dress with the vinaigrette.

Kale with Lemon and Garlic (V)

(Prep + Cook Time: 15 minutes | Servings: 4)

Ingredients:
- 1 pound kale, cleaned and then stems trimmed
- 1 tbsp olive oil
- ½ cup water
- ½ lemon, juiced
- ½ tsp kosher salt
- 3 cloves garlic, slivered
- Freshly ground black pepper

Directions:
1. Set the Instant Pot to SAUTE. Pour in the oil and stir in the garlic.
2. Heat the oil for about 2 minutes or until the garlic is just fragrant.

3. Stir a big handful of kale into the oil and garlic and then start packing the remaining kale into the pot. The pot will be filled. Don't worry because the kale will quickly wilt – just pack the kale enough to close the pot lid. Sprinkle with salt and then pour water over the top of everything.
4. Close and lock the lid. Set the PRESSURE to HIGH and cook for 5 minutes.
5. When the timer beeps, turn the steam release valve to quick release the pressure. Carefully remove the lid.
6. While still in the pot, squeeze the lemon juice over the kale and stir in the freshly ground pepper.
7. With a tong or a slotted spoon, scoop out the kale from the pot, leaving as much liquid as possible in the pot. Serve.

Sweet and Sour Spicy Savoy (V)
(Prep + Cook Time: 15 minutes | Servings: 4)

Ingredients:
- 2 tbsp peanut oil
- 1 tbsp shallots, diced
- ½ cup leeks, sliced
- 2 cloves garlic, crushed and minced
- 1 tbsp fresh grated ginger
- 2 tsp crushed red pepper flakes
- 1 head savoy cabbage, sliced
- 1 cup vegetable stock
- ¼ cup rice vinegar
- ¼ cup brown sugar
- 1 tbsp soy sauce
- 1 tbsp garlic chili paste

Directions:
1. Place the peanut oil in the Instant Pot and turn on the SAUTE setting.
2. Add in the shallots, leeks, garlic, ginger and crushed red pepper flakes.
3. Sauté for 2 minutes, add the cabbage.
4. In a large bowl combine the vegetable stock, rice vinegar, brown sugar, soy sauce and garlic chili paste.
5. Mix well and pour into the pressure cooker.
6. Cover and lock the lid. Select MANUAL and cook at HIGH pressure for 3 minutes.
7. Use the natural release method to release the steam from the pressure cooker before serving.

Stuffed Eggplant (V)

(Prep + Cook Time: 20 minutes | Servings: 4)

Ingredients:

- 2 eggplants
- 6 tbsp lentils, cooked
- 8-10 cherry tomatoes, softened
- ½ white onion, diced
- ½ tsp salt
- 1 tbsp paprika
- 1 green pepper
- 1 green chili
- Few sprigs mint and parsley
- 1 cup water

Directions:

1. Pour 1 cup of water and place the steam rack in the Instant Pot.
2. Put the eggplant and the green pepper on the steam rack.
3. Close and lock the lid, select MANUAL and cook at HIGH pressure for 4 minutes.
4. Meanwhile, dice the onions and sauté until soft. If you have caramelized onions on hand, then feel free to use it instead.
5. Mix in the onions with the lentils. Set aside.
6. When the timer beeps, quick release the pressure. Carefully open the pot and take out the eggplants and the green peppers.
7. Carefully slice the eggplant lengthwise into halves. Scoop out the meat. Cut the eggplant meat into smaller pieces.
8. Cut the green peppers, cherry tomatoes, green chili into smaller pieces.
9. Mix the eggplant with the green peppers and season with salt and paprika. Into the hollowed out eggplants, scoop the lentils, dividing equally between the 4 halves.
10. Add the eggplant mix on top of the lentil layer.
11. Top with the herbs, softened cherry tomatoes, and, is using, feta cheese. Serve.

Eggplant with Carrots, Tomatoes, and Bell Peppers (V)
(Prep + Cook Time: 30 minutes | Servings: 4)

Ingredients:
- 1 eggplant, chopped
- 1 onion, chopped
- 2 bell peppers (1 green, 1 red), deseeded and chopped
- 1-2 tomatoes, chopped
- 2 carrots, peeled and chopped
- 1-2 fresh garlic cloves
- Salt and pepper to taste
- Olive oil, for sautéing

Directions:
1. Prepare all the vegetables and chop them. You can use a vegetable chopper to do this.
2. Set the Instant Pot to SAUTE. Grease the bottom of the inner pot with olive oil. Add the onions, carrots, and tomatoes.
3. Sauté until slightly browned. Add the eggplant.
4. Add the tomato sauce and then the garlic, salt and pepper.
5. Press CANCEL to stop SAUTE function. Close and lock the lid.
6. Select MANUAL and cook at HIGH pressure for 10 minutes.
7. When the timer beeps, quick release the pressure.
8. Serve and enjoy.

Corn Cob (V, E&S)
(Prep + Cook Time: 15 minutes | Servings: 6)

Ingredients:
- 6 ears corn
- 1 cup water, for the pot

Directions:
1. Shuck the corn and then cut off the pointy ends. Pour the water into the Instant Pot and then put the steamer basket inside.
2. Layer up to 6 ears, arranging them in a crisscross pattern in the steamer basket. Close and lock the lid.
3. Press MANUAL, set the pressure to HIGH, and set the timer to 3 minutes.
4. When the timer beeps, open the valve and use a quick release.
5. Remove the corn from the steamer basket.
6. Top your corn with salt, butter, or your choice of toppings.

Five Spice Eggplant (V, E&S)

(Prep + Cook Time: 15 minutes | Servings: 4)

Ingredients:

- 2 tbsp coconut oil
- 4 cups eggplant, peeled and cubed
- 2 cups fresh spinach, torn
- 1 tsp salt
- 1 tsp black pepper
- 1 tbsp five spice powder
- 1 cup vegetable stock
- ½ cup coconut milk
- Fresh scallions for garnish

Directions:

1. Place the coconut oil in the Instant Pot and set to the SAUTE setting.
2. Add the eggplant and sauté for 1-2 minutes.
3. Add in the spinach and season with salt, black pepper and five spice powder.
4. Pour in the vegetable stock and coconut milk. Mix well.
5. Cover and lock the lid. Set PRESSURE to HIGH and cook for 4 minutes.
6. Use the natural release method to release the steam from the pressure cooker.
7. Garnish with fresh scallions before serving.

Spice-Rubbed Cauliflower Steaks (V)

(Prep + Cook Time: 25 minutes | Servings: 4)

Ingredients:

- 1 large head cauliflower about 2 pounds
- 2 tbsp extra-virgin olive oil
- 2 tsp paprika
- 2 tsp ground cumin
- ¾ tsp kosher salt
- 1 cup cilantro fresh, chopped
- 1 lemon quartered

Directions:

1. Insert the steam rack into the Instant Pot. Add 1½ cups of water.
2. Remove the leaves from the cauliflower and trim the core so the cauliflower sits flat. Place on the steam rack.
3. In a small bowl, combine the olive oil, paprika, cumin, and salt. Drizzle over the cauliflower and rub to coat.

4. Lock the lid. Select MANUAL and cook at HIGH pressure for 4 minutes. Use the quick release method to vent the steam, then open the lid.
5. Lift the cauliflower onto a cutting board and slice into 1-inch-thick steaks. Divide among plates and sprinkle with the cilantro.
6. Serve with the lemon quarters. Enjoy!

Beets with Blue Cheese

(Prep + Cook Time: 35 minutes | Servings: 6)

Ingredients:

- 6 beets (about 1½ pounds)
- ¼ cup crumbled blue cheese
- ½ tsp kosher salt
- ½ tsp fresh ground black pepper
- 1 cup water, for the pot

Directions:

1. Trim the leaves from the beets, making sure not to cut the root off or into the beet. Rinse and remove any dirt.
2. Pour the water into the Instant Pot and set a steam rack. Put the beets on the rack. Close and lock the lid.
3. Press PRESSURE, set the pressure to HIGH, and set the time for 20 minutes.
4. When the timer beeps, turn the valve for quick pressure release. If you have time, you can let the pressure go down naturally.
5. Carefully open the lid and transfer the beets onto a cutting board.
6. Let them cool down for 1-2 minutes. Using a paper towel, peel off the skin and then pull off the roots.
7. Cut the beets into halves, then into quarters.
8. Sprinkle them with salt and pepper, then transfer into a serving bowl. Top with the crumbled cheese and serve.

Vegetable Pasta Salad

(Prep + Cook Time: 25 minutes | Servings: 10)

Ingredients:

- 8 oz pasta
- 3 cups vegetable stock
- 1 cup bread crumbs
- ½ cup cream cheese
- 3 medium cucumbers
- 1 tsp oregano
- ½ cup spinach
- 2 tomatoes
- 1 red onion
- 1 tsp paprika

Directions:

1. Put the pasta in the Instant Pot and add vegetable stock. Close the lid and cook the pasta at HIGH pressure on the MANUAL mode for 10 minutes.
2. Then rinse the pasta with the hot water. Place the cooked pasta in the mixing bowl.
3. Peel the red onion and slice it. Wash the spinach carefully and chop it. Chop the tomatoes and cucumbers.
4. Add the sliced onion, chopped spinach, tomatoes, and cucumbers in the pasta bowl.
5. Sprinkle the salad with the oregano and paprika.
6. Add cream cheese. Mix up the mixture until you get homogenous mass.
7. Then add bread crumbs and stir the salad.
8. Serve it immediately.

Wheat Berry Balsamic Basil Salad (V)

(Prep + Cook Time: 45 minutes | Servings: 6)

Ingredients:

For the wheat berries:

- 1½ cups wheat berries (hard red winter wheat kernels)
- 1 pinch salt
- 4 cups water
- 1 tbsp olive oil

For the salad:

- 1 cup grape tomatoes, halved
- 1 large handful fresh basil, chopped
- 1 large handful fresh parsley, chopped
- 1 tbsp balsamic vinegar
- 1 tbsp olive oil
- ½ cup Kalamata olives, chopped
- 1-2 green onions, chopped
- 1-2 oz feta cheese

Directions:
1. Set the Instant Pot to SAUTE. Pour in the olive oil and heat.
2. When the oil is hot, add the wheat berries and cook for about 5 minutes on medium sauté, stirring frequently until the wheat berries are fragrant.
3. Pour the water and add the salt. Press CANCEL. Close and lock the lid. Press the MANUAL button. Set the pressure to HIGH and the timer to 30 minutes.
4. When the timer beeps, let the pressure release naturally for 10 minutes. Turn the steam valve to release any remaining pressure. Open the lid.
5. Drain the wheat berries in a colander. Rinse under running cold water to cool and transfer in a large-sized bowl.
6. Toss the wheat berries with the remaining ingredients (for the salad) and season to taste with salt and pepper.

Spinach Potato Taco Filling
(Prep + Cook Time: 25 minutes | Servings: 6)

Ingredients:
- 2 Yukon gold potatoes, large-sized, cut into small dice
- 1 package (8 oz) frozen spinach
- 1 medium onion, diced
- ½ cup diced chipotles tomatoes, plus
- ½ cup tomato juice from can
- 2 tsp garlic granules
- 2 tsp ground cumin
- ½ cup nondairy milk, unsweetened, unflavored
- 1/3 cup water
- 3 tbsp nutritional yeast
- Sea salt and freshly ground black pepper
- 12 corn tortillas, for serving

Directions:
1. Put the potatoes, 1/2 bag frozen spinach, cilantro, 1/2 cup chipotle tomatoes with 1/2 of its juice, spices, and season with salt and pepper to taste.
2. Add 1/3 cup water. Close and lock the lid. Select MANUAL and cook at HIGH pressure for 2 minutes.
3. When the timer beeps, use a quick release.
4. There will be excess liquid in the pot. Press SAUTE mode and cook until the excess liquid off.
5. Add the milk and yeast. Cook until thick.
6. Serve with corn tortillas or tortilla chips or nachos.

Caramelized Onion (V)

(Prep + Cook Time: 50 minutes | Cup: 1)

Ingredients:
- 3 tbsp unsalted butter
- 3 large onions, halved and then sliced into 1/8-inch pieces
- ½ tsp kosher salt
- ¼ cup water

Directions:
1. Press the SAUTE button of the Instant Pot.
2. Add the butter and melt.
3. Add the onions and while sautéing, sprinkle with the salt. Occasionally stirring, sauté for 8 minutes or until the onions are soft and slightly browned.
4. Add the water and close the lid. Press the MANUAL button. Set the pressure to HIGH and set the timer to 20 minutes.
5. When the timer beeps, use a quick release. Press SAUTE and constantly stir the onions for about 5-8 minutes to reduce any liquid.
6. Let cool completely and store in an airtight container. Keep in the fridge for up to 1 week.

Notes: Caramelized onions add great flavor and texture in salads, burgers, deli-style sandwiches, pizza, tart, pasta dishes, dips, quiche, or frittatas, and base for French onion soup.

Spaghetti Squash (V)

(Prep + Cook Time: 20 minutes | Servings: 4)

Ingredients:
- 1 whole winter squash
- 8 fluid oz water, chilled

Directions:
1. Cut squash in half lengthwise and remove and discard seeds using a spoon.
2. In the Instant Pot pour water and then insert a steamer basket.
3. Place squash halves in the steamer and secure pot with lid. Select MANUAL and cook at HIGH pressure for 7 minutes.
4. When the timer beeps, use a quick release.
5. Then uncover the pot, transfer squash from the pot and gently pull of the flesh from the skin as strands using a fork.
6. Serve squash spaghetti immediately with your favorite main dish or sauce.

Sweet and Sour Red Cabbage (V, E&S)

(Prep + Cook Time: 35 minutes | Servings: 4)

Ingredients:

For the sauté ingredients:

- 4 cloves garlic, minced
- ½ cup onion, minced
- 1 tbsp mild oil, OR use broth for oil-free

For the Instant Pot:

- 1 cup water
- 1 cup applesauce
- 1 tbsp apple cider vinegar
- 6 cups cabbage, chopped
- Salt and pepper to taste

Directions:

1. Press the SAUTE key of the Instant Pot and select the Normal option for medium heat.
2. Add the oil/ broth into the pot. Add the onion and sauté until they become transparent. Add the garlic and sauté for 1 minute.
3. Add the Instant Pot ingredients. Press the CANCEL key to stop the SAUTÉ function. Cover and lock the lid. Press the MANUAL key, set the pressure to HIGH, and set the timer for 10 minutes.
4. When the Instant Pot timer beeps, press the CANCEL key. Use a quick release.
5. Unlock and carefully open the lid. Serve.

Barbecue Cabbage Sandwiches

(Prep + Cook Time: 25 minutes | Servings: 6)

Ingredients:

- 1 head cabbage cored, chopped
- 1 small yellow onion thinly sliced
- 2½ cups barbecue sauce
- 6 buns whole wheat or gluten free, paleo buns work too for dietary restrictions

Directions:

1. Press SAUTÉ function to heat inner pot.
2. When display reads "Hot", add 2 tablespoons of water to the bottom of the inner pot.
3. Add cabbage and onion; sauté until cabbage begins to soften, about 4 minutes.
4. Stir in barbecue sauce, continue cooking until sauce is heated through, about 3 minutes.
5. Press CANCEL to stop SAUTÉ function.
6. Toast buns then fill with a heap of barbecue cabbage. Serve hot. Enjoy!

Border Corn with Squash and Zucchini (V, E&S)

(Prep + Cook Time: 20 minutes | Servings: 4)

Ingredients:

- 2 tbsp olive oil
- 1 cup red onion, diced
- 1 tbsp jalapeno pepper, diced
- 4 cups fresh corn kernels
- 1 cup red bell pepper diced
- 1 cup summer squash, cubed
- 1 cup zucchini, cubed
- 2 cups tomatoes, diced
- 1 tsp salt
- 1 tsp black pepper
- 1 tsp cumin
- ¼ cup fresh cilantro, chopped
- 1½ cups vegetable stock

Directions:
1. Place the olive oil in the Instant Pot and turn on the SAUTE setting.
2. Add in the red onion and jalapeno pepper. Sauté for 2 minutes.
3. Add in the corn kernels, red bell pepper, summer squash, zucchini and tomatoes.
4. Mix well and then season with salt, black pepper, cumin and cilantro.
5. Pour in the vegetable stock.
6. Cover and lock the lid. Set the pressure to LOW and cook for 5 minutes.
7. Use the natural release method to release the steam from the Instant Pot.

Boiled Peanuts (V)

(Prep + Cook Time: 1 hour 20 minutes | Servings: 4)

Ingredients:
- 1 pound large raw peanuts
- ¼ - ½ cup sea salt
- Water

Optional:
- 2 tsp Cajun seasoning with garlic, jalapeno peppers, etc.
- 1 tbsp BBQ seasoning
- 1 tsp sugar

Directions:
1. Rinse the peanuts under running cool water.
2. Remove any roots, twigs, or material that does not belong. Put into the Instant Pot. Add the salt and add enough water to cover.
3. Put a trivet on to hold the peanuts down. Close and lock the lid. Select MANUAL and cook at HIGH pressure for 70 minutes.
4. When the timer beeps, let the pressure release naturally and let sit for 30 minutes.
5. If the peanuts are still too hard for your liking, just cook more.

Easy Seitan Roast Server (V)

(Prep + Cook Time: 30 minutes | Servings: 4)

Ingredients:

- 1½ cups vital wheat gluten
- 1 cup veggie broth
- ⅓ cup tapioca flour
- 3 tbsp nutritional yeast
- 2 tbsp coconut aminos (or soy sauce)
- 1 tbsp olive oil
- 1 tbsp vegan Worcestershire sauce
- 1 tsp garlic powder
- ½ tsp dried thyme
- ½ tsp dried rosemary
- ¼ tsp black pepper
- ¼ tsp sea salt
- 3 cups veggie broth
- 2 cups water
- ¼ cup coconut aminos
- 2 tbsp vegan Worcestershire
- 1 tsp onion powder

Directions:

1. Let's start with the first list of ingredients. Whisk all the dry ingredients together.
2. In a separate bowl, mix the wet ones. Pour the wet into the dry. Fold first with a spoon, and then knead by hand for a few minutes.
3. Form into a round shape, pulling at the top, and then rolling under so it's smooth. Shape into a more oblong loaf and roll tightly in cheesecloth, tying off the ends.
4. Put the roast in your Instant Pot. Pour in all the ingredients in the second ingredient list. Lock and seal the lid.
5. Select MANUAL and cook at HIGH pressure for 25 minutes.
6. When time is up, press CANCEL and wait 10 minutes before quick-releasing the pressure.
7. Slice and serve!

Notes: When you slice seitan, it should have a meaty texture - not too soft, and not too chewy.

Steamed Asparagus (V)

(Prep + Cook Time: 25 minutes | Servings: 4)

Ingredients:
- 1 pound asparagus, cleaned and 1-inch snapped from the woody, tough stalk
- 1 cup water
- 1 tbsp onion, diced
- 2 tbsp olive oil
- Mediterranean sea salt
- Freshly milled pepper

Directions:
1. Pour the water into the Instant Pot and then put the steamer rack. Put the asparagus on the rack.
2. Drizzle with the olive oil and sprinkle with the onion. Close and lock the lid.
3. Press STEAM and set the timer to 2 minutes.
4. When the timer beeps, turn the valve to quick release the pressure.
5. Transfer the asparagus into a serving plate.
6. Sprinkle with salt and pepper.

Sesame Bok Choy

(Prep + Cook Time: 5 minutes | Servings: 4)

Ingredients:
- 1 medium head of bok choy (with leaves separated)
- 1 cup water
- 2 tsp sesame seeds
- 1 tsp soy sauce
- ½ tsp sesame oil
- Salt and pepper to taste

Directions:
1. Pour water in the Instant Pot and place the steamer basket into the pot. Stack leaves, with the thickest leaves on the bottom. Close and seal the lid.
2. Select MANUAL and cook at HIGH pressure for 4 minutes.
3. When time is up, turn off cooker and use a quick release.
4. Move the bok choy to a bowl and dress with the sesame oil, sesame seeds, and soy sauce.
5. Season to taste with salt and pepper.

Rice Pudding

(Prep + Cook Time: 30 minutes | Servings: 6)

Ingredients:

- 1 cup basmati rice
- ¾ cup heavy cream OR coconut cream
- 2 cups milk, your choice (soaked nut milk OR raw milk)
- 1/8 tsp sea salt
- ¼ cup maple syrup
- 1 vanilla bean scrapings OR 1 tsp vanilla extract
- 1¼ cups water

Directions:

1. Put the rice in a fine mesh colander.
2. Rinse well with several changes of water. Transfer into the Instant Pot.
3. Add the milk, water, sea salt, and maple syrup in the pot. Briefly stir. Cover and lock the lid.
4. Press the PORRIDGE key and let cook on preset time of 20 minutes.
5. When the Instant Pot timer beeps, press the CANCEL key and unplug the Instant Pot. Let the pressure release naturally for 10-15 minutes or until the valve drops. Unlock and carefully open the lid.
6. Add the cream and the vanilla.
7. Stir well until mixed. Serve with optional toppings.

Notes: You can top this rice pudding with berry jam, cream, dates, raisins, nuts, cinnamon, maple syrup, chocolate chips, and butter. This dessert is best served while still warm, but you can pour it into individual mason jars, top with choice of topping, and pack into lunch boxes.

Pumpkin Pudding

(Prep + Cook Time: 50 minutes | Servings: 6)

Ingredients:

For the pumpkin pudding:

- ¾ cup pumpkin, packed OR pumpkin puree, homemade, well-drained
- 2 tsp gelatin, sustainably-sourced
- ¼ tsp ground cloves
- ½ tsp sea salt
- ½ tsp ground nutmeg
- ½ tsp ground ginger
- ½ tsp allspice
- ½ cup coconut sugar
- ½ cup coconut milk OR raw milk
- 1 tsp ground cinnamon
- 1 egg, pastured
- 1 cup water

For the coconut-ginger glaze:

- ¾ cup coconut cream, at room temperature
- 1/16 tsp stevia
- 1 tsp ground ginger

Directions:

1. Pour the milk into a saucepan. Sprinkle with the gelatin. Turn on the heat to medium-low to gently heat.
2. Whisk to dissolve the gelatin and then remove from heat. In a medium-sized mixing bowl, combine the milk-gelatin, coconut sugar, pumpkin, egg, salt, and spices.
3. Whisk until smooth. Pour the milk-gelatin mix into a well-greased 3-cup jello mold, soufflé dish, mini bundt pan, or bowl.
4. Place a trivet in the Instant Pot and pour in 1 cup of water. Put the mold/ pan/ dish/ bowl on the trivet. Cover and lock the lid.
5. Press the MANUAL key, set the pressure to HIGH, and set the timer for 30 minutes.
6. When the Instant Pot timer beeps, press the CANCEL key and unplug the Instant Pot. Use a quick release.

7. Unlock and carefully open the lid. Carefully remove the mold/ pan/ dish/ bowl from the pot and let cool to room temperature – do not disturb while it cools.
8. When cool, put the mold/ dish/ bowl in the fridge and chill for about 4-6 hours or until completely set.
9. When chilled, run a butter knife around the edge of the pudding and turn over onto a cake stand or a plate.
10. In a small-sized bowl, combine the glaze ingredients until smooth.
11. Drizzle over the pudding. If desired, garnish with crispy walnuts. Enjoy!

White-Chocolate Lemon Pudding
(Prep + Cook Time: 40 minutes | Servings: 6)

Ingredients:
- 6-ounces of chopped white chocolate
- 4 whisked egg yolks
- 1 cup heavy cream
- 1 cup half-and-half
- 1 tbsp white sugar
- 1 tbsp finely-grated lemon zest
- ¼ tsp lemon extract
- 2 cups water

Directions:
1. Pour half-and-half and cream into a stovetop saucepan and heat until tiny bubbles appear on the edges.
2. Quickly pour over white chocolate in a bowl, and whisk until smooth. Add in whisked egg yolks, lemon extract, lemon zest, and sugar.
3. Pour liquid pudding into six, ½-cup ramekins that are pressure-cooker safe, and wrap tightly in foil.
4. Pour 2 cups of water into the Instant Pot and place the steamer basket, with the ramekins inside it, and not stacked right on top of each other. Close and lock the lid.
5. Select MANUAL and cook at HIGH pressure for 15 minutes.
6. When the timer beeps, use a natural pressure release.
7. Unwrap the ramekins and let them rest on a cooling rack before eating.
8. For a chilled pudding, store in the fridge for no longer than 3 days.

Apple Crisp (V)

(Prep + Cook Time: 15 minutes | Servings: 4)

Ingredients:

- 5 medium sized apples, peeled and then chopped into chunks
- 4 tbsp butter
- ¾ cup old fashioned rolled oats
- 2 tsp cinnamon
- ¼ cup flour
- ¼ cup brown sugar
- ½ tsp salt
- ½ tsp nutmeg
- ½ cup water
- 1 tbsp maple syrup

Directions:

1. Put the apples into the bottom of the Instant Pot. Sprinkle with nutmeg and cinnamon.
2. Pour in the water and drizzle with the maple syrup.
3. Melt the butter. In a small-sized bowl, mix the butter with the flour, oats, brown sugar, and salt.
4. By spoonful, drop the mix on top of the apples.
5. Close the lid of the pot and make sure the valve is closed. Set to MANUAL, the pressure to HIGH, and the timer to 8 minutes.
6. When the timer beeps, let the pressure release naturally and let sit for a couple of minutes to allow the sauce to thicken.
7. Serve as a warm breakfast.

Baked Apples (V)

(Prep + Cook Time: 40 minutes | Servings: 6)

Ingredients:

- 6 apples
- 4 oz white sugar
- 1 tsp cinnamon powder
- 1 oz raisins
- 8 oz red wine

Directions:

1. Rinse and core apple and place in a 6-quarts Instant Pot. Sprinkle with sugar, cinnamon, and add raisins and red wine.
2. Secure pot with lid, then position pressure indicator, select MANUAL option and cook at HIGH pressure for 10 minutes.
3. When the timer beeps, switch off the Instant Pot and let pressure release naturally for 10 minutes and then do quick pressure release.
4. Then uncover the pot and scoop out apples.
5. Serve apples with the cooking liquid.

Cranberry Apple Steel Cut Oats

(Prep + Cook Time: 50 minutes | Servings: 6)

Ingredients:

- 1 ½ cup fresh cranberries (dried cranberries or cherries)
- 1 cup yogurt (or 1 cup milk or part whey)
- 1 tsp fresh lemon juice
- ½ tsp nutmeg
- ½ tsp salt
- ¼ cup maple syrup
- 1-2 tsp cinnamon
- 2 cups steel cut oats
- 2-4 tbsp butter and/ or virgin coconut oil
- 3 cups water
- 4 apples, diced (or 1-2 cups applesauce)
- 2 cups milk
- 2 tsp vanilla (optional)

Directions:

1. Grease the bottom of the Instant Pot container with butter/ oil.
2. Except for the salt, maple syrup, and vanilla, put the rest of the ingredients into the pot; let soak overnight.
3. In the morning, add the salt, maple syrup, and, if using, vanilla; Press the PORRIDGE button and cook for about 35-40 minutes. Be sure to close the valve.
4. When the timer beeps, turn the steam valve to quick release the pressure.
5. Serve with your favorite milk.

Notes: The Instant Pot will automatically switch to warm and naturally release the pressure when the timer beeps.

Apple Dumplings

(Prep + Cook Time: 35 minutes | Servings: 6)

Ingredients:
- 8-ounces crescent rolls
- 1 big peeled and cored green apple cut into 8 wedges
- 4 tbsp butter
- ¾ cup apple cider
- ½ cup brown sugar
- 1 tsp ground cinnamon
- ½ tsp vanilla extract
- Pinch of ground nutmeg

Directions:
1. Turn your Instant Pot to SAUTE.
2. Roll the crescent dough out flat, and wrap around the apple wedges, so one wedge gets one roll. Add butter to your cooker and press CANCEL.
3. Mix in vanilla, brown sugar, cinnamon, and nutmeg, and stir until the remaining heat melts everything together.
4. Put the dumplings in the cooker and pour over the cider. Close and seal the lid.
5. Select MANUAL and adjust time to 10 minutes on HIGH pressure.
6. When time is up, press CANCEL and use a natural release.
7. Remove the dumplings and let them cool for a few minutes.
8. Serve with the cider syrup from the pot poured on top.

Lemon-Ruby Pears (V)

(Prep + Cook Time: 40 minutes | Servings: 4)

Ingredients:
- 4 ripe Bosc pears
- 3 cups grape juice
- 1 cup currant jelly
- 1 lemon
- ½ split vanilla bean

Directions:
1. Remove the core from the pears, but leave the top of the pear and stem intact.
2. Pour grape juice and jelly into the Instant Pot.
3. Press SAUTE and heat until jelly melts.
4. Grate the lemon into the pot, and then squeeze the juice, as well. Add vanilla bean.
5. Cut out four squares of foil, to wrap your pears in. Before wrapping, turn the pears in the cooker sauce.

6. Wrap pears in foil tightly and put in your steamer basket. Insert basket into cooker.
7. Seal the lid. Press MANUAL and cook at HIGH pressure for 11 minutes.
8. When the timer beeps, press CANCEL and quick-release the pressure.
9. Unwrap the pears, put in a baking dish, and pour over sauce.
10. Wait till pears are room temperature before storing them in the fridge overnight and then serve!

Stewed Pears (V)
(Prep + Cook Time: 40 minutes | Servings: 6)

Ingredients:
- 6 pears, peeled
- 16 oz brown sugar
- 1 tsp ground cinnamon
- 1 tsp ginger powder
- 4 whole cloves
- 1 bay leaf
- ½ cup basil leaves
- 26 oz red wine

Directions:
1. Pour red wine in the Instant Pot and stir with cinnamon, ginger, cloves and bay leaf. Add pears and secure pot with lid.
2. Select MANUAL and cook at HIGH pressure for 4 minutes.
3. When the timer beeps, switch off the Instant Pot and let pressure release naturally for 10 minutes and then do quick pressure release.
4. Then uncover the pot and pull out pears and set aside. Turn on the pressure cooker, select SAUTE and simmer cooking liquid or until reduced to one-third of the actual amount.
5. Drizzle pears with this cooking liquid, sprinkle with basil and serve.

Stuffed Peaches (V)

(Prep + Cook Time: 35 minutes | Servings: 6)

Ingredients:
- 5 peaches, organic, medium-sized OR 6 peaches, small-sized
- 2 tbsp butter, grass-fed
- ¼ tsp pure almond extract
- ¼ cup maple sugar, sucanat, mascobado
- ¼ cup cassava flour (I used Otto's)
- ½ tsp ground cinnamon
- Pinch Celtic sea salt

For the Instant Pot:
- ¼ tsp pure almond extract
- 1 cup water

Directions:
1. Slice ¼-inch off from the top of the peaches; discard the cut off top.
2. With a sharp paring knife, cut around the pits and remove them so the peaches are hollowed out – leave at least ½-inch of flesh from the skin so they stay intact.
3. If the peaches are very firm, use a spoon to help loosen and scoop out the pit and the flesh around it. Set aside.
4. In a shallow dish or a mixing bowl, put the cassava flour, your choice of unrefined sweetener, cinnamon, butter, sea salt, and almond extract.
5. Using clean hands, mix until the mixture is crumbly. Fill the hollowed peaches with the crumble mix until full.
6. Put a trivet in the Instant Pot and pour 1 cup of water.
7. Add the almond extract. Carefully put the filled peaches onto the trivet. Cover and lock the lid.
8. Press the MANUAL button, set the pressure to HIGH, and set the timer for 3 minutes.
9. When the Instant Pot timer beeps, press the CANCEL button and unplug the Instant Pot. Use a quick release. Unlock and carefully open the lid.
10. Carefully lift and remove the trivet and put in a dish.
11. Let the peaches rest and cool for about 10 minutes.
12. Serve with vanilla ice cream.

Notes: Use firm peaches and not overripe ones.

Tapioca Pudding (V)

(Prep + Cook Time: 30 minutes | Servings: 4)

Ingredients:

- 1¼ cups almond milk
- ½ cup water
- ⅓ cup sugar
- ½ split vanilla bean
- ⅓ cup seed tapioca pearls

Directions:

1. Rinse tapioca pearls. Pour 1 cup of water into your Instant Pot.
2. In a bowl (safe for pressure cooker), add tapioca, water, milk, sugar, and vanilla and mix.
3. Place the steamer basket into the pot.
4. When the sugar has dissolved, place the bowl in the steamer basket.
5. Select MANUAL and cook at HIGH pressure for 8 minutes.
6. When time is up, press CANCEL and use a natural release. This will take about 15 minutes. When pressure is released, wait 5 minutes before opening the lid. Stir.
7. Serve warm or cool in a fridge (covered with cling wrap) for at least 3 hours.

Chai Rice Pudding

(Prep + Cook Time: 45 minutes | Servings: 8)

Ingredients:

- 5 cups 1% milk
- 1½ cups Arborio rice
- 1 cup raisins
- 1 cup half-and-half
- 2 eggs
- ¾ cup sugar
- 1 ½ tsp pure vanilla extract
- ¾ tsp ground cinnamon
- ½ tsp ground cardamom
- ½ tsp ground allspice
- ½ tsp salt

Directions:

1. Mix rice, sugar, milk, and salt in your Instant Pot.
2. Turn on to the SAUTE setting and stir until it comes to a boil and the sugar has dissolved. Once the liquid is boiling, immediately seal the lid.
3. Select MANUAL and cook at LOW pressure for 16 minutes.
4. In the meantime, whisk vanilla, eggs, and half-and-half.
5. Once cooking is complete, use a natural release for 10 minutes, before quick-releasing.
6. Stir the rice before adding half-and-half mixture. Select SAUTE and cook until it begins to boil again.
7. Turn off the cooker right away, add raisins and chai spices and stir. Serve right away or chill in the fridge until cold.

One Step Arroz Pina Colada

(Prep + Cook Time: 25 minutes | Servings: 8)

Ingredients:
- 1 cup Arborio rice
- 1½ cups water
- 1 cup condensed milk add more for a sweeter taste
- 1 can coconut milk full fat, divided, 14 ounce can
- 2/3 cup pineapple crushed, in juice
- 1 tbsp cinnamon

Directions:
1. Combine water and rice in the Instant Pot.
2. Select MANUAL and cook at LOW pressure for 12 minutes.
3. When time is up, quickly release the pressure and add the condensed milk, half of the coconut milk, cinnamon and the can of pineapple with juice. Mix well and taste.
4. Let the pudding cool for a bit and absorb all the liquid, swelling and thickening as it does so.
5. Use the remaining half a can of coconut milk to thin the pudding to your taste after it has cooled.
6. Serve and enjoy!

Pina Colada Rice Pudding

(Prep + Cook Time: 35 minutes | Servings: 8)

Ingredients:
- 1 cup Arborio rice
- 1½ cups water
- 1 tbsp coconut oil
- ¼ tsp salt
- 1 can coconut milk, 14 ounce can
- ½ cup sugar
- 2 eggs
- ½ cup milk
- ½ tsp vanilla extract
- 1 can pineapple crushed, well drained and cut in half, 8-ounce can

Directions:
1. In the Instant Pot, combine rice, water, oil, and salt. Lock the lid. Select MANUAL and cook at HIGH pressure for 3 minutes.
2. When beep sounds turn off pressure cooker and use a natural pressure release for 10 minutes. After 10 minutes, release any remaining pressure with a quick pressure release.

3. Add coconut milk and sugar to rice in pressure cooking pot; stir to combine.
4. In a small mixing bowl, whisk eggs with milk and vanilla. Pour through a fine mesh strainer into pressure cooking pot.
5. Select SAUTÉ and cook, stirring constantly, until mixture just starts to boil. Turn off pressure cooker. Stir in pineapple tidbits.
6. Pour into serving dishes and chill. Pudding will thicken as it cools.
7. Served topped with whipped cream, toasted coconut, and a maraschino cherry if desired. Enjoy!

Blueberry Pudding
(Prep + Cook Time: 55 minutes | Servings: 4)

Ingredients:
- ½ pound blueberries
- 1 cup flour
- 1 beaten egg
- 5 ounces milk
- ½ cup white sugar
- ½ cup butter, cubed ½-inch
- 2 ½ tbsp breadcrumbs
- 1 ½ tsp baking powder
- ½ tsp salt
- Hot water as needed

Directions:
1. Grease a 4-6 cup pudding basin, or baking dish. In a large bowl, sift the baking powder, salt, and flour. Add the butter.
2. Mix in the breadcrumbs and sugar.
3. Add milk and egg, blending together, before adding blueberries.
4. Pour into your baking dish ¾ of the way full.
5. Cover the top of the dish with a piece of buttered parchment paper, tying with some kitchen string so it stays secured.
6. The paper should have a little pleat in it, so when the pudding rises, it has room.
7. Pour 2-inches worth of hot water in your Instant Pot. Place the trivet in the pot.
8. Put the dish on top and close - not seal - the lid. You're going to just STEAM the pudding for 15 minutes.
9. When that time has passed, now seal the lid.
10. Select MANUAL and cook at HIGH pressure for 35 minutes.
11. When time is up, press CANCEL and quick-release.
12. Take out the pudding and cool for a few minutes before inverting on a plate.

Pumpkin-Spice Brown Rice Pudding with Dates (V)

(Prep + Cook Time: 65 minutes | Servings: 6)

Ingredients:

- 3 cups almond milk
- 1 cup pumpkin puree
- 1 cup brown rice
- 1 stick cinnamon
- ½ cup maple syrup
- ½ cup water
- ½ cup chopped pitted dates
- 1 tsp vanilla extract
- 1 tsp pumpkin spice
- ⅛ tsp salt

Directions:

1. Pour boiling water over your rice and wait at least 10 minutes. Rinse.
2. Pour milk and water in your Instant Pot.
3. Turn on cooker to SAUTE and when boiling, add rice, cinnamon, salt, and dates.
4. Close and lock the lid. Select MANUAL and cook at HIGH pressure for 10 minutes.
5. Once pressure cooking is complete, use a natural release. This will take about 15 minutes. Open the lid.
6. Add pumpkin puree, maple syrup, and pumpkin spice.
7. Select SAUTE and stir for 3-5 minutes until thick. Turn off cooker.
8. Pick out cinnamon stick and add vanilla. Move pudding to a bowl and cover in plastic wrap, so the plastic touches the top.
9. Wait 30 minutes to cool. Serve warm or chilled.

Sticky Toffee

(Prep + Cook Time: 45 minutes | Servings: 8)

Ingredients:

- 1¼ cups finely-chopped dates
- 1¼ cups flour
- 1 egg
- ¾ cup brown sugar
- ¾ cup boiling water
- ⅓ cup room temperature butter
- ¼ cup blackstrap molasses
- 1 tsp baking powder
- 1 tsp vanilla extract
- ¼ tsp salt
- 2 cups water

Caramel Sauce:

- ⅔ cup packed dark brown sugar
- ⅓ cup whipping cream
- ¼ cup butter
- 1 tsp vanilla extract

Directions:

1. Grease 8 ramekins. In a bowl, mix boiling water, molasses, and dates, and wait to cool.
2. In a separate bowl, mix baking powder, flour, and salt.
3. Cream brown sugar and butter with a mixer till fluffy. Add eggs and vanilla, and mix.
4. Divide batter into ramekins. Wrap ramekins tightly with buttered foil.
5. Pour 2 cups of water into your Instant Pot and lower in the rack. Put the ramekins on the rack.
6. They can stack on top of each other, but not directly on top. Close and lock the lid.
7. Select MANUAL and cook at HIGH pressure for 25 minutes.
8. While the pudding cooks, make caramel sauce by mixing brown sugar, butter, cream, and vanilla in a saucepan.
9. Bring to a boil, stirring, so the sugar dissolves. Reduce heat and simmer for 5 minutes.
10. Remove from heat when thickened.
11. When the pudding is done, press CANCEL and use a quick release.
12. Unwrap the ramekins and let the pudding cool a little before serving with the caramel sauce on top.

Tapioca with Fresh Berries (V)
(Prep + Cook Time: 20 minutes | Servings: 4)

Ingredients:
- 2 cups almond milk
- 2 cups fresh berries
- ½ cup small pearl tapioca
- ¼ cup organic sugar
- 1 tsp pure vanilla

Directions:
1. Rinse tapioca under cold water for half a minute.
2. Pour milk into the Instant Pot, and then add the tapioca.
3. Close and lock the lid. Select MANUAL and cook at HIGH pressure for 4 minutes.
4. When time is up, press CANCEL and wait 10 minutes before quick-releasing leftover pressure.
5. Mix in sugar and vanilla. To make it a parfait, spoon 2 tablespoons of berries in a glass, followed by tapioca, and then berries, and so on. Serve.

Simple Egg Custard
(Prep + Cook Time: 25 minutes | Servings: 6)

Ingredients:
- 6 big eggs
- 4 cups milk
- ¾ cup sugar
- 1 tsp vanilla extract
- ¼ tsp cinnamon
- Pinch of salt

Directions:
1. Mix the eggs in a bowl.
2. Add the salt, sugar, vanilla, and milk until just mixed. Pour into six ramekins and wrap in foil.
3. Poke a few holes in the foil. Pour 1½ cups of water into your Instant Pot and place the trivet. Put the ramekins on top of the trivet. Seal the lid.
4. Select MANUAL and cook for 7 minutes at HIGH pressure.
5. When time is up, press CANCEL and use a natural release. This will take about 10 minutes.
6. Then release any leftover pressure and let the custard cool for 2 minutes, unwrapped.
7. Dust with cinnamon before serving.

New York Cheesecake

(Prep + Cook Time: 55 minutes | Servings: 12)

Ingredients:

16 ounces cream cheese

15 Oreo cookies

1 tbsp vanilla

1 cup sugar

2 eggs

2 tbsp butter, melted

1 cup water

Equipment: 7-inch spring-form pan

Directions:

1. Put the Oreo cookies into a food processor and process until crumbled. Add the melted butter and stir.
2. Transfer the Oreo cookie mix into the spring-form pan and press into an even layer.
3. In a medium-sized to large-sized bowl, put the eggs, cream cheese, vanilla, and sugar; mix until creamy and smooth.
4. Transfer in the spring-form pan and spread into an even layer. Put a trivet in the Instant Pot and pour 1 cup of water.
5. Take a long piece of foil and fold it lengthwise to create a strip long enough to allow you to lower the cheesecake onto the trivet and retrieve it later when the cooking time is done. Using the foil sling, lower the pan onto the trivet. Cover and lock the lid.
6. Press the MANUAL key, set the pressure to HIGH, and set the timer for 40 minutes.
7. When the Instant Pot timer beeps, press the CANCEL and use a quick release. Unlock and carefully open the lid.
8. Using the foil sling, carefully remove the cheesecake from the pot. Chill for about 1 hour. Top with your favorite topping or fruits.

Cookies and Cream Cheesecake

(Prep + Cook Time: 70 minutes | Servings: 8)

Ingredients:
- 16 ounces cream cheese
- ¼ cup sour cream
- ½ cup sugar
- 1 tsp vanilla
- 1 bag of bite-sized Caco Chocolate sandwich cookies
- 2 eggs
- 2 tbsp butter, melted
- 1 cup water

Equipment: 7-inch springform pan

Directions:
1. Use a rolling pin or any other heavy tool to convert ½ your cookies into sweet crumbs.
2. Mix crumbled cookies with the melted butter and press the mixture into the springform pan.
3. Put the eggs, cream cheese, sugar, and sour cream into a mixer. Mix until well combined.
4. Crumble the remaining cookies and then add into the mixture.
5. Transfer the batter into the pan and spread into an even layer.
6. Cover the spring-form pan with unbleached parchment paper, top it with foil, and secure around the edges.
7. Put a trivet in the Instant Pot and pour 1 cup of water. Take a long piece of foil and fold it lengthwise to create a strip long enough to allow you to place the cheesecake onto the trivet and retrieve it later when the cooking time is done.
8. Using the foil sling, place the pan onto the trivet. Cover and lock the lid.
9. Press the MANUAL key, set the pressure to HIGH, and set the timer for 40 minutes.
10. When the Instant Pot timer beeps, press the CANCEL key and unplug the Instant Pot. Let the pressure release naturally for 10-15 minutes or until the valve drops. Unlock and carefully open the lid.
11. Using the foil sling, carefully remove the cheesecake from the pot.
12. Put on the counter and let cool completely. Slice and serve.

Chocolate Fondue with Coconut Cream (V)

(Prep + Cook Time: 5 minutes | Servings: 4)

Ingredients:
- 2 cups water
- 3.5 oz 70% dark bittersweet chocolate
- 3.5 oz coconut cream
- 1 tsp sugar

Directions:
1. Pour 2 cups of water into your Instant Pot and insert trivet.
2. In a heatproof bowl, add chocolate chunks.
3. Add coconut cream and sugar.
4. Put the bowl on top of the trivet. Close and seal the lid.
5. Select MANUAL and cook at HIGH pressure for 2 minutes.
6. When time is up, press CANCEL and use a quick release.
7. Carefully remove bowl and whisk with a fork until it becomes smooth. Serve!

Chocolate Zucchini Muffins

(Prep + Cook Time: 35 minutes | Servings: 24)

Ingredients:

- 1 cup water
- 1 cup flour
- 1 cup grated zucchini
- 2 eggs
- ¾-1 cup cane juice
- ½ cup coconut oil
- ⅓ cup chocolate chips
- 3 tbsp cocoa powder
- 1 tbsp melted butter
- 2 tsp pure vanilla extract
- ¾ tsp cinnamon
- ½ tsp baking soda
- ¼ tsp salt

Directions:

1. Mix cane juice, eggs, coconut oil, and vanilla.
2. In a separate bowl, mix melted butter with cocoa powder.
3. Add to the egg mixture and mix. Add dry ingredients (flour, baking soda, cinnamon, and salt). Add the chocolate chips and zucchini.
4. Pour 1 cup of water into your Instant Pot and lower the trivet.
5. Select SAUTE to preheat the pressure cooker.
6. Fill silicone muffin cups ⅔ of the way full with muffin batter. Put cups in the pressure cooker.
7. For the second layer, separate with a piece of parchment paper, foil, and another trivet.
8. Finish layering muffins, and cover again with parchment paper, foil, and then a plate. Close and seal the lid.
9. Select SAUTE and cook at HIGH pressure for 8 minutes.
10. Once cooking is complete, press CANCEL and wait 15 minutes. Then quick release any leftover pressure.
11. If a toothpick comes out clean from the muffins, they're ready!

Chocolate Custard

(Prep + Cook Time: 55 minutes | Servings: 6)

Ingredients:
- 13-ounces chopped dark chocolate
- 6 whisked egg yolks Just over
- 1 cup cream (1.2 cups)
- 1 cup whole milk
- ½ cup sugar
- 1 tsp vanilla extract

Directions:
1. In a saucepan, simmer milk, cream, vanilla, and sugar until sugar has dissolved.
2. Take the pan off the heat and add chocolate.
3. When melted, slowly add whisked egg yolks, being careful that they don't cook. Pour into an 7.2-8 -inch baking dish.
4. Pour 4 cups of water into your Instant Pot and insert trivet. Put the custard pan on the trivet and seal the lid.
5. Select MANUAL and cook at HIGH pressure for 30 minutes.
6. When time is up, press CANCEL and let the pressure release naturally for 10 minutes before quick-releasing.
7. The custard will have a wobbly center, like a jelly. Serve hot or cold.

Two-Ingredient Chocolate Fondue

(Prep + Cook Time: 5 minutes | Servings: 4)

Ingredients:
- 3.5-ounces of dark chocolate (minimum 70% cocoa)
- 3.5-ounces of cream

Directions:
1. Pour two cups of water into the Instant Pot and lower the trivet.
2. Put chocolate chunks in a ceramic, heat-proof container that fits into the pressure cooker, and pour over the cream.
3. Put into the Instant Pot. Close and lock the lid. Select MANUAL and cook at HIGH pressure for 2 minutes.
4. When time is up, press CANCEL and carefully quick release the pressure.
5. Open the lid and remove the container.
6. Whisk quickly until the chocolate becomes smooth.
7. Serve right away!

Chocolate-Chip Banana Cake

(Prep + Cook Time: 75 minutes | Servings: 6)

Ingredients:

- 1½ cups flour
- 2 eggs
- 2 ripe bananas
- ½ cup milk + 1 tbsp
- ⅔ cup water
- ⅓ cup dark chocolate chips
- ¼ cup honey
- 3 tbsp coconut oil
- 1 tbsp vinegar
- 1 tsp baking soda
- ½ tsp cinnamon
- ⅛ tsp ground nutmeg

Directions:

1. Grease the 3-cup Bundt Pan.
2. Pour vinegar into milk and let the bowl sit until the milk curdles and turns to buttermilk.
3. In a separate bowl, mix bananas, honey, vanilla, eggs, coconut oil, and nutmeg.
4. Add buttermilk. When combined, add the cinnamon, baking soda, and flour.
5. With a spatula, fold the chocolate chips into your batter.
6. Pour batter into your Bundt Pan.
7. Pour ⅔ cup of water into the Instant Pot and place the trivet. Put the Bundt Pan on top of the trivet. Close and seal the lid.
8. Select MANUAL and cook at HIGH pressure for 25 minutes.
9. Once cooking is complete, use a quick release. Take out the Bundt Pan and cool for 10 minutes.
10. Invert the cake and wait until fully cooled before serving.

Rich Chocolate Pudding

(Prep + Cook Time: 35 minutes | Servings: 6)

Ingredients:

- 1½ cups whipping cream
- 4 ounces bittersweet chocolate chopped
- 4 egg yolks
- 1/3 cup brown sugar packed
- 1 tbsp unsweetened cocoa powder
- 1 tsp Vanilla
- ¼ tsp salt
- 1½ cups water

Directions:

1. Heat cream to a simmer in medium saucepan over medium heat. Remove from heat. Add chocolate; stir until chocolate is melted and mixture is smooth.
2. Whisk egg yolks, brown sugar, cocoa, vanilla and salt in large bowl until well blended. Gradually add hot chocolate mixture, whisking constantly until blended.
3. Strain into 6- to 7-inch (1½ -quart) soufflé dish or round baking dish that fits inside Instant Pot. Cover dish tightly with foil.
4. Pour water into Instant Pot. Place soufflé dish on rack; lower into pot using handles of rack.
5. Close and lock the lid. Select MANUAL and cook at LOW pressure for 22 minutes.
6. When cooking is complete, use natural release for 5 minutes, then release remaining pressure.
7. Use handles of rack to remove dish from pot. Remove foil; cool to room temperature. Cover and refrigerate at least 3 hours or up to 2 days.

Apple Crumb Cake
(Prep + Cook Time: 55 minutes | Servings: 6)

Ingredients:
- 6 small red apples
- ¾ cup melted butter
- ½ cup sugar
- 1½ cups water
- ⅔ cup dry bread crumbs
- Juice and zest from ½ lemon
- 2 tbsp flour
- 1 tsp cinnamon
- 1 tsp ginger

Directions:
1. To make the filling, mix bread crumbs, sugar, cinnamon, melted butter, ginger, lemon juice, and lemon zest.
2. Core the apples, leaving the peels on, and slice very thin.
3. Grease your baking dish with butter and coat with a dusting flour. Lay down the apple slices in fan shapes.
4. Add a layer of the crumb filling, followed by apples, and keep going until everything is used up.

5. Wrap the dish tightly in foil. Pour 1½ cups of water into your Instant Pot and lower in the trivet.
6. Put the wrapped dish on top and seal the lid.
7. Select MANUAL and cook at HIGH pressure for 23 minutes.
8. Once cooking is complete, press CANCEL and wait 10 minutes before quick-releasing.
9. Take out the cake and remove the foil.
10. Flip the cake on a dish. To finish, sprinkle raw sugar on top and broil for just 3 minutes, or until the sugar caramelizes. Serve!

Mango Cake
(Prep + Cook Time: 50 minutes | Servings: 8)

Ingredients:
- 1¼ cups flour
- ¾ cup milk
- 1 cup water
- ½ cup sugar
- ¼ cup coconut oil
- 1 tbsp lemon juice
- 1 tsp mango syrup
- 1 tsp baking powder
- ¼ tsp baking soda
- ⅛ tsp salt

Directions:
1. Grease a baking pan that will fit in your Instant Pot.
2. Mix the sugar, oil, and milk in a bowl until the sugar has melted.
3. Pour in mango syrup and mix again.
4. Pour all the dry ingredients through a sieve into the wet.
5. Add lemon juice and mix well.
6. Pour into the baking pan.
7. Pour 1 cup of water into the Instant Pot and place a trivet in the pot.
8. Lower the baking pan into the cooker and close the lid.
9. Select MANUAL, and cook at HIGH pressure for 35 minutes.
10. When time is up, press CANCEL and let the pressure release naturally.
11. Check the cake for doneness before cooling for 10 minutes.
12. Serve!

Apple-Ricotta Cake

(Prep + Cook Time: 45 minutes | Servings: 6)

Ingredients:

- 2 cups water
- 1 cup ricotta cheese
- 1 cup flour
- 1 egg
- ¼ cup raw sugar
- ⅓ cup sugar
- 1 sliced apple
- 1 diced apple
- 3 tbsp olive oil
- 1 tbsp lemon juice
- 2 tsp baking powder
- 1 tsp baking soda
- 1 tsp vanilla extract
- ⅛ tsp cinnamon

Directions:

1. Pour water into your Instant Pot and lower in steamer basket or trivet.
2. Mix your diced and sliced apple in lemon juice.
3. Put a piece of wax paper on the bottom of a 4-cup baking dish (shallow and wide), and oil it, and then dust it with flour.
4. Sprinkle in raw sugar before laying down the apple slices. In a bowl, whisk ricotta, sugar, olive oil, vanilla, and egg.
5. Sift in the cinnamon, flour, baking soda, and baking powder. Stir in the diced apples and then pour into your baking dish. Seal the lid.
6. Select MANUAL and cook for 20 minutes at HIGH pressure.
7. When time is up, press CANCEL and wait 10 minutes before quick-releasing any leftover pressure.
8. To test for doneness, poke a toothpick in the middle.
9. If batter sticks to it, put back in the cooker and bake another 2 minutes under pressure.
10. To serve, chill or eat warm.

Vanilla Sponge Cake

(Prep + Cook Time: 1 hour 10 minutes | Servings: 6)

Ingredients:

- 1½ cups powdered sugar
- 2 room temperature eggs
- 1¼ cups flour
- ½ cup milk
- ½ cup canola oil
- 1½ tsp baking powder
- ¾ tsp vanilla extract

Directions:

1. Grease a 6-inch square pan with butter and a dusting of flour.

2. In a mixing bowl, beat eggs and sugar until frothy. Sift in the flour.
3. Add milk and canola oil, and blend. Last, add the vanilla and baking powder.
4. Turn your cooker to SAUTE and wait 10 minutes for the pot to warm up.
5. Fill the square pan with batter to the ½-way mark and put in the Instant Pot on top of the trivet.
6. You are not bringing the cooker to pressure, so you don't add water.
7. Remove the gasket (the silicone) ring from your pot's lid before putting it on the cooker (or use the glass lid).
8. Let the heat from the cooker "bake" the cake for 40 minutes.
9. Check the cake when that time is up.
10. A few crumbs on the toothpick is perfect.
11. Wait 10 minutes before removing the cake and serving.

Molten Lava Cake
(Prep + Cook Time: 25 minutes | Servings: 2)

Ingredients:
- ½ cup semi-sweet chocolate chips
- ¼ cup powdered sugar
- 4 tbsp room temperature butter
- 2 tbsp flour
- 1 room temperature egg
- 1 tsp vanilla extract
- 2 cups water

Directions:
1. Prep your Instant Pot with 2 cups of water and place the trivet.
2. Grease your cake mold/ ramekin with butter.
3. Melt the chocolate and mix in egg and vanilla, making sure the egg doesn't cook. Add in sugar and flour.
4. Fill your ramekin halfway-full and place on the trivet in the cooker. Close and seal the lid.
5. Select MANUAL and cook at HIGH pressure for 7 minutes.
6. When time is up, press CANCEL and wait for a natural pressure release. Serve and enjoy!

Cranberry-Pear Cake (V)

(Prep + Cook Time: 55 minutes | Servings: 6)

Ingredients:

- 1 cup chopped pears
- ½ cup fresh, chopped cranberries
- 1¼ cups whole-wheat flour
- ½ tsp baking soda
- ½ tsp baking powder
- ½ tsp ground cardamom
- ⅛ tsp salt
- ½ cup unsweetened almond milk
- ¼ cup agave syrup
- 2 tbsp applesauce
- 2 tbsp ground flax seeds
- 1½ cups water

Directions:

1. Grease a 7-inch Bundt pan.
2. Mix dry ingredients in a bowl. Mix wet ingredients (except water) in a separate bowl. Mix wet into dry before folding in pears and cranberries.
3. Pour batter into pan and wrap in foil.
4. Pour water into your Instant Pot and lower a trivet or a steamer basket, then place the pan.
5. Close and lock the lid. Select MANUAL and cook at HIGH pressure for 35 minutes.
6. When time is up, press CANCEL and let the pressure release naturally.
7. Take out the pan and throw away the foil.
8. Cool before serving.

Fudge Brownie for Four

(Prep + Cook Time: 45 minutes | Servings: 4)

Ingredients:

- 2 cups water
- 2 eggs
- 1 cup sugar
- ¾ cup flour
- ½ cup melted butter
- ¼ cup unsweetened cocoa powder
- 1 tbsp honey
- ¾ tsp baking powder
- ¼ tsp salt

Directions:

1. Mix melted butter with the cocoa powder.
2. In another bowl, mix the flour, sugar, salt, and baking powder.
3. Add honey, eggs, and the melted butter/ cocoa mix, making sure it has cooled a little, so it doesn't cook the eggs.
4. When the batter is mixed well, pour it into a greased 8-inch round pan.
5. Wrap completely in foil. Pour 2 cups of water into your Instant Pot and lower the trivet.
6. Put the wrapped brownie pan on top. Seal the lid.
7. Select MANUAL and cook at HIGH pressure for 35 minutes.
8. When time is up, press CANCEL and carefully quick release the pressure. Serve warm or chilled.

Raspberry Jam

(Prep + Cook Time: 30 minutes | Servings: 4 cups)

Ingredients:

- 2 pounds fresh raspberries
- 1½ pounds light honey.

Directions:

1. Pour raspberries and honey into your Instant Pot. Turn the cooker to the KEEP WARM setting and stir for 3 minutes until the honey has become liquid.
2. Turn to SAUTE and stir until the pot begins to boil. Close and seal the lid immediately. Select MANUAL and cook at HIGH pressure for 2 minutes.
3. When the timer beeps, press CANCEL and let the pressure release naturally.
4. Take the lid off and select SAUTÉ, bring the jam to a boil again until it reaches 220F.
5. Pour jam into clean half-pint jars and screw on the lids. Jam will keep in the fridge for 4-6 weeks.

Triple-Berry Jam

(Prep + Cook Time: 1 hour 25 minutes | Servings: 2 cups)

Ingredients:

- 8-ounces raspberries
- 8-ounces halved strawberries
- 8-ounces blueberries
- 1 cup sugar
- ¼ cup honey (optional)
- 2 tsp lemon juice
- 1 tsp grated lemon zest

Directions:

1. Add sugar and raspberries to your Instant Pot.
2. Let the mixture marinate (called macerate) for at least 15 minutes, but no longer than 1 hour.
3. After that time, turn the Pot on to SAUTE and bring it to a boil for 3 minutes. Close and seal the lid.
4. Press MANUAL and adjust time to 8 minutes on HIGH pressure.
5. When time is up, press CANCEL and wait 10 minutes for a natural pressure release.
6. Take off the lid and press SAUTE again. Add lemon zest and juice.
7. Taste the jam (it's hot, so be careful) and add up to ¼ cup honey if you want the jam to be sweeter. Boil for 3-4 minutes, stirring, until the jam gets that gel-like consistency and reaches 220F.
8. Press CANCEL. If you like smooth jam, mash it all together.
9. Transfer to clean Mason jars and screw on the lids.
10. When cool, move to the fridge for 3 weeks, or a freezer, for up to 6 months.

Pine Nuts Honey Mousse

(Prep + Cook Time: 45 minutes | Servings: 6)

Ingredients:

- 2 eggs
- 1¼ cup pine nuts
- 1¼ cup coconut cream
- ½ cup honey
- 1 tbsp coconut oil
- Chocolate Ganache Topping, optional

Directions:

1. Using a paper towel, coat the inside of a springform cake pan or oven proof casserole pan with coconut oil.
2. Line the bottom and sides of the pan with parchment paper and set aside.
3. Put the eggs, cream, and honey into a blender and mix, scraping down the sides as needed, until completely smooth. Pour the mixture into the pan.
4. Pour 1 cup of water into the Instant Pot and place the trivet inside. Place the pan on top of the trivet and close the lid tightly.
5. Select MANUAL and cook at HIGH pressure for 25 minutes. Once pressure cooking is complete, use a natural release.
6. Open the lid and carefully lift out the trivet and place the pan on a cooling rack for 30-45 minutes.
7. When cooled, invert the pan onto a platter, carefully lift out the parchment paper from the side.
8. Invert it again onto another platter, loosely cover and refrigerate overnight.
9. If you are using chocolate ganache topping, you can make it before serving, let it cool a little and cover the Pine Nuts Mousse and serve immediately.
10. Alternatively, you can cover with coconut crème fraîche and top with roasted pine nuts! Enjoy!

Carrot-Raisin Bread with Walnuts

(Prep + Cook Time: 1 hour 50 minutes | Servings: 6)

Ingredients:
- 2 cups flour
- 1⅓ cups sugar
- 1½ cups cold water
- 2 grated carrots
- 1 cup chopped walnuts
- 1 cup raisins
- 2 tbsp butter
- 2 tsp baking soda
- 1 tsp cinnamon
- ½ tsp allspice
- ¼ tsp nutmeg
- ¼ tsp salt

Directions:
1. Boil the water, sugar, raisins, butter, and spices on the stove for 10 minutes.
2. Let it cool completely, storing in the fridge to speed up the process.
3. When cool, add the flour, salt, baking soda, carrots and nuts.
4. Stir to combine right away and then pour into a greased baking dish.
5. Pour 1 ½ cups of water into your Instant Pot and lower a trivet.
6. Put the dish on top and seal the lid.
7. Select MANUAL and cook at HIGH pressure for 1 hour and 10 minutes.
8. When time is up, press CANCEL and wait 10 minutes before quick-releasing. Test the cake with a toothpick.
9. Cool a little while before removing the cake to cool completely.

Carrot Halwa

(Prep + Cook Time: 35 minutes | Servings: 6)

Ingredients:
- 2 tbsp ghee (the ghee butter can be subbed for a vegan butter to make the recipe vegan)
- 10 cups carrots, peeled and grated
- 1 cup almond milk, unsweetened
- ¾ cup sugar
- 1 cup almond meal
- 2 tsp cardamom powder
- 2 tbsp raisins
- ½ tsp saffron
- 2 tbsp almonds or pistachios, sliced (for garnish)

Directions:

1. Turn Instant Pot to SAUTE mode and adjust to HIGH heat. Add ghee and grated carrots. Cook for 2-3 minutes with the glass lid on.
2. Add almond milk and close the lid with the pressure value set to sealing. Set Instant Pot to cook on MANUAL and adjust to HIGH pressure for 5 minutes. Quick release pressure when time is up.
3. Add sugar, almond meal, cardamom powder, raisins and saffron. Mix well.
4. Turn Instant Pot to SAUTE on HIGH heat again and cook for 5-7 minutes, until most of the liquids are evaporated.
5. Garnish with sliced almonds or pistachios. Serve hot or chilled. Enjoy!

Almond Fudge Drop Candy

(Prep + Cook Time: 30 minutes | Servings: 30 pieces)

Ingredients:

- One 14-ounce can of sweetened condensed milk
- 12-ounces semi-sweet chocolate chips
- 2 cups water
- 1 cup chopped almonds
- 1 tsp vanilla

Directions:

1. Add milk and chocolate chips into a cooker-safe bowl and wrap in foil.
2. Pour water into your pressure cooker and add the trivet.
3. Put bowl on top of trivet and seal the lid.
4. Select MANUAL and cook at HIGH pressure for 5 minutes.
5. When time is up, press CANCEL and use a quick release.
6. Unwrap the bowl and add the nuts and vanilla.
7. With a teaspoon, drop candy pieces on a wax-paper lined cookie sheet.
8. Freeze for 20 minutes.

Creme Brulee

(Prep + Cook Time: 55 minutes | Servings: 6-8 cups)

Ingredients:
- 2 cups fresh cream
- 6 egg yolks
- 5 tbsp white sugar
- 1 tbsp vanilla extract
- 4 tbsp raw sugar for caramelizing

Directions:
1. Prepare the Instant Pot by adding 2 cups of water and the trivet (or steamer basket).
2. In a mixing bowl, combine the egg yolks and sugar, whisking until the sugar is dissolved.
3. Add the cream and vanilla to the mix, whisking until just combined (do not overmix and whip this).
4. Pour the mixture slowly through a strainer into a spouted container - this will make pouring the mixture into the ramekins or cups easier.
5. Pour the mixture into ramekins, covering them all tightly with foil. Arrange the ramekins in the steamer basket, ensuring all ramekins are sitting straight.
6. Close and lock the lid. Select MANUAL and cook ay HIGH pressure for 9 minutes. For smaller cups like espresso cups, simply set it so 6 minutes.
7. When time is up, open the cooker using natural pressure release.
8. Open the pressure cooker and carefully lift out the custards.
9. Open the first one and jiggle it to see if it is ready. They should be nearly solid and firm, not liquidy. If they are still liquid, pressure cook for an additional 5 minutes.
10. Remove the custards and leave to cool uncovered for about 30 to 45 minutes. Once cooled, cover them in plastic wrap and place them in the refrigerator to chill for 3-4 hours or overnight.
11. Before serving, remove the custards from the refrigerator and sprinkle with a thin even layer of raw sugar. Melt the sugar with a culinary torch or place under the broiler for about 5 minutes in the oven to caramelize. Enjoy!

Fruity Yogurt
(Prep + Cook Time: 12 hours | Servings: 4)

Ingredients:
- 5 2/3 cups milk, organic, reduced fat or whole
- 4 tbsp sugar, all natural, divided
- 4 tbsp dry milk powder, non-fat, divided
- 2 cups fresh fruit, chopped
- 1½ cups water, for the pot
- 4 tbsp yogurt culture, plain, divided

Equipment:
4 wide mouth pint jars

Directions:
1. Pour the water into the Instant Pot and then put a rack or a grate in the pot.
2. Pour 1 1/3 cups into each jars and the cover the jar loosely with their lids. Put the jars onto the rack/ grate.
3. Set the Instant Pot to PRESSURE Cycle and set the timer to 2 minutes; this will heat the milk and kill any pathogens that might be in the milk.
4. When the cycle is done, turn the steam valve to quick release the pressure.
5. Open the pot lid and with a jar lifter, remove the jars from the pot. Put the jars into cool water and carefully remove the jar lids.
6. Once the milk is below 100F, add 1 tablespoon yogurt culture, 1 tablespoon dry milk powder, and 1 tablespoon sugar into each jar; stir until well mixed.
7. Carefully add about 1/2 cup of fresh fruits into each jar; do not over fill them and leave at least 1/ 8-inch clear from the top each jar. Return the jar lids back.
8. Check and make sure that there is still 1½ cups of water in the bottom of the Instant Pot.
9. Put the jars back onto the rack/ grate. Press the yogurt cycle and set the timer for 8-12 hours.
10. When the cycle is complete, put the jars in the refrigerator; this will cool them down and stop the cooking process.

Notes: Making the yogurt in jars enables you to make plain or different flavored yogurt at the same time.

Made in the USA
Middletown, DE
26 December 2017